To my dear wife, the best thing
that ever happened to me . . .

THE CO-OP'S GOT BANANAS!

A MEMOIR OF GROWING UP IN THE POST-WAR NORTH

HUNTER DAVIES

**SIMON &
SCHUSTER**

London · New York · Sydney · Toronto · New Delhi

A CBS COMPANY

First published in Great Britain by Simon & Schuster UK Ltd, 2016
A CBS COMPANY

1 3 5 7 9 10 8 6 4 2

Simon & Schuster UK Ltd
1st Floor
222 Gray's Inn Road
London WC1X 8HB

www.simonandschuster.co.uk

Simon & Schuster Australia, Sydney
Simon & Schuster India, New Delhi

The author and publishers have made all reasonable efforts
to contact copyright-holders for permission, and apologise
for any omissions or errors in the form of credits given.
Corrections may be made to future printings.

A CIP catalogue record for this book
is available from the British Library

Hardback ISBN: 978-1-4711-5340-2
eBook ISBN: 978-1-4711-5342-6

Typeset in the UK by M Rules
Printed and bound by CPI Group (UK) Ltd, Croydon, CR0 4YY

MIX
Paper from
responsible sources
FSC® C020471

Simon & Schuster UK Ltd are committed to sourcing paper
that is made from wood grown in sustainable forests and support the Forest
Stewardship Council, the leading international forest certification organisation.
Our books displaying the FSC logo are printed on FSC certified paper.

CONTENTS

Intro

On the morning of 9 October 1954, I woke up in a Norman castle. Quite a change from the previous eighteen years of my life which I had spent in a grim, unheated, crowded council house sharing a bed with my brother. We did have a bath and, no, we did not keep coal in it, but the bathroom was too cold to enter and anyway we had no hot water.

Quite normal, for those post-war years. Millions of us were in the same austerity boat and around half the population lived in rented or council property. My family circumstances were perhaps a bit bleaker and sadder than some, not that I was really conscious of it. It was just how it was, living like most of the neighbours seemed to live.

But now I had found myself in a suite of well-appointed rooms in an historic building, once the splendid home of Prince Bishops, today a World Heritage site. I had a bedder to make my bed, maids to serve me meals in the Great Hall, new words and phrases to understand, such as buttery, battels, Senior Man, JCR, SCR, sconcing, 'oaks up'. A new life to learn, a new life to live. And it was all free. Even my train fare from Carlisle the day before had been paid for.

What was happening to me was not at all normal for an eighteen-year-old in the 1950s, a period when only 4 per cent of the population went to university. But again, I was not really conscious of this, of being in any sort of elite. It just seemed how it was, what you did.

All the same, I was a bit dazed and confused, not quite sure how I had got there. I just seemed to wake up that morning, my first day as an undergraduate at University College, Durham, open my eyes, and find myself there.

At breakfast in the Great Hall I tried to identify the accents of the others. I had not heard a southern accent before, not in the flesh, only on the radio, nor even Birmingham or West Country, and certainly never come across anyone who had gone to a public school. I wondered if my accent stood out.

The second and third year chaps seemed so grown-up, knowing all the ropes, swapping banter with Eddie the butler, flirting with the maids. Many did look incredibly mature, having done their national service, seen the world, fired guns, probably shot people. That was one thing hanging over me – the thought of national service. At least I had three years ahead, safe in an ivory tower.

Carlisle and home was already another world, receding fast in my mind. Would I lose contact with my parents, my sisters and brother, move away emotionally, socially and culturally, forget all those eighteen years at home? Perhaps even be embarrassed by them?

When you are one of only a tiny percentage of lucky beggars you can't expect the remaining 96 per cent of the population to understand or sympathise with you. Not like today. Everyone and their aunty seems to go to 'uni' today.

I was aware it could afford me opportunities and experiences denied to my own parents, and all their parents before them. Let's hope I didn't muck it up, fail my exams. Oh, the shame and ignominy for my mother.

At dinner that night, in the Great Hall, wearing my gown, listening to the Latin grace being read by one of the scholars, I was on a table with about twelve other first years, first days, all my age. I realised, looking round and listening, that they were mostly like me. From their conversations about their sixth forms and A-levels, they appeared to have come from the same sort of grammar schools. Despite one or two being louder and more boastful than the others, they were apprehensive, nervous.

It suddenly struck me, seeing myself in them, as them, that for the first time in my whole life I was with people all beginning at square one. We were all equal, more or less, poised on the same starting block. Until then, for various reasons, I had always felt an outsider, behind the others.

Surely that had to be a good thing. But where might it lead, if I survived my student years? Would I manage to find something to do with my life? Six years ahead, say, at the end of the decade, finally fleeing the fifties, what would have happened to me? In 1960, what would I be, who would I be, where would I be living, and with whom?

1

FAMILY BACKGROUND

'I am going back to the Highlands,' my mother used to say towards the end of her life. She never lived in the Highlands, but only visited now and again as a child, so I can't believe she had many memories, just images she had been told about, fantasies which had gathered in her mind.

'I am going back to Australia,' she also used to say, right towards the very end. She had never been to Australia, so goodness knows where that had come from.

There are places we remember from our lives, some have changed, some are gone, some might not even have existed.

I have decided, at long last, that I am going to go back to the place where I was born. So, obviously I have been there, in my life. I am now aged eighty, yet I have never been back to my birthplace – which was Johnstone. I have been to other parts of Scotland, to Edinburgh for example, loads of times over the decades. And it's not far, really, just a few hours on the train. What has been stopping me?

Is it prejudice, something I have against the place I was born? But how can it be, when I have never been and don't really know anything about it. When asked, I always say I am Scottish, because I am proud of it, pure Scots on both sides. And if Scotland had become independent in 2014 I would have applied for a Scottish passport, if they had ever got round to such things.

I suppose it is partly because I don't really know where it is that I was born. I know that factually I was born on 7 January 1936 in Johnstone in the county of Renfrewshire, which is near Paisley, not far from Glasgow. I have no image of Johnstone, let alone any memories. In my mind all these years I have seen Johnstone as a dot somewhere on the edges of the Greater Glasgow sprawl, part of the old urban, industrial Clydeside shipping heartland, once so dominant in Scottish and British life but now decaying and sad-sounding. Who would want to go there, unless they had to? After all, I left it when I was four. My family were just passing through.

If, of course, I had been born somewhere more exotic or glamorous or interesting and exciting and famous, then I am sure I would have had occasions over the years to pop in, poke around and say, 'Hi, you don't know me, but I am one of yous, oh yes, I mean och aye.' We don't pick our own birthplace, no more than we pick our parents. It's all chance, there is nothing you can do about it.

One advantage is that it is a blank slate; if you have left that place as young as I did, nothing has been painted or marked on it. I won't be able to stand around and say, 'When I was a lad, these were all fields, goodness the views from here were sublime' or, more likely, 'This street was full of factories, the smoke and the noise were awful and the poverty, my dear the poverty.' For I remember nothing. Johnstone just happens to be the place where I came into the world.

*

My father, John Hunter Davies, was born in 1906, so was thirty when I came along, quite old for those days. His father, Edward Davies, was some of sort of engineer, not a professionally qualified one, more probably a fitter who looked after various machines in the steelworks.

The family lived in Cambuslang, which is on the other side of Glasgow. They were upper working class, as far as I can make out, for they owned their own house on the Hamilton Road, where I spent many holidays when I was growing up. I loved staying there. It seemed so huge, with little attic rooms on landings and bedrooms which were holes in walls and a wooden pulley suspended over the kitchen table with clothes drying.

My father had a sister Jean and three brothers, Eddie, Alex and Jim. Jean went to Glasgow University and became a teacher at Hamilton Academy, which was unusual for women from that background and at that time, but then Scotland always prided itself on its education system, offering more chances of higher education compared with the English system. Alex also became a teacher. Jim, the youngest of the family, became some sort of clerk and then a rent collector but considered himself a poet and playwright. He did once have a play performed at the Byre Theatre in St Andrews. It was in Scots dialect, Lallans, the old language of south and central Scotland, and was called *The Hands of Esau*. I was once forced, as a teenager, to stay up late while he read it aloud to me and found it excruciating. Till I fell asleep.

My mother, Marion Brechin, came from Motherwell and her family were less educated, less cultured, and rather looked down upon by the Davies clan. Her father was from the

Highlands and had been an engine driver, which my mother always said was the aristocracy of the working class, the best job any ordinary working man could aspire to, a job for life, with great status. So she always maintained. But if this were true, why had they never managed to buy their own house, like my Davies grandparents? All families have little secrets, mostly piddling, minor mysteries about which you never ask till it is too late and they have all gone. I suspect Grandpa Brechin was not in fact an engine driver but a fireman, assisting the engine driver, but it did mean he got free travel on the railways.

As a child, up to the age of ten or so, I spent some of my summer holidays living with my Brechin grandparents. They lived in an upstairs council flat on the Bellshill Road in Motherwell. I never looked forward to it, compared with my Cambuslang relations. It was cold and cramped and my Grandma Brechin was very bossy. She had a yappy Highland terrier called Sheila who ran round the little flat, barking to be taken out. She would go mad if my grandmother forgot to take her hat off and ran around in a frenzy, convinced she was about to go for a walk.

Grandma Brechin used to make crowdie, pouring sour milk into a muslin bag, tying it up and leaving it overnight to drip over the sink. In the morning for breakfast you scraped out the white cheese, like goat's cheese, which had formed in the muslin bag. It was surprisingly delicious spread on toast.

My grandfather didn't speak, even when we played Ludo together. He would sit and stare out of the window, emitting a constant breathy whistle which had no notes, no tune, clearly unaware of what he was doing. His other activity was unfankling – i.e. unravelling – endless bits and balls of string which he had picked up in the street.

My mother had three sisters. The oldest, Aunt Maggie, emigrated to Canada when quite young. Then there was Bella, who lived nearby in the Buildings and was broad Glasgow, with an even stronger accent than my mother. Jean, the youngest, was very pretty and quite refined, but delicate and always ill, resting on a day bed whenever I was taken to see her. Which I thought was my fault, as I was always being told to pipe down when I was young.

Her husband Tom was a hero in the war, a chief petty officer on the submarine that was the first to break the German blockade of Malta when the island was on the brink of starvation, for which he received a medal. They had one daughter, Sylvia, who was my age so they tried to get us to play together, but she was very serious and solemn. Last I heard of her she had become a nun and gone off to Africa.

'Oh, I loved school. Don't you love school, Hunter? Oh, I loved school.' That was one of my mother's constant refrains throughout my childhood. I never thought about school as being something to be loved or not loved. It was simply there, a place you had to go. But my mother insisted her schooldays had been nothing but wonderful.

If she had loved school so much, and was good at all her lessons, so she said, why had she left at fourteen and not stayed on longer? That was one question I often asked her, when I got a bit older. She would look puzzled. 'Oh, I don't know. Did I leave at fourteen? I suppose I did.'

In 1922, aged fourteen, she went into service for the next few years, as a live-in domestic, a tweeny, with a series of

Church of Scotland ministers and their families. She always reminisced how one day she had taken the Reverend Eric Liddell breakfast in bed when he came to visit the minister she was working for. Before entering the Church of Scotland, Eric Liddell had been a famous Scottish runner, appearing at the 1924 Olympics. His strong religious beliefs meant he refused to train or run on Sundays, as was portrayed in *Chariots of Fire*, the 1981 film about him.

When my parents met, my mother had stopped working as a domestic servant and was serving in the NAAFI in Perth. My father was in the RAF. Over a cup of excellent NAAFI tea, their eyes met. Presumably.

During the war there were always jokes on the radio about the awful food and tea in the NAAFI, but I never quite understood what this 'Naffy' was. It stood for Navy, Army and Air Force Institutes and was created by government in 1921 to run recreational services for the British armed forces, selling goods to servicemen and their families. It ran clubs, bars, shops, supermarkets, launderettes, restaurants, cafés and other facilities on most British military bases, and also canteens on board Royal Navy ships. Commissioned officers were not usually supposed to use the NAAFI clubs and bars, since their messes provided these facilities.

I don't know at what age my father joined the RAF, or what he did beforehand, if anything, or if he joined as a boy from school. I have photos of him in RAF uniform, and also playing in his RAF football team. He once told me that the squadron leader, sitting in the front row of one group photo, was the Duke of Hamilton, or perhaps later became the Duke of Hamilton. Most families, however humble, have pet stories they trot out over the years in which they worked with, or met or saw or just passed in the street or nearly almost met someone who later became well known. Celebs, as we call them today.

My parents got married in Motherwell in 1934. My dad was twenty-eight and my mother twenty-six. I don't think the Davies family were exactly thrilled by the arrival of my mother into my father's life, a mere NAAFI girl, tall and rather bony, who seemed nervous and awkward. My father had apparently been engaged to or going out with a teacher, who was greatly liked and approved of by all his family. Something had gone wrong; possibly she dumped him, which was why he married my mother on the rebound. Who knows the truth about these situations – or if the people ever know it themselves.

My mother had also had a long relationship. He was a soldier called Ronnie. I once found a photo of him – in full uniform, complete with kilt – in my mother's drawer. He had inscribed it to Marion – and signed it 'Ever Thine Ronnie'. That became his name in our family legend – Everthineronnie, as if it was one word. My mother, on special occasions, used to wear his engagement ring. So, my parents got married rather late for the times and, it would appear, both on the rebound from someone else. And two years after they got married, I was born.

2

A Jaunt to Johnstone

As an amusement for myself, a detour before I get started on
my own exciting life, I decided to visit the place where my
parents happened to be living when I was born. I took maps
and guidebooks, emergency rations and crampons (okay,
that is a silly joke), and headed for Euston station to catch
the Virgin Trains Pendolino that would take me to Glasgow
Central. It did feel like going on a safari, to unknown areas
not yet mapped.

When I was born, my father was a clerk, so it says on my
birth certificate, but he was still attached to the RAF. He was
working as a civilian at a base at Abbotsinch, as some sort of
pay clerk, giving out the wages each week. The Abbotsinch
airbase had been created in 1932 as an overspill from the bigger
airbase at Renfrew. He must have been posted there sometime
around 1934, after my parents had got married, and they took
rented quarters not far away at The Bungalow, Inchinnan
Road, in Johnstone.

My birth certificate also says I was born in Thornhill
Maternity Hospital – which sounds private, perhaps even
posh. Why was I not born at home as most babies were in the

1930s, pre-NHS? Who paid for it? Is the hospital still there? Is there a plaque saying 'Hunter was born here'?

Those were the only two addresses I had, when I set off. Both of them might well have disappeared long ago. Eighty years is a long time in politics. In life, it is, well, a lifetime.

A Google search seemed to suggest that Inchinnan Road was a whopper, stretching for miles, most of it now dual carriageway, probably part of the M8 motorway, so fat chance of finding any little cottage called The Bungalow. Must have been flattened, blown away decades ago. Like my mother and father, long gone.

At Glasgow Central, I caught the local train to Johnstone, just fifteen minutes away. The destination on the board was Largs – which immediately sparked off memories I never knew I had. My parents once took me to the seaside at Largs, or was it Troon? I have a photo somewhere of me, aged about three or four, on an Ayrshire beach with my parents, which I was always led to believe was Troon, or Largs. Should I go and see both places? Might be nice, but what on earth would I learn there, about me, now?

After Paisley, the countryside grew green and sylvan and I could see proper fields and hills in the distance, which was a pleasant surprise. I had expected either industrial wasteland or built-up areas and council estates all the way to Johnstone, which was how it had appeared on the map. As we approached Johnstone, I could see low-flying planes, heading for Glasgow airport.

Johnstone railway station was small, neat and tidy, quite attractive. On the platforms, I noticed that the signs also had the name in Gaelic – 'Baile Iain', literally 'John's town'. It is

THE CO-OP'S GOT BANANAS!

a recent wheeze by the triumphant, all-conquering Scottish National Party to add the Gaelic name to every station in the whole of Scotland, despite the fact that most of these places never had a Gaelic name or people who ever spoke Gaelic.

At the 2015 general election, there was a massive local victory for the SNP, defeating the MP for Paisley and Renfrewshire South, Douglas Alexander, who had been in the Labour cabinet under Tony Blair and then shadow foreign secretary. What a surprise and humiliation it must have been for him, having been one of the important Labour figures. But perhaps the bigger surprise was the person who beat him: a 20-year-old Glasgow University student called Mhairi Black, who became the youngest MP in the House of Commons since the 1660s. She is a keen tweeter, making no secret of her drinking and use of strong language, or of her football allegiance: 'I hate fucking Celtic,' so she announced to her followers.

I did a quick internet search and discovered that Gordon Ramsay, the chef, was born in Johnstone in 1966 – and, like me, in Thornhill Maternity Hospital. Not that I would recognise him if I met him in my porridge, which was a saying of my mother's. I don't watch TV, except football, and I would never in a million years watch anything to do with cooking.

Renée Houston also came from Johnstone, born there in 1902, and was an actress and comedian, very popular in the prewar and post-war years. My mother was awfie fond of her. I should think today she is forgotten, even in Scotland, by anyone under sixty. Other famous Johnstonians include the footballer Jim Leighton and Sir George Houstoun Reid, who in 1904 became the fourth prime minister of Australia. Quite a mixed bunch, with only their birthplace in common, but I suppose that's true of any place, anywhere.

I stood for a long time outside the railway station, asking people if they knew where The Bungalow, Inchinnan Road, was. People had heard of the road but didn't seem to know where it began. I have a family snap somewhere of me in a garden of The Bungalow and the house looks like a shack, a sort of wooden chalet. Must be long gone, so I decided to give up.

I then asked people how far Renfrew was, the town itself, as I wanted to look at the parish church where I was baptised. They all said it was miles away. I Googled it on my iPhone to see if it still existed, and found it was still there – but for sale. It looked interesting, sort of mock Gothic, not the usual dour-looking Scottish church. The asking price was £88,000 and had been 'heavily discounted for an early sale'. The estate agent blurb said it was just fifteen minutes from Glasgow and perfect for being turned into twelve luxury apartments – 'subject to relevant consents'. Consent is, of course, the relevant word with all conversions.

I did have my cheque book with me, but I thought no, not worth the bother. Best to stick to Johnstone itself. That was where I was born.

So I headed for Thornhill Maternity Hospital, not far from Johnstone station – but I was a bit late. It closed in 1986. But the gate posts and wall of the entrance to the old hospital are still there. It now leads into a rather superior housing estate called Thorndene, with eighty-two smart houses in all, lush lawns, conservatories, large garages, winding round a cul-de-sac. I got a passer-by to take a photo of me on my phone, leaning against the front, low wall at the entrance. I could see that there had once been iron railings along the top of the wall – presumably taken down during the last war and melted into guns or bullets. All over Britain you can still see the remains of once handsome iron railings at the front of houses and buildings and public places which were savagely cut down and never replaced.

I walked round the estate several times without spotting any humans. All in perfect condition, well-kept, but it was as if all the houses had been abandoned. It reminded me of various villages in Sussex I passed through one afternoon when I was walking along disused railway lines for a book. It felt as if a sudden plague had cleared out all the inhabitants, but I imagined there must be some house-bound mothers, holed up inside, or some secret assignations taking place behind those closed curtains.

On my third circuit I spotted a man coming out of his front door to get into his car – so I pounced. I talked rapidly, trying to explain my project, knowing that the normal reaction when approached by a total stranger, who does not talk in a local accent, is to assume they are selling something, looking for houses to burgle, or they are potty.

'I was born here,' I explained. 'Eighty years ago . . .'

He looked a bit puzzled as I rambled on, but when I started asking him questions, he became helpful and amused. His name was Alastair Wilson and he and his wife bought their house exactly twenty-five years ago, moving into it when it was new. He is now retired, after thirty-eight years working for the Bank of Scotland. I asked how much he paid for his house, thinking he might not tell me. People can be funny about money, almost like asking about their sex life or politics. He said he paid £124,000 in 1990. Today he thought it would be worth £330,000. Not quite the vast increase over twenty-five years had he bought in London, but still a good investment.

He often met people wandering round his little estate who said they had been born in Thornhill Maternity Hospital. The hospital had been going since 1934 and was run by Renfrew county council, which was why my parents had not had to pay, who passed it over to the NHS in 1948. Thousands of people must have been born there over the decades, before it finally closed in 1986.

Houses were still going up when Alastair and his wife first looked at the estate. His initial general impression of Johnstone itself was depressing. 'There seemed to be so many empty factories and disused buildings. A bit of a dump really. It was the view that did it, making us fall in love with the house.'

He took me round the back of his house. From his neat back garden he could look as far as the eye could see at green fields and hedges, across the Firth of Clyde. In the far distance I could see clearly a range of mountains. 'Er, what is that, Alastair? I know I'm Scottish, but you will have to identify it for me.'

'Ben Lomond – can't you recognise it? Marvellous view, don't you think? I get pleasure out of it every day.'

A low-flying jumbo jet came over his house heading for Glasgow airport, just five miles away. 'The planes don't bother me. I've got used to them. It helps to identify the wind direction. If they are coming in directly over our house, it means there is an easterly wind. Very handy to know that.'

I had never expected such a splendid view as the one from Alastair's back garden. I wondered if the ward I was born in had looked out on it. Was it the first thing I gazed out at when I was born? In those days, babies were kept in maternity wards for up to ten days, unlike today. So my eyes must have opened.

I then went into Johnstone, just a mile away, to see the sights, to explore the burg, as they say in the States. It is, in fact, an ancient Scottish borough – hence the name of their local football team, Johnstone Burgh – with a population today of 15,000.

I asked for the town hall and was directed to a low, modern, concrete building across the square, boring and grim outside, but quite spacious and attractive inside. No, they didn't have a tourist office. But I was told there was a Johnstone museum. I love museums so I got the address and rushed to see it.

It turned out to be out of town – inside Morrisons. Yes, Morrisons, the nationally known supermarket in which I have ten shares.

Alas, I had come on a Monday. Johnstone History Museum is only open on Wednesday, Friday and Saturday. A Morrisons management man tried to get me a key, but was unable to contact anyone. I peered through the door of the tiny one-room museum, tucked away at the far end of the store, just past the café. I could see some badges, books, booklets and photos, presumably all about Johnstone, but, though tantalisingly near, I was unable to get in and devour them. Would I have learned more about my birthplace if I had broken the door down, set off alarms and had every Morrisons security person for miles around rushing to apprehend me? I'll never know.

Back on Johnstone station, I got talking to a woman on the platform. I thought she must be about my age. Which is what I do all the time, then they turn out to be fifty-eight. Is it my vanity, my self-delusion, that I imagine I must look their age? Or is it that once people get over fifty-five they all seem to meld into the same generation . . .

I told her why I had come to Johnstone, and mentioned Thornhill hospital. No, she had not been born there, but she had had an operation there some years ago.

'Och, must be twenty-five years ago. Let me think now, Sandy is twenty-eight, Annie is twenty-seven, Wee Callum is twenty-five. So, yes, it must have been back in the 1980s.'

'And what was the operation?' I asked, hesitantly.

'Oh, it was where I was sterilised. I was told I was the last women to be sterilised in Thornhill hospital before it closed.'

And what nicer place to have it done. I hope she enjoyed the view.

3

HUNTER'S RECORD

One of the few things my mother left me was a booklet called 'My Record Book', which for several months in 1936 she faithfully filled in. It is a sixteen-page, full-colour, very pretty production with nice little illustrations and attractive typography in which you were supposed to enter all the details of your baby's first months. I see I was born at 2.35am, the doctor who delivered me was called Dr Mackay and the nurse was Nurse Waddell. I weighed 7 pounds 13 ounces and was 21 inches long. Quite long for a baby, I think, though what do I know?

On one of the pretty pages you have to list the gifts of money the baby has received, 'Which shall go into the Bank to build a Savings Account so that some day the baby shall go to College'. My mother has carefully written in ink that I got £1-5-0 from Grandma Brechin, £1 from Grandma Davies and £1-2-6 from aunties and uncles.

On turning over the attractive booklet I see it is copyright '1927 Imperial Granum, New York'. It does seem a very American production – hence the reference to 'going to College'. I wonder where they got it from? I can't believe it was on sale in the local Woolworths in Johnstone. We had no relatives in the USA, as far as I know, but we did have some in Canada, courtesy of my mother's eldest sister Maggie.

On the front page of 'My Record Book' it gives my full name: Edward Hunter Davies. I have gone through life keeping my first name quiet, mainly because for most of my growing-up years I never knew I was really an Edward. From the moment I was born, my parents always called me Hunter. I assume it began with the fact that there were already two Edwards in the immediate family – my father's father and one of his brothers. Hunter had been a family name for many generations, usually stuck in the middle, as in my father's case.

It wasn't till I was about ten and at primary school that I realised. The school nit nurse came round and said, 'Stand up, Edward.' I looked around, thinking what poor sod is called Edward. And it was me. It's only on things like medical records that the truth comes out. Otherwise I deny it.

I have enjoyed going through life as Hunter, with almost everyone being unaware that it is not my true first name. With new people, I do get called David Hunter, or David Hunt, till they get it straight. I have never met another person called Hunter, though there have been a few in the USA, such as Hunter S. Thompson, the writer, and the golfer Hunter Mahan.

When Paul McCartney came to have a holiday with us in Portugal in 1968, my first name happened to come out – and he started laughing and mocking. I pointed out his real first name was James, not Paul, so he should mind himself. He then went off to the lavatory with his guitar and came back with a song called 'There You Go Eddie'. I did hear him playing it to John later on the *Let It Be* sessions, but it never made it as a Beatles song. One of the disappointments of my life.

While I have liked being called Hunter I would have preferred not to have the surname Davies. Much better if I had
been called Hunter McGregor, then everyone would know
where I really came from. Davies is, of course, Welsh, one of
the most common names not only in Wales but also in England.

According to one of my Canadian relations, who has done
some genealogical research, the first Davies in our lineage did
come from Wales in 1815. He was at the Battle of Waterloo
and decided to change sides. No, not joining the French, but
leaving his Welsh regiment for a Scottish one, becoming a
batman to the Duke of Argyll. After the battle he moved to
Scotland, settled down and married, spawning a long list of
Scots called Davies, most of whom eventually moved to the
Glasgow area for work. Or, in my father's case, to Johnstone.

I do have some photos of my mother and father when they
were living in Johnstone, and some earlier ones from their
courting days. When I was growing up, and looking at these
old snaps, I did find it hard to believe they were ever young.
My mother even looks vaguely fashionable, with her bobbed
hair, nice frocks, stylish hats, although my main memory of
her, from when I was a schoolchild, was of someone with
no interest in clothes. My dad, walking down some street
in Johnstone, arm in arm with my mother, is wearing a suit,
carrying a coat, and also looks rather smart. I have only one
photo of me and him when I was very young; he's holding me
as a baby, rather warily.

I have no memory of him ever looking after me, or holding me, or showing any interest in me. This was the normal
pattern for fathers at the time, working class or otherwise.

They were not involved in child rearing. I do know he played football as a young man, for I have photos of him in his various RAF teams. I even have a medal which he won when playing with a team called Hearts. I used to pretend it was Heart of Midlothian, the famous Edinburgh club.

My first memory in life is of being pushed in my pram to see the *Queen Mary*, or it might have been the *Queen Elizabeth*, being launched on Clydeside. I can see me in the pram, and have visions in my mind of the mud and all the people, all very clear and vivid – but I think this is nonsense. I couldn't possibly remember stuff that happened to me in my pram. I know some people say they can, but I don't believe them. So it must be a received memory, based on what I was later told.

Now I look at the record, I see the *Queen Mary* was launched in 1934, so I could not have seen that, but the *Queen Elizabeth* was not launched till 1938. We were still living in Johnstone, so I might well have been taken to see that when aged two.

I do have one happy, fun memory of my father when he once took me out in an RAF jeep. This might have been while we were still living in Johnstone, and he was based at Abbotsinch airfield – which, I know now, became Glasgow airport.

His job involved visiting various RAF bases and handing out the men's wages, and he was accompanied by uniformed servicemen, guarding him and the money. We stopped several times on the way because it was Grand National Day and they all wanted to hear the latest on the race. My father was not a betting man, as far as I ever knew, but listening to the Grand National was a national event. Being out in a motor vehicle, that was an excitement in itself.

*

While we were still living in Johnstone, my twin sisters, Marion and Annabelle, were born. They came three years after me, in 1939, in the same maternity hospital. Not long after their birth, I tried to drown them. They were having their bath and my mother left the bathroom for a moment. She came back to find that I was pushing their heads under the water. Quite common, I suppose, for a first born to be resentful when a younger sibling arrives – and even worse when it is two of them. My father was carried round his RAF base on the day they were born, as if it was somehow a triumph for him.

We left Johnstone a year later, in 1940, when I was four years old, so I have no other memories, real or imagined, of my Johnstonian years. Would I have been a different person if I had remained living in Johnstone all my life, if my parents had not moved and I had gone to a local school and college, as my baby record book predicted? Would I have been looking around while in Johnstone for the people I sat beside at school, the first pub I went to, the girls I took out? My Scottish accent would certainly be intact today, which would be good, as I have gone through life with a nondescript accent which no one can place.

I would obviously not have married the same woman, as I would never have met her, or had the same children, or ended up in the job I wound up in. Decisions and developments would not have been the same, so, yes, my life would have been totally different. And yet I would still have been me, presumably.

4

ON THE MOVE

When we moved in 1940 it was to a foreign country – England. I don't know why. It just seemed to happen. Aged four, no one is going to explain things to you. I now realise it was to do with my father's job. He was still doing some sort of clerical work as a civilian, connected with the RAF, but now he was being moved to 14 MU in Carlisle, an RAF mainte-nance unit. Was it demotion, promotion, or just bureaucracy, moving people around for no reason?

As a child, you never think of asking such things. You are more concerned with playing with your friends or stuffing your face. Everything else you just accept. A bit like adults really, when it comes to wartime. You are there not to reason why there is a war, just to do what you are told.

Our arrival in Carlisle was one of the moments my mother often spoke about later, which was not like her. She never moaned or complained, blanking out anything unpleasant, but it clearly had a great effect on her.

We arrived in the winter of 1940, just before Christmas, in the freezing cold. The three successive winters from 1940 to 1942 were incredibly cold, a sequence of nightmare winters that have not been equalled since. They went down in folklore, all over Europe, because it was not just in England that the effects were felt. It was the height of the war, so ships got stuck, despite the icebreakers, troops could not move, supplies got frozen.

My mother came down to Carlisle on the train from Glasgow, clutching me by the hand and struggling with the twins, who were then eighteen months old, plus bags and bundles of belongings. My father was nowhere to be seen. He did not figure at all in my mother's memory of the arrival, nor did she explain why he was not with her. At work, still in Johnstone, or what? He just never seemed to be there at vital, domestic or family, times. Which, of course, was pretty typical of men in those days.

She did have her father with her, that thin, silent, weird-looking, whistling man whom I can barely remember. He had a free pass for the railway, as a railway worker, and probably for my mother as well, which would explain why we all came on the train.

We arrived in the dark to this empty council house in a strange town, with my mother knowing nobody. There was no heat, no fire, no furniture and no lights. Electricity existed, but the previous occupants, long since gone, had taken all the bulbs. My mother staggered around, with the three of us crying and moaning, while she herself began to feel sick and ill. Our little pathetic, refugee-like family must have been spotted by the next-door neighbour, a cheerful cockney woman called Mrs Dembow, who after an hour or so, hearing us clattering around and the children crying, came in with a pot of tea and some lightbulbs. So my mother could at last see the full horror of the new home.

I, of course, can recall nothing of our arrival, or how distraught my mother was, but I do remember those dreadful early winters in Carlisle. It became quite exciting and dramatic – the whole street blocked in by snow, which didn't melt for months. Standpipes appeared in the street, as in every house the pipes had frozen solid. Our school was closed, so we played in the snow every day.

For my mother, though, there was no fun, no amusement or novelty in being frozen in. Even worse when she realised the cause of her sickness. She was pregnant once again, without having been aware of it.

In Carlisle, they turned out to speak a different language, or at least with a very different accent. Yet Carlisle is only just in England, ten miles over the border, an ancient border city, where the Romans built a fort and through which Hadrian's Wall ran. Then, when they left, it was fought over for centuries by both English and Scots and was part of Scotland at one time. Carlisle's history has therefore always been bound up with Scotland's. There shouldn't really be such cultural and social and linguistic gulfs.

Most people in the UK are not quite sure where Carlisle is – wondering if it is in Scotland or perhaps Wales. Its uncertain and remote location makes Carlisle feel that it gets ignored by most of the rest of England. It has a chip on its shoulder about being cut off, so far from London. Unless there are floods, then it makes the TV news.

I was not aware of any of that at the time. It just seemed we had landed somewhere abroad, where we were the migrants. I had not realised till then that my mother's accent was so broad.

People from Motherwell are considered, even in Scotland, to have a very broad if not rough accent. I have her on tape, Super 8 and video films, so I know what she sounded like, but I have no sound recording of my father. He didn't say enough for me to remember his voice, but Scottish, obviously. When he did talk to me, he seemed to be doing a lot of shouting, ordering me to pipe down. He maintained my voice annoyed him, gave him a headache. Bloomin' cheek, as my mother used to say, which was the worst, unkindest remark she ever made about anybody.

We took a little bit of Scotland with us when we moved to Carlisle, as immigrants usually do. My mother joined a church with lots of Scottish members – Warwick Road Presbyterian – and at home we managed to get the BBC Scottish Home Service on the radio, read the Scottish *Daily Express* during the week and the *Sunday Post* at the weekend.

There was, naturally, a large Scottish community in Carlisle, but I don't remember any Scottish people in our street. We seemed to be surrounded by cockneys or Geordies, families like us who had been moved from elsewhere to work on the RAF unit.

We lived on the St Ann's Hill council estate on the north side of the city at 25 Deer Park Road. Doesn't that sound idyllic, which I suppose it was, as we had a whole semi-detached house with two bedrooms and there were woods to play in not far away.

About half the whole nation at the time lived in rented accommodation, most of it council housing. The movement for better housing started after the First World War, the government deciding that the only adequate solution to the housing question was to build houses specifically for the poor.

Carlisle was one of the earliest councils to make use of the government subsidies and their first council houses opened in 1922. As more estates were added, they provided a variety of styles and accommodation. Some had bay windows, some parlours, some proper indoor bathrooms and indoor lavatories. They were desired and occupied by many lower white-collar workers who might well at other economic periods have tried to save and pay a mortgage to acquire their own house.

The city architect credited with this enormous expansion was Percy Dalton. He is still remembered in a street named after him on the Raffles estate, Dalton Avenue. I used to think he was the same person who made the peanuts. I felt quite proud that someone from Carlisle had done so well. Alas, that was another Percy Dalton.

The St Ann's estate was built in the 1930s, so was quite new when we moved in. It was council owned, and we paid council rent, but its main purpose was to house workers from 14 MU, which had been created in 1938, when the RAF took over the old Kingstown aerodrome. Almost all the fathers around us worked at the site.

There were seven RAF maintenance units spread all over the UK and each carried a complete range of stock and equipment, from paperclips to aircraft engines, just in case any of the units got hit during an air raid or infiltrated and wiped out by some of our nasty enemies. They were heavily guarded and all classified as secret, which meant no outsiders ever got in or knew what went on inside.

At one time, at the height of the war, there were 4,300 people working at Carlisle 14 MU – 784 uniformed airmen and the rest civilians – it was enormous, spread over seven different sites with massive hangars and thirteen miles of its own railway track. A good half of the workers were women, who had replaced the men during the war years.

I never found out what my father did there. I think his days of taking round the wages to other sites were over and he now sat at a desk shifting bits of paper or counting paperclips. He did sometimes bring home pads of MU notepaper and pencils, so there were some perks.

I started at the local primary school, Stanwix, when I was five. It wasn't all that local, as I had to get a bus there, up a steep hill. Stanwix – pronounced with the 'w' silent – was considered 'clarty posh', meaning posh in an ostentatious and vulgar way. It was full of the lower, ambitious middle classes in private semi-detached houses and Victorian terraces. The council house kids who came up the hill from the St Ann's estate tended to stick together. We did feel envious of people who lived in their own homes and had a garage and, even more fortunate, so it seemed to me, their own front-door bell. Council houses always had knockers. Tenants trying to get above their station could not build their own garage but installed their own bell.

Not long after we moved to Carlisle, in February 1941, my mother gave birth to her fourth child, John, always known as Johnny, to differentiate him from my father John. Johnny was the sole English person, living with five Scots, as we liked to tease him as he got older.

I suppose my mother must have taken me to Stanwix school in the early days, but in my recollection I always went on my own, or with my best friend, Reggie Hill. He lived in the next street, Fraser Grove. His street had been named after the father of the author George MacDonald Fraser, who had been a well-known doctor in the town. In the 1930s there were four Dr Frasers who had come to practise in Carlisle, which shows the Scottish connection had always been there – and also how good Scotland had always been at producing doctors.

Reg's dad, like mine, worked at 14 MU, having originally come across from the Northeast. His father, also called Reg, had at one time been a professional footballer for Hartlepool United before being transferred to Carlisle United. I found this hard to believe when I was first told. Football to me seemed the most glamorous possible profession, yet he seemed to be an elderly, shambling, burly figure who never spoke. But then dads didn't in those days.

There were family sports held each year at 14 MU, for the children of all the people who worked there, with real money as prizes. One year, Reg and I trained for weeks in our streets in the dark, determined to win something, but we never did. So we put our hopes in collecting up as many empty pop bottles as possible, left over from various picnics. You had to pay a penny deposit on soft drinks and you got the money back when you returned the bottles. It was a boiling hot day and we were totally exhausted carrying all these bottles back from the wilds of Kingstown to Clark's, the local shop on our council estate. When we got there, triumphant, they refused to give us a penny for any of them. Said the bottles had not been bought from their shop and were a different brand anyway. Bastards.

Reg seemed to be about my height as well as my exact age when I first met him, but then suddenly he started to shoot up, leaving me behind, feeling like a midget. His family had nicknamed him Toddles, because he used to toddle along when he first learned to walk, but as he got older he hated the name. I would use it, just to annoy him. Once he got stronger than me, he would beat me up if I dared call him Toddles, especially in front of other people.

On the way back from school each day, Reg and I would wait for our favourite bus, letting others go past just because we wanted to catch the Dummy. This was a small, single-decked bus, rather a funny shape, as if it had a bit cut off the front. All the school kids loved it as it was so unusual.

We got on it one day, pushing our way to the back, which was considered the best place to stand. We were right up against the rear emergency door, which had a huge handle and a sign saying it was not to be touched. As we were bumping away down Etterby Street, a cobbled hill leading down from Stanwix towards our council estate, the back door of the bus flew open. It could have been our own fault, or perhaps some other kids had been playing with it.

Reg and I fell out – right into the path of a lorry that was following behind. Goodness knows how it managed to brake and avoid us. I have no memory of what happened, as I had been knocked unconscious. I came to sometime later to find I was lying in a ward at the Carlisle infirmary.

The first our mothers knew about it was when a policeman arrived at their front door, to inform each of them we were in hospital. My mother then had to catch a bus into town and make her way to the infirmary on Wigton Road. Going into Carlisle was always an ordeal for her, as she had no sense of direction. I never did ask my mother about what happened when she heard the news, how she had reacted, how she had got herself to the hospital, what she must have been dreading.

When we eventually got back to school, none the worse, it made us something of local heroes, having survived what could have been a serious accident, if not death. It helped to cement our friendship, me and Reg, something we had in common, a shared experience.

But then the bond was suddenly broken. Once again, out of the blue, we were on the move. In 1943, after three years in Carlisle and with me now aged seven, we were moving back over the border to Scotland. Reg and I promised to write to each other, and we probably did, for a few weeks, but then it all petered out as I got to grips with being in yet another foreign country, even though it was one from whence I had come.

5

BACK TO SCOTLAND

Dumfries has a similar sort of history to Carlisle: Roman occupation, lots of battles and castles, cross-border looting, till eventually it settled down. It is about a third the size of Carlisle, population around 32,000, not a city like Carlisle, as it has no cathedral, but it is a royal burgh, having been given that honour in 1186.

In school in Dumfries I learned only Scottish history, a lot of it totally foreign to English schoolchildren, about William Wallace – portrayed by Mel Gibson in the film *Braveheart* – defeating the English, and also Robert the Bruce. It was in Dumfries that Robert the Bruce slew his rival the Red Comyn, giving him an extra stab to make sure he was dead and shouting, '*I'll mak siccar!*' I remember learning this phrase but never really knew what it meant, which of course is 'I'll make sure'.

Dumfries's most famous resident was Robert Burns, who lived there from 1788 till his death in 1796. My mother endlessly recited Burns poetry, as most Scottish people of her generation did, and knew all his songs, which I also learned.

People from Dumfries, and followers of their football team,

Queen of the South, are known as Doonhamers. The phrase is said to have originated in the nineteenth century in Glasgow, when lots of Dumfries folk went up there to work on the railways, dreadfully missing their hometown, always wanting to go back '*doon hame*'.

My father had been forcibly moved to Dumfries to do the same sort of job as he had done in Carlisle. So there must have been some sort of RAF presence, yet I don't recall the name of any local aerodrome or RAF maintenance unit ever being mentioned. In Carlisle, 14 MU was referred to all the time, a legend throughout the city.

I can remember my father talking about the American servicemen he was working with, and on one famous occasion – famous in our family – him coming home with a tin of fruit. Inside were pineapple chunks, oh joy!

Wouldn't it be wonderful if after all these years he turned out to have been an undercover government agent, engaged on some secret work, reporting on our so-called allies, the Americans. Or could he have been some sort of go-between involved in that mad, farcical meeting between Rudolf Hess and the Duke of Hamilton? Hitler's deputy flew to Scotland on his hopeless peace mission in May 1941, when we were living in Scotland, and of course my papa did know the Duke of Hamilton, so he once boasted.

These ridiculous thoughts have only just struck me now, but as children during the war we had such mad fantasies all the time, convinced that spies and agents were everywhere, constantly watching us. If someone we didn't like was horrid to us, told us off, well then he or she must be a spy. They could be anywhere, so we were led to believe. Government posters warned us that walls have ears, careless talk costs lives, you must always beware, never reveal any possible information, not even your name or address in case, er, I am not quite sure what might have happened. We followed anyone acting suspiciously, like *Emil and the Detectives*, making notes on their movements, taking it in turns to observe them, ready to report them to, well, we never got that far.

One of the wartime rumours that spread though our school was that the Germans were dropping parachutists in local woods – disguised as nuns. So what you had to do if you saw any nuns suddenly running around was to check if their legs were hairy. Then you would know they were up to no good.

The real reason I was never aware of any actual RAF station or maintenance unit in Dumfries, and so never knew where my father went, was that we lived out of town, not among other families with fathers doing the same job, as in Carlisle. We were not on a council estate this time, but renting accommodation over a disused shop on a busy thoroughfare, the Annan Road, leading out of Dumfries.

Hmm, that does sound suspicious. Even more suspicious was the fact that below us, where the shop had once been but was now boarded up, lived a strange single man with a limp and a frightening face who had a foreign accent. We could hear him wandering around in the night, talking to himself in an unfamiliar language. Sending radio messages to Berlin on a transmitter made out of biscuit tins? That was my first suspicion, which I immediately related in a whisper to my twin sisters. Didn't bother telling Johnny. He was too young and too English.

My mother eventually informed us that he was a Polish

pilot who had fought on our side and been very brave, but had been badly burned and invalided out. So we should be nice to him. Polish airmen, of course, did play an important in the last war.

The house was called Nancyville. It made it seem as if we had achieved a slight social step up, living in a house with a name not a number. Beside us were other private houses, lived in by very nice people. One of whom, a genteel elderly lady, knocked on our door the moment we arrived and brought us soup. 'Wasn't that awfie nice?' said my mother. We never saw her again. I think it was the sight and sound of four screaming kids under the age of seven that put her off.

For a while we had a cat, called Peter, the only time in my growing-up family life, in Carlisle or Dumfries, that we ever had a pet, despite begging our mother. She had enough to worry about. This cat once disappeared, didn't come back for weeks, and we were sure it was a goner, then one morning it reappeared from over the fields behind our house, dragging behind it a large trap. Its foot had been caught and mangled so much it had to be amputated. Until the end of its life, we could hear Peter wandering round in the middle of the night going pad pad pad thump, pad pad pad thump, as every fourth step his gammy stumpy leg hit the lino.

You entered the house downstairs at the side, into a kitchen, then beyond into a living room. Upstairs were just two bed-rooms. We four children slept in one bedroom and our parents slept in the other.

Our bedroom was at the front of the house overlooking the busy Annan Road. All night long there were military convoys roaring past on the way to Carlisle and the South. Every few minutes their headlights pierced our bedroom dark, despite the blackout blinds, brilliantly illuminating the four of us, burrowing down in our beds, blankets over our little heads, trying to sleep.

Before bed every night, our mother would make us kneel down beside the bed, put our hands together, close our eyes and say the Lord's Prayer. This was followed by 'Bless Mum and Dad, Annabelle, Marion and Johnny, our grandmothers, all our uncles and aunts, all our airmen, soldiers and sailors, politicians, the royal family . . .' The Polish war hero down below would often get a mention, or anyone else my mother was currently concerned about, such as Peter the cat.

Having coaxed us all into bed, she would then get us up again and put each of us on the potty. She had a fetish that we each had to perform before bed, either a number one or number two. So we would strain and stretch and pretend we had performed, till our little bottoms were indented with deep cold rings, not wanting to be given the dreaded senna pods or syrup of figs or whatever pet laxative she currently believed in. The entire nation's mothers were in a continual panic about bowel movements, which is strange, considering that our whole diet during the war consisted of the roughest of roughage, the sort of diet you would now pay extra for.

When eventually the praying and potty rituals were over, as the oldest I would try to create some discipline in the bedroom, attempting to get us all to sleep.

'One, two, three, goodnight,' I would say, which was the signal for no more talking. Then one of them would talk, forgetting. I would have to start all over again.

'One, two, three, GOODNIGHT!'

·This could go on for ages, with me shouting, and them winding me up by starting to talk again.

During the day, if the American convoys were still rumbling past, all the local kids would stand in the gutters making a 'V for Victory' sign at them. I could never manage to get my fingers arranged the right way, so my mother would have to come out in the street and do it for me.

The object was to shout, 'Got any gum, chum!' at the Yanks, smile and wave, pathetically but appealingly, in the hope that they would chuck out some sweets or chewing gum. They often did, which led to a mass stampede as we rushed into the road, trying to avoid the oncoming jeeps and trucks, pushing and shoving each other to secure the treasures.

I went to the local primary school, Noblehill school, just along the road from Nancyville, on the same side. I remember it as being enormous but in fact there were only three classes. While I was there, sometime between 1943 and 1947, there was a tremendous fire in the school, with large parts burned to the ground, which of course meant we couldn't go there for several weeks.

I had a fight in the playground one day. Some brute was bullying me, probably for having an English accent. He had been doing it for some days and I had put up with it, being a scaredy-cat and always willing to please and appease, but this time I couldn't bear it any longer. He was taller and bigger than me and I was small and weedy and wheezy, but from somewhere I summoned the willpower and strength to lash out like a wild animal, screaming and shouting, punching and kicking him. Everyone stopped their playground games and rushed over, shouting 'FIGHT FIGHT FIGHT!' He was so surprised at what he had unleashed that he backed away. And never bothered me again.

I also got teased a bit about my buck teeth and the fact that there was a slight gap in the middle. (Apparent on the front jacket photo of this book, if you put on your best specs.) I had not really been aware of it, till some sweet girl in the class pointed it out, then of course others joined in. The teacher must have heard all this, for at the end of the lesson she called me over, on my own. 'I always think there is something attractive about uneven teeth.' Wasn't that kind, wasn't that thoughtful. I immediately forgot about it from then on. The gap, such as it was, disappeared anyway with age. Oh, if only all unpleasant and unattractive things we worry about could disappear with age.

When I was about nine or ten, in the top class, I went on a school outing to Glengonnar camp, in the Leadhills. It seemed miles and miles away, but was probably only about an hour's distance, up in the hills beyond Moffat, an area where once there had been lead mines. We stayed in wooden huts which had dormitories, went on nature trails and had campfires. My twin sisters and younger brother – then aged around six and four – were incredibly jealous that I should be so favoured, going away on such an adventure.

For some reason, I can still remember a song we sang by the campfire, to the tune of 'Oh My Darling, Clementine'.

To Glengonnar, to Glengonnar,
Came the children with a will
From St Michaels and St Josephs
Larry Now and Noblehill.

These were the names of other local Dumfries schools that were also at the camp. Larry Now stood for Laurieknowe Primary School.

Back home, I taught Marion, Annabelle and Johnny the words of this fairly pathetic song and we all used to sing it in the dark in our beds to get ourselves to sleep before the next convoy woke us all up. Who said we didn't have fun in wartime . . .

I had a good friend in the Annan Road called Bertie Williamson. His family had a wood yard beside their house where we used play. It was quite dangerous, as the logs could fall on you and bury you underneath. His father was a barber in the middle of the town, a small asthmatic man, who used to work bent over his customers so you could see his skinny, weedy bottom. He cut my hair for free, which was why I went there. I think he took pity on our family as my mother was very often ill. Something to do with varicose veins. She was always being told she needed an operation.

I used to go to town on my own every Saturday, running messages for the neighbours, going on the bus clutching shopping bags, shopping lists and the money. I can't have been more than ten at the time, yet I was sent off alone, given such responsibility. I don't think my own children were allowed on the bus on their own till they were grown-up, well, till they were teenagers. Parents were so trusting. There was no talk of paedophiles and loonies, muggers and knifemen wanting to harm you or dodgy people trying to spirit you away. Obviously they existed, but we were not warned about them. Perhaps our parents were as innocent as we were.

The shops I went to were right in the middle of the town, in the High Street, mainly grocers like Lipton's, the Home and Colonial or the Co-op, the same sort of grocery stores we had in Carlisle. I loved watching the pulley devices which whizzed across the shop floor carrying little metal canisters. They would end up in a hidden cubicle where someone would open them, check the order and the money, then put the change back in the canister and whiz it back to the relevant counter. I found it fascinating and exciting, like watching an aerial train set, but really, what a nonsense, what a palaver. Why did they do it? Could they not trust individual shop assistants to handle money?

Smaller shops never had such fancy technology and the shopkeepers would do it all in their heads or on the back of a paper bag, instantly adding up 19/11, 12/6 and 5/7, often with halfpennies and farthings thrown in. Today you see dopey assistants in a panic when they have to add £7 and £4 together, using expensive electronic calculating machines.

My mother did have to go into hospital for an operation and for several weeks it was my job to look after my brother and sisters after school, till my father came home from work. I made them their tea, which always consisted of the same thing – toast. Sometimes I spoiled them and boiled them potatoes as well. They used to moan and groan as the toast was burned and the spuds half-raw. I would slap it down and say, 'That's all you're getting, eat up or shut up.' I don't think Health and Safety would allow any child of ten to look after three younger ones – and have pans of boiling water on a stove.

*

In 1947, when I had just turned eleven, and after only four years in Dumfries, we were on the move once again, leaving Dumfries for good.

Last time I was there our old house Nancyville had been converted back into a shop. Noblehill school was still there, but now has an additional building – a mosque. Who could have imagined that in 1947?

I now also know, which I didn't at the time, that Dumfries did have an aerodrome, which opened in 1938, and then, on 18 June 1940, an RAF maintenance unit was inaugurated, 18 MU. I was never aware of either at the time. That must have been why we moved, to help out at a new MU, my father being a dab hand by now at moving paperclips and pencils around.

One of my abiding memories of living in Dumfries is of a condom, not that I realised then what it was. One Sunday morning, when I was about eight, I went to the lavatory, which was at the top of the stairs, and there floating in the water was what I thought was a balloon. I picked it up and went with it into my parents' bedroom.

'Look, Mam, someone has left a balloon in the lavvy. I bet it was that Marion.'

I can still see her face, a mix of shock and worry, panic and embarrassment. She glared at my dad on the other side of the bed, who turned over and went back to sleep. She got out of bed and took it gingerly from my outstretched hand. Strange how that scene stuck in my mind, without knowing what the object was. It seemed to haunt me for some years, trouble me, without understanding why. Perhaps it was my mother's reaction to me appearing with it, the atmosphere it created, which registered on my innocent young mind.

I am now old and in that way quite innocent. I have somehow managed to reach the age of eighty without ever using a condom. I now realise, of course, that the last thing my mother would have wanted at the height of the war, with four young children and her poor health, was to have another child.

6

ME AND THE WAR

One day in 1947 in Dumfries we woke up and were told a furniture van was coming, so we had to get ready. As the oldest, I was being allowed to travel in the back of the van with the furniture. My dad sat in the front with the driver and his mate. My mother, sisters and brother were going on the train.

I was thrilled to be allowed to sit in the back of the removal van, as rides in any sort of vehicle were rare. After a few miles, I began to feel sick. I couldn't get my dad's attention, as he was chatting away to the driver. When we got to Carlisle, and drew up once again in the St Ann's council estate, I was violently sick. Welcome back to England.

Yes, we had returned to Carlisle. Not very exciting or foreign this time, but on the other hand it did feel a bit like coming home, even though I had lost my English accent.

And in Carlisle we stayed from then on. Which meant that all my wartime years were spent in either Carlisle or Dumfries, well away from any front-line bombing. Nevertheless, the effects of the war were felt wherever you were, whatever your situation. But at the time, it just seemed sort of normal, how it was. I had only known wartime, being only three years old when the war started in 1939. When I did come across examples of prewar life, such as the fat, colourful comics that children of my age read back in the thirties, I could not believe comics had ever looked like that. Thanks to my relations in Canada, we sometimes did get sent a Yankee comic. They were like fantasy publications.

When I had been listening to the convoys at night, while lying in bed, I did not understand fully what was going on, where they were going. It was just heavy traffic. It was only being at school that I began to pick up roughly what the war was all about.

One day at school in Dumfries the teacher got each of us to knit a square. She then stitched them all together to make one big blanket. She then explained that they were going to be sent off to cover our brave soldiers who were freezing and filthy out there somewhere in the trenches. I always felt sorry for the poor sod who got any of my squares in his blanket. They were always a funny shape, lots of holes, stray ends hanging out, which if you pulled the whole square unravelled.

I did learn needlework, which all the boys in my class did, sewing on my own buttons. I also darned my own socks when they got a hole, using a large wooden mushroom over which you pulled the sock tight while you darned the offending hole. I rather enjoyed this simple technology, feeling I was a real craftsman. I still do my own sewing and putting-on of buttons, when needed, which is rare these days. Everything is disposable, nothing is meant to last.

My mother had a sewing machine, but she wasn't very good at it, unlike my Grandma Brechin, who was a whiz on her Singer, the sort of machine that was a piece of furniture in itself, a table with a treadle underneath. You pedalled away on it like a bicycle, turning wheels and pulleys, giving off a constant hum as if a couple of million wasps had got into her bedroom. I was not supposed to touch it. Too precious. I did once secretly have a go and mucked it up, stitching some vital piece of clothing she had been working on all the wrong way, then in trying to right it I broke the needle.

In wartime, it was a case of make do and mend, with nothing new to buy in the shops, so everyone was constantly stitching and repairing, ripping up old items and remaking them. Even my father did his bit, at least he tried to when we were very young, repairing our shoes, like all good wartime dads. You bought packets of these little steel studs, which you hammered on to the toes or heels of shoes to make them last longer. More complicated was replacing a whole new rubber sole, which you had to stick on with glue, then perhaps shave with a Stanley knife if it had been fitted badly. Did we have a Stanley knife in those days? My dad was useless at such jobs. Halfway to school the sole came loose and flip-flapped till you had to rip it all off. The steel studs usually stayed on, but you made a sound like a carthorse, clanking along the pavements. Useful in fights, though, for kicking people.

At primary school one day in Dumfries all those children whose father was a prisoner of war had to put up their hands. They came out to the front and each was given a food parcel. I was so jealous.

'Why aren't you a prisoner of war, Dad?' I accused him when I got home. 'It's not fair.'

We endlessly collected wastepaper to help the war effort. In all the comics, such as they were, thin and weedy specimens on rubbish grey paper, there was always a drawing of a massive pile of wastepaper, getting bigger and bigger in each issue, with the word 'BERLIN' written on the top. Somehow, so it seemed to suggest, we would get to Berlin, knock the Nassies out, if only we could save enough wastepaper. Were we going to spread it out across the Channel and walk there? Or make paper darts and throw them at Hitler?

The Nazis were always called the 'Nassies', at least among most of the kids at primary school, in Carlisle or Dumfries, and probably elsewhere as well. I assumed it started with not knowing how to pronounce the letter 'z', or perhaps we were just being satirical. The Germans as a nation were always Jerries, which in a way was quite affectionate.

I didn't particularly hate them. They were just the enemy, baddies we had been fighting for as long as I could remember, the way it has always been, would probably always be. The dreaded Japs, they were much more scary and fiendish.

Our heroes in life were the American soldiers. They looked so handsome and healthy whenever you saw them, with square jaws, clean sparkling teeth, great smiles, terrific crew-cut hair, all wearing neat, smooth uniforms made of excellent cloth, both ordinary soldiers as well as officers, so unlike the horrible itchy, cheap, rough serge that all our brave lads had to wear. They always had goodies coming out of their pockets – gum for the kids, nylons for the young women. No wonder the girls fell at their feet. Poor old Tommies.

It is often said that the biggest influence on our post-war popular culture, right through the fifties and sixties, was American music and films. I think it was the chewing gum and the nylons, that's what started it, made us all swoon, made us followers of their fashion, envy everything that they had.

We knew about Hitler. He had a funny moustache and only one ball and we sang that rude song about him. Adults and kids were forever pretending to be Hitler, putting one finger along their upper lip and goose-stepping in a funny walk, making everyone laugh. We didn't know about the concentration camps. Probably would not have believed it, even if we had been told.

The Queen has recently been revealed in a home movie, when young during the war, making a Nazi salute – we all did. It was satirical, a cheap laugh. We adored the royal family, they could do no wrong; all children were brought up to respect and honour them, always standing for the national anthem. Boys as well as girls knew all about the Little Princess, had seen photographs of the corgis and that wonderful doll's house they had. We were given glossy books about them as presents, bought cheaply through the *Daily Express*, but gold bound, which was very rare in wartime, and we had to wash our hands when turning over the pages.

We were not quite sure where London was, or what the Blitz actually meant, but we knew our royal family had stayed in Buckingham Palace and not fled to the country or abroad, and the Queen was always smiling and waving her hand when she visited bombsites.

I was always very proud, and still am, that I have lived through four royal reigns. I tell my children and my grand-children this, as of course they have only ever known one monarch. I only just caught George V – he died on 20 January 1936, just thirteen days after I was born. Then Edward VIII didn't last long – he abdicated after just 326 days. That same year, on 11 December 1936, George VI took over. So that was three different kings in one year, not that I was paying much attention. George VI then had a good run, till his death in 1952, and our dear Queen Elizabeth II succeeded him – going on to have the longest reign of any British monarch, ever. And I have been there all the time.

The moment the war started, all citizens, of all ranks, had to have blackout curtains on all the windows. Wardens would come round and knock at your door and tell you off if a crack of light was shining through. Despite not being within range of any bombers, even the odd one that might have got lost, most people had an air-raid shelter. In Carlisle we had a metal one under the dining table, a Morrison shelter, made of steel and incredibly heavy. It was very cramped and you were always banging your head getting into it and out again. The other sort was an Anderson, which you had in your garden, semi-dug into the ground, with a roof of curved corrugated iron, on top of which you would put soil which soon turned to grass. I longed for one of those. What a great camp it would have made, playing there with your chums. I suppose it was considered that neither Carlisle nor Dumfries would be in the front line, so there was no need to excavate the gardens. The Morrison shelter was much cheaper and quicker to install.

At school we all got fitted with gas masks, which were hellish to wear. You could hardly breathe and they smelled awful. We had practice days in case of an emergency when we had to put them on and rush out into the playground. We would all stand around, giggling, making faces, then be counted and sent back in. Now and again we would be marched in a crocodile through the streets and taken into a large communal air-raid shelter. The smell of urine was disgusting. We all hated going there.

The gas masks came in a strong cardboard box complete with string to help you carry them. Later, some of them had an extra filter added to make them safer – in case arsenic smoke bombs were dropped, so we were told. The extra filter made them too big for the original cardboard boxes, so we were given a tall blue cylindrical tin. We were told to carry some cotton wool to put in our ears and a piece of rubber to place between our teeth, if ever we had to use our gas masks. This was to avoid damage to our ears and swallowing our tongues if we were knocked unconscious.

Water tanks appeared in streets, and many houses were given stirrup pumps, the idea being that if we were bombed and houses set on fire, we would try to put the flames out on our own. People donated saucepans, pots and kettles to the war effort and iron railings disappeared from the fronts of the smarter houses and public buildings, all to be used to make guns and aircraft, though I never quite understood how. Concrete blocks appeared on bridges to delay traffic. Out in the country, road signs vanished. That would fool the Nassies, if they ever landed in Carlisle or Dumfries, har har, they would be totally lost. Weather forecasts were banned, as we didn't want the enemy to know whether it was going to be sunny or cloudy, another fiendish ruse to confuse them.

A survey during the war revealed that the biggest grumble among adults was the blackout, which surprises me. I would have expected that rationing was the greatest bugbear for all parents. From my perspective, as a child, the biggest grumble was the rationing of sweets.

Food rationing began in January 1940 and from then on each person was allowed only a small amount of sugar, butter, bacon, ham each week. Our government had had the ration books printed and ready as early as 1938, which was smart. Sweet rationing started in July 1942. Eventually almost everything was rationed, from clothes to furniture, paper to petrol. And many items remained rationed for years, long after the war had finished, into the 1950s, finally finishing in July 1954 when you didn't need a ration book any more for any form of meat or food.

Vegetables, of the sort grown in Britain, were never rationed, nor fish, but huge queues appeared whenever there was a smell of fresh fish. Strangely enough, bread was not rationed during the war – that started after the war, in 1946. All the wartime bread seemed to be grey and horrible.

My whole childhood, from the age of four to eighteen, was therefore lived under rationing and I could not remember a non-rationing time. You lived by counting points, recognising As and Bs and Cs and the different coloured coupons. When I used to run messages as a nipper in Dumfries I had to take with me a pile of ration books, along with the money and shopping lists. From memory, E and D were sweet coupons.

You did hear in the papers and on the radio about the black market, about spivs and wide boys with thin moustaches selling dodgy items from the inside pocket of their raincoats. I don't remember seeing any of them in Carlisle or Dumfries, but they were joke figures, really, cartoon characters, all of them cockneys. So we believed.

So many factories were turned over to munitions work that lots of items manufactured prewar were no longer produced, or were in very short supply – such as pianos, bikes, lawn-mowers, cutlery, fountain pens. You could only get utility furniture, which was like a joke form of furniture, similar to utility sweets, made of cardboard and tasting much the same. Priority for utility furniture was given to newlyweds or those who had lost their homes through bomb damage.

The thing about rationing was that it affected all of us, rich and poor, middle and lower class, north and south, and we all accepted it and abided by the rules. We didn't, of course, actually know any middle-class people, but we accepted that they did not break the rules or practise any fiddles. After all, we were told that even the King and his family had a ration book. My mother constantly informed us that the King him-self took his bath in only five inches of water. I've stuck to that till fairly recently, thinking what the hell, I'm old now.

Wartime and post-war Christmases were pretty dire, with no turkeys and no sweets, no fruits or other goodies – not that our family missed Christmas all that much. Being Scottish, our big celebrations were held on New Year's Eve, Hogmanay, when we went first-footing. Someone in the family with black hair, i.e. me, would take a piece of coal to the neighbours and be invited in for a drink of homemade ginger wine.

We did have a stocking each, which we hung up, and in the foot of it there might be an apple and perhaps some utility sweets tasting of cardboard. We always looked forward to get-ting a proper present at Christmas from our so-called wealthy relations in Cambuslang, such as Aunt Jean, the teacher, but all she ever seemed to send us was vests. Ugh, who needs them? Perhaps Liberty bodices for my sisters.

The big excitement was the arrival of a parcel from our Canadian relatives – which was not allowed to be opened till Christmas Day. One year, when torn open, it was found to contain not sweets or comics as we'd hoped – but paper curtains. Paper curtains! No one had ever heard of them here and certainly didn't know what to do with them. You can't eat paper curtains.

I was always longing to see a real warplane. We did not get any actual bombing but there were often stories of enemy bombers being shot down or crashing in some local wood, on the way to Liverpool or Glasgow to do real damage. One of our own planes, a Lancaster bomber, came down in the fells not far from Carlisle and all the locals rushed to see it. Miraculously, the pilot climbed out of it.

All small boys knew about Spitfires and Hurricanes, could tell the difference, and rather revered the Messerschmitt, however deadly it might be. In the primary playgrounds, we would rush round pretending to be a Spitfire in a dogfight, arms out, bending sideways and backwards, giving a loud hum, and then a rat tat tat tat, imitating the sound of a real Spitfire, so we thought.

At the entrance to my father's workplace at 14 MU, they had an old Spitfire inside the front gates, on a plinth, set in a lawn, surrounded by large cobbles which had to be constantly painted bright white. I liked to think it proved my dad really was involved in war work not just pushing pencils.

The biggest contribution towards the war by remote towns like Carlisle was taking in evacuees. Next door when we were in Deer Park Road arrived a family of cockneys whose accent I could not understand. We didn't have any evacuees staying with us. We were already considered overcrowded, with four children, but of course hundreds of thousands of families did.

It is often forgotten that more children – 827,000 – were evacuated at the beginning of the war than the whole of our armed forces serving abroad. 'It is an exodus bigger than that of Moses,' said Walter Elliot, the health minister. 'It is the movement of ten armies, each of which is as big as the whole Expeditionary Force.' And like the servicemen, the children did not know where they were going or when they would return.

Most of the ones who came to Carlisle were from the Northeast. Out in the country, in rural Cumberland, they got a higher class of evacuee. In Keswick, many of them were billeted in the railway station – now gone – and in the handsome railway hotel next door. Roedean was one of the schools that moved to Keswick, from miles away on the Sussex coast. When a whole school arrived in a new place, they often had to share premises with the existing schoolchildren, doubling up the size of the classes, sometimes doing shifts, one school starting early and the other taking over later.

Children who grew up in London, or Glasgow or Liverpool, have much more dramatic memories of the war, with houses in their street being bombed, children missing from school the next day, loved ones being killed. On the other hand, they do have fond memories of playing in bombsites, going into the street after a heavy raid and picking up bits of shrapnel as souvenirs.

As for the servicemen and women, later in life a lot of them admitted that it had been an exciting time, recalling the camaraderie, the normal constraints and social inequalities being for a time forgotten or ignored.

There was an elderly lady called Joan who lived beside us in Loweswater in the Lake District, wife of the local vicar, a magistrate, pillar of the community, who had been a driver during the war. I happened to be in her house one day when an old friend was visiting from the South, who had served with Joan in the ATS (Auxiliary Territorial Service, later the Women's Royal Army Corps). They were having hysterics about some incident in a pub in London's West End during the war.

They had picked up two Yankee officers, been taken with them to a smart bar, plied with endless gin and tonics which they scoffed down. After a couple of hours, when the Yanks were getting a bit too familiar, suggesting some hotel they might all go to, Joan and her chum excused themselves, saying they had to powder their noses. They then climbed through the toilet window, out into the back yard, on to the road and jumped on a passing bus. The bus, by chance, drove round the pub they had just left, slowly going past the front door, where they could see the two Americans standing, looking up and down the street, very puzzled – and quite miffed. One of them spotted Joan and her friend on the top deck. Joan immediately waved back.

Joan and her chum made a habit of this, as presumably many young women did, allowing themselves to be chatted up by handsome Yanks, accepting the free drinks, perhaps some nylons, then giving nothing or little in return.

Some of course did, which led to the German propaganda department dropping leaflets on our poor lonely Tommies in the front line, showing pictures of handsome Yanks back in Britain, taking advantage of half-naked English girls in their bedrooms, the wives and girlfriends of our soldiers. A fiendish trick to lower their morale and make them want to pack up and go home.

What surprised me about the tricks of Joan and her friend was not that they did it, but that they never forgot it. 'Oh, it was the best time in our lives, wasn't it Joan?'

'Such fun,' Joan agreed. 'Never had such fun since.' And they would dissolve again into hysterics.

However, I did eventually witness some real front-line action, for reasons that were never quite explained.

One school holiday, when I was about eight or so, my mother put me on the bus to go and stay for a few weeks with our Cambuslang relations. Looking back, I assume now she must have been ill, her varicose veins playing up again – yet why did she send me all that way to such a dangerous place at the height of the bombing? My sisters got farmed out to neighbours. Perhaps no one had any room for me – or maybe I insisted on going to Cambuslang, which I always loved.

The London Blitz was well known to everyone in England but the Glasgow Blitz never received as much publicity, at least outside Scotland. Yet on the nights of 13 and 14 March 1941 the Luftwaffe dropped hundreds of bombs on Glasgow, killing 528 people, injuring 617, destroying 4,000 homes and making 35,000 people homeless. In just two nights. They came straight over the North Sea from Germany, heading for the shipyards, such as John Brown's, where the famous liners had been launched, and also the steelworks and the munitions factories.

I was, in fact, sent to Cambuslang twice, while my mother was ill, but don't know which years. But I do remember lying in bed watching the night sky through cracks in the blackout blinds, looking out for loud flashes and bangs and searchlights crisscrossing the darkness. Then the sirens would sound and I would be wrapped in a blanket and taken down to the shelter at the bottom of the garden where we stayed all night.

Next day, or when that particular raid was over, we would venture out into the street, perhaps taking the tram to visit other relations. I was always totally amazed by the barrage balloons. You came across them suddenly, round a corner, corralled into odd open spaces, tied down securely with stout cables on a platform. They were enormous, out of all proportion to their surroundings, and totally unreal. It was like coming across an elephant in your bathroom. There was often an anti-aircraft position nearby, or as part of the same installation, with big mounted gun carriages that swivelled round.

When Jerry planes were spotted, or expected, the balloon would be let loose, float high up in the air, but remain secured on its cables. The theory was that the Jerry planes would bang into them or their dive bombers would be dissuaded from coming too low. By 1944, there were 3,000 barrage balloons in all, a third of them in London, but also in Glasgow and other big industrial cities.

The Germans devised a cutting device on the wings of their planes which could sever the cables and detach the balloons. Meanwhile, our boffins installed little explosives on the balloons, which would detonate if a German plane hit them. War does create ingenious solutions to new problems.

I found it all incredibly exciting and stimulating. It was frightening yet awesome to see and hear aeroplanes fighting each other in the night skies, or the low-flying bombers humming on the horizon, making their deadly way, carrying instruments of mass destruction, then witnessing the pyrotechnics and noises and smells and explosions and lights of real warfare. I never thought of the danger, but then you don't as a child. You accept you will always be safe, as you have always been so far.

When it was all over, in 1945, we celebrated victory in Europe on 8 May, and then victory over Japan on 15 August – and yet I don't remember either event. In London, a million people were out on the streets for VE Day, in Trafalgar Square and the Mall, and I assume there were endless photographs in the newspapers, but I don't recall looking at them. There was, of course, no TV. I didn't know, nor did anybody at the time, that the two royal princesses, Elizabeth and Margaret, had sneaked out of Buckingham Palace to join the crowds, anonymously, as they danced and sang in the streets.

The whole country, we are now told, had street parties, but not in Dumfries, or at least no one invited me or anyone in my family. Was it something we had said? And when we arrived in Carlisle two years later, no one seemed to have enjoyed street parties there either.

But on 8 June 1946, I did get a letter from the King. 'I send this personal message to you and other boys and girls at school. For you have shared in the hardships and dangers of a total war. I know you will always feel proud to belong to a country which was capable of such a supreme effort.' It was on stiff coloured paper, with the royal coat arms in colour on the top, and a little ribbon so you could hang it up above your bed. It had a handwritten signature – *George RI.* I still have it, but now I look at it, I see it must have been duplicated. Drat it. And I thought it was just for me.

The event that signalled the end of the war as far as I was concerned, and one which has stayed in my memory ever since, occurred one day when I was playing in Noblehill Park in Dumfries, not far from our house. I was in the middle of a game of football when I heard a cry go up from the other side of the park: 'THE CO-OP'S GOT BANANAS!' In Dumfries, we pronounced Co-op as 'Cope', as if it was just one word, which did make it easier to chant. We all stopped playing, listening carefully, checking to make sure we had heard the words correctly, then we took up the same refrain: 'THE CO-OP'S GOT BANANAS!'

We rushed out of the park, down the hill, and were joined on the way by gangs of other kids till we were a large crowd, all chanting what we had just heard: 'The Co-op's Got Bananas!'

And it was true. The Co-op had received its first supply of bananas in living memory, at least to those whose conscious memory like mine only stretched back seven years to the beginning of the war. I rushed home to tell my mother, as I had no money on me. She queued up and was allowed to buy three bananas – enough for us to have half a banana each, or a sliver a day for a week, if we sliced our share really thin.

That evening, my mother ceremonially peeled and carefully cut the three bananas in front of us, giving us a half each. The twins and Johnny immediately ate their share but I cut my half into thin slices, determined to spin it out for the rest of the week, to make them all jealous, not knowing that a banana, once peeled, goes brown and mushy.

Over the previous year or so, my mother had often given us mashed boiled parsnip, squashed up on a plate, telling us it was bananas. Then, as she didn't lie, telling us that it was a joke, but reassuring us that, really, bananas did taste like that anyway. So now we had the real thing in front of us at last. I felt like Christopher Columbus testing some of the exotic fruits of the New World which Europeans had never tasted before. Or Sir Walter Raleigh, having his first cigarette.

The texture of my small sliver of banana was interesting, but the taste was a bit strange and rather disappointing. Didn't taste at all like mashed parsnips, which really, on reflection, I think I preferred . . .

7

THE DREADED ELEVEN-PLUS

When we returned to Carlisle in 1947, we came back to the same council estate at St Ann's Hill, but to a different house in a different street, 28 Caird Avenue, where we lived from then on, happy ever.

We were happy in the sense that at last we were settled. Our family then stayed in Carlisle, without another move, and I look upon Carlisle as my hometown. But so many of my memories of Carlisle throughout the fifties are shrouded by greyness, dreariness, dust, noise and smoke. And being cold all the time.

Was this the fault of the fifties, with its ongoing rationing, austerity and deprivation, despite the triumph of our so-called victory? With open coal fires the only form of heating, and often the only form of cooking or boiling the kettle, no wonder the dust and dirt never settled. Or is my memory clouded by entering my teenage years, when you become dissatisfied, start wanting to move away, from wherever you are? Or was it because of Carlisle itself?

In the fifties, Carlisle was a factory town, which visitors might find hard to believe now, since it has all been cleaned

62

up and prettified. There were many thriving textile factories which continued until very recent times – such as Dixon's, Buck's, Morton Sundour and Ferguson's. Dixon's factory chimney, 320 feet high, was said to be the tallest in the land when the factory was opened in 1836. The chimney is still there, one of the city's landmarks, though they have chopped a bit off the top. Later came the heavier industries, such as Cowans Sheldon who made cranes.

Perhaps the best-known factory among the general public is Carr's of Carlisle, the oldest biscuit works in the world, where the manufacturing of biscuits by machinery, as opposed to by hand, was begun by Jonathan Dodgson Carr when he opened his first factory in 1837. In the 1950s, Carr's employed around 2–3,000 workers, mostly women.

All these factories, churning out their products, night and day, meant that the smoke and dust seemed constantly to hang over the centre of the town. All British towns with any industrial presence were like that. And there was no escape from the dust, the noise of the lorries and the factory hooters.

If by chance you went 'up street' – as we said in Carlisle, meaning going into the town – at a time when a shift was finishing and all the gates opened, you were swept aside in a sea of humanity, hordes of workers in their boilersuits and headscarves, desperate to get home. The main bus terminal, where I got my bus home to St Ann's Hill, was in the centre of the town, opposite the Old Town Hall, so if you hit the end of a shift, the queues stretched for miles and you might as well walk.

And yet, despite all this activity and workers swarming around, the town always seemed to be dead after five o'clock.

Everything closed. That was it. Most provincial towns in the UK were like that in the fifties. Shutters went up, shopkeepers went home. Cafés and restaurants, of which there were few, locked their doors. Thursdays were even worse, for that was half-day closing in Carlisle. Oh God, it was depressing.

During that decade growing up in Carlisle, I was totally unaware that the place had any historic heritage. I knew we had a cathedral, but never visited, and a medieval castle, but it seemed cut off from the town. The Old Town Hall was right in the middle, but was little more than a dark blob behind the bus shelters, with the public lavatories in front. I just never knew it was an eighteenth-century gem. Today, it has been cleaned up and revealed to be a rather gorgeous gentle pink. Pink! Round the corner, I used to go regularly to Tullie House, a grim and dour and forbidding building which housed the public library. Now, the world can see that it is a magnificent Tudor building set in immaculate gardens. Who knew? Not me. I think I must have been in a dream in the fifties, or lost in an industrial haze. Or too busy living my own little life.

Our house in Caird Avenue had three bedrooms, so that was an improvement, with an indoor lavatory and bathroom, but an outside washhouse. We even had a front parlour. At the back of the house were the 'lotties' – the allotments – which had probably been thriving during the war but had now been left largely to grow wild, waiting for the next round of council estate building. Johnny and I created a hole in the back hedge and went into the lotties most days after school to play. It was a bit rough for football, as the ground was ridged and uneven, but made a great adventure playground.

When we arrived back in Carlisle in 1947, I immediately re-entered Stanwix school, the primary school I had been at four years before. This time, though, I had a Scottish accent and was known in the playground as Scotty. But I wasn't bullied or victimised for it, or picked upon in any way. Gradually, after a year or so, I lost my Scottishness and was speaking like all the other kids.

At school, I had some problems at first with maths because in Scotland we had recited our times tables in a different way. Same tables, of course, with the same results, but different wording.

I picked up again with Reg Hill, my old friend from Deer Park Road, going on the bus to school with him as in the past. Which was handy. Not just having a friend, but someone from the same council estate among all the Stanwix upper classes – or so I imagined them at the time.

I remember being scared of Miss Tinn. Teachers who were scary or notorious always do seem to have great names. Miss Tinn had a grey bun and was thin and steely and as sharp as a tack.

I have two school reports from my earlier spell at Stanwix school, from 1942 and 1943, when I was aged six and seven. I see my teacher in Class 2 was P. Cooke. Was it a she? Must have been. All the male teachers were away. I got 10 out of 10 for arithmetic, which surprises me, as I don't remember being any good at that stage, but only 5 out of 10 for composition. Bloomin' cheek. For spelling I got 4 out of 10. Under conduct in the first report it says, 'Rather talkative'. In the second it says, 'Fairly good, rather talkative'.

I also have a report card from my Dumfries years at

Noblehill and it is interesting to see the list of the subjects we were studying during the war. Apart from English, arithmetic, history and geography, our Scottish curriculum included nature study, handwork or sewing, drill and singing. At Stanwix, there was a separate category for spelling.

I was rubbish at spelling, and still am. I can go into a trance wondering whether it should be sow or sew, disappoint or dissapoint – appalling, isn't it, after all these years and all these words I have shifted, or do I mean apalling . . .?

As for my handwriting, that is also awful. I make notes all the time when I am out and about, ideas for my various columns, but I can't read them, unless I write them out carefully and neatly in capitals the moment I get home. At primary school, particularly in Scotland, they were very hot on handwriting. I used to have to sit for ages writing out exercises with a scratchy pen – a nib on the end of a piece of wood which usually splayed the minute you pressed on it. You dipped it in an ink well in your desk, usually splattering ink all over the page. I often had to write the same few words, page after page, not just to spell them right, but to form them all in decent lettering. Otherwise I would be kept behind after school. Yet I never seemed to improve or get neater.

I see that there were forty-nine in my Stanwix class, out of whom I was ranked fifteen in 1943. At Noblehill, my class had forty-four pupils, but there is no ranking order. The size of each class surprises me, yet I don't have the impression of the classrooms being crowded, either in England or Scotland. Today, of course, you hear moans from local parent groups if their precious little treasures are in classes of more than thirty. And yet in the forties and fifties, there were no teaching assistants, no one helping out the class teacher, listening to the slow ones reading or blowing their noses. The class teacher was on her own. I don't personally think class size is the vital factor – it's what happens inside that matters.

The teachers coped on their own with such large numbers thanks to all the rote learning, and by putting the fear of God into us, giving everyone a sound clip round the ears if they misbehaved or got their sums wrong. The worse pain was being grabbed by the ear, hoicked out of your little wooden desk, then dragged down the aisle to be humiliated in front of the whole class. If they couldn't be bothered to drag you out they rapped you across the knuckles with a wooden ruler or hit you with a blackboard duster. That was agony.

But, of course, no one complained. All our parents had been through the same regime when they were at school. It was how children learned. Some teachers were less brutal than others, and would rarely hit you, but corporal punishment of some sort was normal. For really awful behaviour you would get taken to the head, who would give you the strap. In Scotland it was called the tawse, a thick leather strap, usually with a few strips at the end, which was brought down hard on your hand. I don't remember it being administered on the bottom in primary school. That was for public schools. We read about that in the comics and chortled when the miscreant put a book down the back of his trousers to lessen the pain.

You recited your times tables and your poems by rote, the whole class speaking aloud in unison, then pupils might be asked questions individually. In most lessons, the whole class would be asked to put up their hands if they knew the answer to a question. Often you put your hand up out of nervousness, not knowing the answer, but not wanting to look stupid or draw attention to yourself, praying you would not be asked. When you did know the answer then you shouted 'ME MISS, ME MISS, ME MISS!', hoping to be asked and be given a star.

There was one really nasty teacher who made the whole class stand up when she was checking our maths. She would go round the room, rattling out the questions – 'Seven times five, boy?', 'Nine times eight, girl?' – and you would have to fire back the answers at once, which most people could. You were allowed to sit down if you got your answer right. The ones who got three answers wrong had to go to the front, where they were poked and pushed with a ruler till eventually they got something right. Oh, the fear and trembling this teacher instilled in the class. And yet to this day I am a whiz at answering my times tables, unlike my dear children and grandchildren, who take forever and then have to get out their calculators.

Stars and badges or some sort of rewards and recognition for good behaviour and performance at primary schools are still with us, for my two younger grandchildren, aged six and seven, are always delighted when they get gold stars or stickers, taking it ever so solemnly and seriously. Let's hope it lasts. It usually does throughout primary school. Most kids are keen to learn at that age, look up to and respect the teachers. The problems come later.

One reward, nay honour, for being good and/or teacher's pet was to be made pencil monitor. You gave out the pencils each day and were in sole charge and had exclusive access to the pencil sharpener. This was not one of those titchy sharpeners the size of a rubber but one of industrial size and strength, clamped to the edge of the teacher's desk. You could very easily have used it for grinding up a whole cow, and have enough mince for the entire school for a year.

Milk monitors also had high status – handing out and collecting up the milk bottles each day. All primary school children during the war and later got a little bottle of milk each, about a third of a pint. In winter, the milk would often freeze so you would have to put the bottles on the radiators to thaw, trying to time it so that they were ready at the right time. In summer they could curdle and no one wanted to drink it; the smell was enough to put you off.

The most responsible job of all at primary school, usually given to a senior child in the top class, which meant it was usually a girl, was to be the savings monitor. All schools had a savings club, run by a teacher, but often they needed a little helper who could be relied upon.

The idea of a national savings scheme was started by Palmerston's government in 1861, to encourage ordinary workers to save and also to provide money for the government. It was called the Post Office Savings Bank at first, then during the two world wars they became known as National Savings and special certificates were issued as an extra incentive.

You brought in a shilling every week to school, were given a savings stamp, then in due course when you had sufficient to make a pound – i.e. twenty shilling stamps – they were exchanged for a real certificate which you stuck proudly in your little blue savings book. The certificate told you that if you kept it for four years it would be worth twenty-five shillings, or something around that figure. It was a way of saving, getting a return on your savings, and also helping the war effort.

There were posters and adverts in the newspapers and on hoardings proclaiming the joys of National Savings, with local committees organising events and drives to raise as much as possible. There were also endless special targets in particular regions. The good people of Carlisle would be told that if they raised £10,000 in a month it would buy six Spitfires, or £100 would be enough for two bombs, or £10 would purchase two bullets. I'm sure our particular shillings did not actually go towards a Spitfire but disappeared into the pot from which the government helped itself.

Some lucky child in some schools, but not all, was given the job each Friday of taking all the shillings to the post office and getting the appropriate number of savings stamps. I am amazed they never got mugged, or ran off with all the money, or lost it. Oh, we were so trusting then.

I have just opened my Noblehill school report again, the one for 1946, and where it says 'Signature of Parent or Guardian' my father has signed it – J. H. Davies. It is in ink and rather spidery, yet done with a flourish. Underneath his signature he has drawn a straight line with two dots under-neath, to finish it off, making his mark.

I don't think I had ever noticed it before but suddenly it brought him back, a solid, physical remembrance, a relic of his life. Now I study it closely, like an archaeological artefact, I can see signs of his hand shaking, which I am sure I was never aware of at the time, not back in 1946. I have also just turned over one of my Stanwix school reports for 1943 and discovered there is a typewritten message on the back. It is not addressed personally to Mr and Mrs Davies, but would appear to be a duplicated message to all parents. I didn't know schools could do photocopying or at least duplicate printing in those days. The message apologises for no school magazine being issued at present – I am surprised they had one at all, as the war was on. It then goes on to give a stern warning, in heavy quotation marks, as if they are quoting from some official directive:

In far too many cases there is a lack of earnestness and concentration despite the possession of brain power. Little individual effort is showing. It has been noticed that some children think it necessary to be spoken to twice or three times. It is such a pity that children with ability should lack the grit to use it. Will you please help by insisting upon immediate and complete obedience in the home.

Oh my God, did they mean me personally? Or was there a group of slackers in my class of seven-year-olds – which included me?

So much for me remembering the fiendish discipline, the rote learning, the ear-pulling and knuckle-bashing, being scared to answer back – yet this is a piece of written proof, one I have never read before, which suggests that some of us, including me, were getting totally out of hand and what we needed was 'complete obedience'. Goodness, I wonder what my parents thought when they read it. My mother never disciplined us at all, as far as I can remember, while my father never seemed to be involved in any family matters. Perhaps I was a right little tearaway when I was seven, but have wiped it from my mind. Or was it teachers being teachers, the same as in every generation, moaning about the lowering standards of behaviour.

It is interesting that I still have these school reports, from over seventy years ago. Obviously my mother must have preserved them, each time we moved, put them in some drawer somewhere, and I eventually inherited them when she died. Yet she was never a person for collecting memorabilia. We had no bookshelves in the house, no space to keep and store anything that wasn't strictly necessary, that didn't serve a prime purpose, such as feeding us or keeping us warm.

School reports tell you so much, establish dates and places and years, when often we forget the sequence of events, and can also give clues to our future interests, strengths and pursuits. Or not, as the case may be.

I think the world divides into people who keep everything and those who don't, whose first reaction is 'straight to the skip'. I am one of nature's hoarders and collectors. Any old rubbish and assorted ephemera. Or, as I call it, treasure.

When I returned to Stanwix school, it took me a few months to realise that things had somehow moved on, new groupings had begun to take place, new bonds were being made, new huddles of excited fellow pupils were discussing things I had never heard discussed before, such as a school uniform. At neither of my primary schools, in England or Scotland, had we worn a uniform.

What I had not been aware of, on arriving back at Stanwix in the spring of 1947, was that I had missed the eleven-plus, or the merit as it was called in Carlisle. In Scotland at the time, there was a twelve-plus, known in Dumfries as the qualifying, which was the stage at which all primary school children were tested and then segregated. It was expected, if I had stayed in Dumfries, that I would go to the Dumfries Academy as I was by then considered to be in the top two or three in the class.

In Carlisle, they had all sat their eleven-plus before I reappeared. Then, when the results came through it was like a little earthquake, the plates immediately started shifting, new movements were formed, there was shaking and tremoring; life was not going to be the same again.

It only slowly dawned on me that I was in a no-man's-land, left on my own, going nowhere. Reg and most of my other friends in the class knew they were bound for Carlisle Grammar School, while a clutch of girls in my class were heading for the Carlisle and County High. I was a displaced person.

My parents were as mystified as me. My mother, intelligent though she was, never really understood how Carlisle worked, always getting lost every time she went shopping up street. She had little idea of the local education system, which was of course different from that in Scotland. Nor did she know or recognise the names of the secondary schools that were now being bandied around at school each day, discussed, rated and ranked by all the pupils and their parents. I didn't know their names either, but slowly I picked up that those who had passed the eleven-plus were the brainboxes, heading for the two best schools.

The eleven-plus exam, dividing up the school population, came in with the Butler Education Act of 1944. (It also raised the school leaving age from fourteen to fifteen, though this

did not come into force till 1947.) The government had envis-
aged a three-tier system, but this had rarely been established
in most parts of the country. Instead, all pupils were strictly
and brutally divided in two, either to the grammar school or
to the secondary modern. In most areas, it was around 15–20
per cent who were the chosen ones, who went to a grammar
school, while 80–85 per cent, the vast majority, the so-called
eleven-plus failures, were condemned to what was being
called a sec mod – a secondary modern school.

For the next thirty years or so, this was the system for millions of English and Welsh and Northern Irish schoolchildren
aged eleven. The exam hung over all primary school pupils in
their last year. Everyone knew that those who failed the eleven-
plus and went to the sec mod were doomed to be second-class
citizens, not just educationally but socially and economically.
Your chances of betterment in life, having a decent, possibly
professional job, had gone. That was it. At eleven years old, you
had already failed the first big hurdle in life.

In Carlisle, for some remarkable reason, a proper tripartite
system had just been established. This had happened only the
year before I arrived back, so I was told later. It meant that in
Carlisle, after your eleven-plus exam, you went one of three
ways: 12½ per cent went to the grammar school or the high
school; the next 12½ per cent went to either the Creighton
School for Boys or the Margaret Sewell School for Girls; while
the remaining 75 per cent, in other words the majority, went
to one of the city's secondary modern schools.

No wonder there was so much chatter and clatter, discussion and expectation, as pupils tried to grasp, compare and
contemplate what was about to happen to them.

Meanwhile, I was left in limbo. I had not been allocated any school because I had not taken the exam. So where was I going to go? What would happen to me?

Somehow my mother eventually worked out that I had been left behind, overlooked, had become a stateless citizen. I am not sure whether she went up to the school to enquire about my situation, or down into the town to the education offices, but one day I found myself called for an interview at the Creighton School. I sat in the headmaster's study, quietly in a corner, and was given a short written test which I completed there and then. I was then asked a couple of questions, one of which was what I would like to do in life. I assumed this meant your fantasy life, your dream job, so I said, 'Footballer, sir.' Which was true, but probably not the answer to impress headmasters with your seriousness.

A few weeks later I heard that I had been accepted into the Creighton School, which was apparently classed as a technical secondary, not one of the dreaded sec mods. It meant, apparently, that I was being considered as having passed the eleven-plus, so jolly well done, then, but alas not at the top level, not up to the standards required for the rigours and wonders of the grammar school.

However, it did mean that, along with everyone else, I now had a secondary school to go to at the beginning of the new school year in September 1947.

8

CREIGHTON AND ASTHMA ATTACKS

The Creighton School was long and low and modern, reddish bricks with lots of glass. The building had opened in 1940 and was clean and bright with lots of tarmacked playground but also green-grass playing areas to the rear leading down to the River Eden. We wore a uniform of dark blue blazers and a badge; we had a school cap; we learned French and the school game was rugby – all immediate and obvious clues to a school with pretensions. What could be more idyllic? How lucky we were in 1947, the post-war generation, about to start our secondary education in such wonderful, modern surroundings. I did feel fortunate to have got in, having been worried that I might be going nowhere.

Next door was our sister school, the Margaret Sewell, a mirror image of the Creighton, same sort of building and layout. My twin sisters, three years later, 'passed' for the Maggie Anne, as it was known in the town, and they too wore uniform and felt quite privileged.

Annabelle, so my mother always maintained, had passed for the high school, and would have gone there, but because her twin sister Marion had done far less well in the eleven-plus, the education authorities decided to keep them together and send both to Margaret Sewell. Our younger brother Johnny, when his time came for the eleven-plus, did not pass at any level. He was sent to what was considered the least favoured of all the sec mods, Kingstown, a small school, just an extension of a primary school, quite far away, almost out in the country. I never knew anyone else who ever went there. Poor Johnny, my mother always used to say, but he seemed perfectly happy and content.

The Creighton and the Margaret Sewell were in the middle of the town, in Strand Road – the same road as the grammar school. It was the next building, in fact, except for some old stables. So near us, yet a world away in status and prestige.

I don't think the majority of Creightonians worried much about the grammar school or felt much jealousy. They were considered stuck-up snobs, grammar cads, who would want to be there, yah boo.

We were not a sec mod, certainly not, we were a sec tech, so lots to be proud of. Although half the boys went on to become apprentices, as plumbers or electricians, much as they would have done, or hoped to have done, at a sec mod, the other half, the A stream, were aiming for more technical, white-collar jobs, such as draughtsman. The favoured job seemed to be something at Laing's, the builders, who were very big in the city, having been founded locally and were soon to go on to become one of the construction giants of post-war Britain.

Only the A stream went on to sit O-levels at sixteen – the General Certificate of Education as it was called. If you man-aged to pass five this would get you into Laing's, or similar, at a fairly good level, possibly junior management.

But at sixteen, you had to leave. The Creighton did not

have a sixth form. At the end of the fifth year, if you lasted that long, and half had left after the fourth year aged fifteen, that was it, you went out into the world of work.

The grammar school had a sixth form, so Reg explained to me, which had fancy names like Upper Alpha or Beta or something like that. They didn't give marks out of 100 for essays or exams as we did but grades with Greek names, alpha, beta and gamma, with rows of plus or minus signs added on to fine-tune your exact grading. All the masters wore gowns, for they all had degrees, and both Latin and Greek were taught.

It sounded like a different world, on a level with the public schools we read about in the comics, yet if I felt this gulf between us and the grammar school, I wondered what it must be like for all those in the nation's real sec mods, damned for decades as third-class citizens.

Being at Big School was such a Big Event in itself, feeling so important in your new blazer with your new pencil box, set square, ruler, compass, protractor, all neatly tucked inside your new leather satchel – out of which you soon took your ruler. Fashion dictated that you stuck your ruler in your sock, can't remember why. Was it to keep your socks up, and mine, like Just William's, were always falling down? Or to show you were ready to rule, if some teacher demanded a quick bit of technical ruling? Or was it the better to smite some bully who was bothering you?

Being at Big School, everyone seems Bigger than you – and not just the teachers. Some of the older boys seemed absolute giants, massive hulks, some with moustaches.

Gradually it became clear which were the totally useless

teachers. The French teacher, for example, I am sure could not speak French, for I never heard him say a word in the language. Instead, he would get us to read out from our French books and he would then correct our pronunciation, without in fact speaking the words himself. I suspect he was lumbered with teaching French because no one else could do it.

At the Creighton very few teachers had degrees, as was obvious at prize-giving when most turned up in their ordinary clothes. The small handful of graduate teachers would display their furs and finery for all to see. Most of them had been in the war, come out and done short-service teaching training courses, encouraged by the government. The country needed more teachers, especially male teachers, ready to cope with the population explosion which was soon expected, now that our brave soldiers were back at home with their wives.

I was put in class 1T for my first year – the T standing for Mr Thompson. The other class, in the two-class intake, was 1P after Mr Potter. They had been divided equally alphabetically, not on any merit system. At the end of that first term, in December 1947, out of our class of forty, I was eleventh. My next report, at the end of my first school year, showed I had jumped to fourth. In the second year, I went into 2A, which comprised the top half of the first year. From then on, I was in the A stream, being clearly totally gifted.

My Creighton report, which naturally I still have, is a proper little book, with lots of pages, as it was to serve you for the whole of your Creighton career, during the next five years, if you stayed that long, so you had to take care of it.

On the cover, the label says Hunter Davies, but inside, at

the top of each annual report, it says E.H. Davies, Edward Hunter Davies and sometimes Edward Hunter-Davies. They could obviously never get my name straight. There was a boy in our year who had a proper double-barrelled name, Norman Heeley-Creed. Who said the Creighton was not a quality school.

My school report is covered in brown paper. We had to do this to all our books each year, whenever we got a new set. It was an annual and agonising ritual in our household when all four of us suddenly announced we needed sheets of brown paper, which of course my mother never had, being unaware the new school year was imminent.

Another ritual at school took place at the end of each term, when we had to take our desks out into in the playground and scrub them with soap and water. We rather liked this, instead of having any more lessons. I don't think the grammar school did it, priding itself on its ancient, ivy-covered, battered desks. At the Creighton, we were a relatively new school, with new fittings, so we were supposed to keep everything clean.

Even though I was in the A stream, I still had to do metalwork, up to the fourth year, and also technical drawing, right up to O-level, as we were a technical secondary. I hated both of them and was utterly useless.

The metalwork classroom was a proper workshop, with lathes, a furnace, soldering irons, very noisy, dusty and dangerous. The master in charge, big and burly and always busy on his own particular creations, hardly bothered us, not in the way of teaching or talking to us. We were given a project and the materials at the beginning of each term, then left to get on with it. If we had any problems we queued up to see him while he was bent over his own work, with his protective goggles and ear pads firmly on, ignoring us.

For four whole years in metalwork lessons I worked on a companion set. This consisted of a poker, a shovel and tongs, plus a stand on which each item was hooked. A wonderful present, so I thought, for my dear mother, won't she be pleased. Like most families, our domestic life revolved around crouching in front of our coal fire with people shouting, 'Shut that bloomin' door!'

All the items in the set were made of wrought iron, which we hammered and heated, bashed and battered, soldered and screwed, hoping recognisable shapes might emerge. Mine, when completed, was absolutely appalling. It was more like a piece of modern art, which Picasso or Salvador Dali might have made when drunk. I did eventually finish it and present it to my mother. I wonder where it is now. Be hard to destroy. Perhaps it's in the Metropolitan Museum of Art.

Technical drawing was at least quiet and clean, but oh-so-boring and tedious. You had to draw plans with side elevations and different angles and I could never get the hang of it, constantly rubbing out my pencil marks, then trying again, ending up with dirty marks, fingerprints, indentations and creases all over the page.

I see I got 50 per cent in the tech drawing exam that first year, which surprises me. Must have been generous marking. There were two boys in the class, Dobbo and Barker, who always got 100 per cent. I hated them, so neat and tidy, not just in their drawings but in their clothes, their school uniforms, their shorts, their everything. I hated neat fuckers.

Not, of course, that I would ever have used such language at the time, not even in my head. People did not swear, not that

I heard, not in public. There was no bad language in books, in films, or in the street. The worst we ever said was bloody and bugger, but never the f- and c-words. I was on a train once, going to see my relations in Cambuslang, when some soldiers got into the crowded carriage. In talking among themselves, one was heard to use the phrase 'bloody hell'. A gentleman beside me in a suit stood up and glared at them. He said there were women in the carriage, who could clearly hear what had just been uttered, so could they kindly desist from using such disgusting language. The soldiers immediately apologised.

Today, if you dared to reprimand anyone for their language you would likely get a right mouthful, if not a good kicking. Or just laughed at. No one would comment, or even register the words spoken, not even any women who might be listening. Everyone swears, in every walk of life, from the cabinet to Buckingham Palace. Prince Philip recently told a photographer to get on with the fucking photograph, so the papers reported. And I believe everything in the papers.

I saw a survey the other day that said that the average adult, men as well as women, from all classes, all ages, uses the f-word twelve times a day and that people swear twenty-seven times more today than they did fifty years ago, back in 1965. Bloomin' heck, is all I can say.

I played rugby for the first year at the Creighton and hated it. I was small and weedy and got knocked over all the time and started wheezing. So I managed to get myself excused, even though that meant I found myself on games afternoons lumped with the lumps, the fatties, the speccy four eyes and the totally uncoordinated, who were herded together behind the goals on a spare bit of grass and left to muck around among themselves or just stand there, doing nothing, staring into space, pathetic specimens, while all the hearties and thugs beat the living shit out of each other.

Yet at home, in the street, in Caird Avenue, I was always playing football. Often I would start wheezing, go red in the face, but I was determined to carry on, as I loved football so much, and would grit my teeth and continue, hoping to overcome the asthma attack. Amazingly, it very often subsided.

At school, though, I decided to use my asthma as an excuse, to get out of rugby, but it was real. It had clouded my early childhood and now, aged about twelve, it had suddenly come back to haunt and humiliate me.

I can't remember when my asthma started. It seems to have been there since I was born. Both my parents smoked, even over my cot as a baby, so I was told by my grandmother. She said she had constantly warned them about it, but it made no impression. Everybody smoked in the thirties and throughout the war. The government even handed out cigarettes to servicemen, as part of their rations. It was glamorous, film stars smoked, the flappers and bright young things smoked, the upper and the lower classes. In advertisements, for cars or clothes, models were always languidly, elegantly smoking.

I never tried, even later as a teenager. Being in the same room in which someone had smoked made me choke. It is hard to believe it now but people smoked in the cinema, causing thick clouds to hang in the air, practically obscuring the screen. They smoked on buses and on trains and in cafés. You could not escape, smokers were everywhere.

I was sent to the doctor, for which we must have paid before the National Health Service arrived in 1945. Our Carlisle doctor, Dr Jolly, was in Portland Square, where several doctors had their surgeries. His waiting room had mahogany furniture and high ceilings and everyone sat in silence and awe, not just in fear and trembling. Medical folk were superior beings and we were grateful to be in their presence, we humble patients. My mother almost bowed when she took me into his surgery.

I was at various times given various pills and potions. There were funny rubber balls which you squeezed and some special air would come out and help you breathe, in theory. Then there was a powder which you ignited and breathed in. None of them worked.

I was once sent to Manchester, God knows how they found the money for the train and presumably the appointment, where a specialist performed a test for allergies. It consisted of having my arm perforated all the way up, so it looked like the edge of a penny stamp, and different things injected, which I might have a reaction to. They found I was moderately allergic to dust. Most people are, so it was a waste of time and money.

I would often be too ill to get up or go to school and would just lie in bed, feeling sorry for myself. If I was really bad in wintertime my mother would bring up some hot coals on a shovel – could it have been the one I made? – and put them in the little fireplace in my bedroom. I would lie there, watching the embers glow in the dark and then slowly fade. Coal was expensive so she could not afford to have a bedroom fire on as well as the one in the living room. I felt privileged and special, being treated like royalty.

My Grandma Brechin had her own pet asthma treatments

which she insisted on when I went to stay with her. One was camphor oil which she rubbed on my back so I smelled like a chemist's shop. Another was to make me wear a silk vest right next to my skin. Both remedies felt nice, but didn't help much.

I came to the conclusion that the main point of all the treatments and medicines, especially the complicated ones involving apparatus, was not to cure or help but simply to amuse the patient, give you something to do, a distraction while you were having an attack. There was no cure, just distractions.

I eventually found that I had more luck with self cures than anything the doctors recommended. This consisted of deliberately distracting myself. Lying in bed, wheezing and doubled up, I would manage, ever so pathetically, in a low, halting voice, to ask my mother to bring me my stamp album. I would then slowly turn over every page, carefully studying each stamp, thinking about where it was from, where each country was on the map, whether I would ever go there. Slowly my mind would move off my asthma, till I realised it had faded, my wheezing had almost stopped.

Or I would ask her to find my football scrapbook. This was a homemade scrapbook, using homemade paste made out of flour, in which I would stick torn-out photos from the pink 'uns of my fave players, most of them Scottish. They would be all soggy and sticky when I stuck them in, but a day later, they would have dried out and become almost three dimensional, sticking out from the pages, having risen from the dead. And again, looking at them, I would feel better.

Patient, cure thyself. Which very often I did. I would then get out of bed, try a few deep breaths, and then rush downstairs, out into the street – and join the football game. My mother, of course, would make a face, sigh and smile, bring down on the shovel anything left of the dying coals. But I had not made it up.

Asthma is partly psychosomatic. Which doesn't mean to say it is not real and awful and physical when you do get an attack, but just thinking about it, fearing you might have one, or being excited and emotional about something, can all bring it on, not just various physical causes, like rushing or running too fast.

I found that itchy clothes could bring it on, even itchy socks, but especially itchy jackets and trousers. In Dumfries I once had a little brown suit, a jerkin top and matching shorts, made by some neighbour. I hated it partly because other kids shouted 'Eyetie!' at me – the reason being that there was an Italian prisoner-of-war camp nearby and you would see the men walking down the Annan Road on the way to the fields wearing a brown uniform, very like my suit. But also because it was itchy and made me wheeze, or I got it into my head that it did, which is the same thing.

I used to maintain that certain hankies made me wheeze, but this could have been an exaggeration. All adults were obsessed by the notion that children should at all times carry a handkerchief, either in the top pocket of your jacket or in your trouser pocket. If you didn't use it yourself, they would grab it out of your pocket and drag it across your nose, whether you were sniffing or not. Just as they were always producing a horrible wet cloth, holding you by the ear, and slapping it across your face, on the pretext that your face was dirty.

Kids did easily get filthy in those days, with all the coaldust, the factory smoke, the outdoor muddy games, climbing trees and stuff, generally doing dangerous unsupervised things, and most of us sniffled most of the time, having no heat in our houses, making mothers obsessive about cleanliness.

The worst thing about their passion for hankies was that you were always getting them as presents, for your birthday or Christmas, from aunts and uncles, often in packs of three. Dear God, save us from vests and hankies, so I used to pray every Christmas. I'd rather have sneezed and wheezed.

I don't think I ever used my asthma as an excuse, to plead for special treatment, except to get out of rugby. If anything I was ashamed. I tried to hide it, not let people see I was suffering, unable to breathe. I didn't know anybody else among my friends or relations who had it, which is strange, considering it is always described as one of the most prevalent childhood illnesses.

In the fifties, there was no effective treatment. Today, the use of those Ventolin inhalers has totally revolutionised the management of asthma. I used to watch Paul Scholes, when he was warming up for Manchester United and England, to see if he was wheezing. Asthma sufferers can always tell the signs, the hunched shoulders, the rise and fall of the chest, when others are in the early stages, even if they are trying to disguise it, or are not even aware themselves. Then I would look out for him in the tunnel taking a sneaky puff of his inhaler. Lucky sod, I used to think. If only I'd had an inhaler when I was young, surely I would have played for Scotland . . .

I was always being told that I would grow out of it, most people did, so they said. Which I hoped would happen to me, as soon as I became a teenager.

9

PROBLEMS WITH MY FATHER

I hadn't been at the Creighton School long when my father started staggering. He would come from work and be seen to be holding on to the hedges in Caird Avenue as if he had had a few. Neighbours would smile, go 'aye, aye' and nod knowingly. He did enjoy the occasional drink and would go up to the Redfern – the local State Management pub on the estate, named after the architect who built many of the government-controlled public houses in the Carlisle area – on a Saturday and have a couple of pints with his chums, mostly blokes of his age who worked at the MU and lived on the estate. I never saw him drunk, or even the worse for wear.

We never had any drink in the house, except at Christmas time, when I would have to go down to the off-licence part of the County Hotel, beside the station, and buy a bottle of British sherry – ugh, sweet stuff, even I wouldn't drink it – and eggnog, which was my mother's favourite, even more horrible. Shops and supermarkets did not sell alcohol in the fifties and there were no wine shops or off-licences, only those attached to hotels or the bigger pubs, at least not in Carlisle, though I am sure there were wine shops in London, a wild, dissipated place which no one I knew had ever visited. We bought drink at Christmas in case people popped in, which they rarely did. The bottle went back in the cocktail cabinet and remained there, going dusty and crumbly, for another year.

So it wasn't drink that was affecting my father. The doctor, when he eventually went to consult him, could see nothing much wrong with him, and so he staggered on, for about another year. He was by then a higher grade civil servant. Not sure what that meant, but I recall him having to go before some sort of board. Probably a higher grade of MU paper-pusher. That sounds patronising, but I never did discover or understand what he did, but then children are not interested in their father's occupation, just accept that he goes out to work.

I do clearly remember one awful scene with him when I must have been about ten. Having tried to mend our shoes from time to time, hammering on the metal studs, he then got it into his head to do something more creative around the house. In the fifties, men were being bombarded by DIY advertisements. Magazines like *Practical Householder* encouraged them to make things, put up shelves, build furniture, assemble your own radio, make your own Hawaiian guitar, make an electric gas lighter. In our house one of the three books we had was *Hobbies Handbook* – the other two were a *Daily Express* book about the royal princess and a medical dictionary, all acquired free or cheap by saving coupons through the *Daily Express. Hobbies Handbook* was 300 pages long and gave hints on a staggering number of things a real husband could do around the house and garden. Advertisements offered fabulous new materials and tools to create these wonders. There was a product called Asbestolux, which was a form of asbestos, which you could cut up and do wonderful things with and it would never catch fire. 'Asbestolux – fire safe board for men in a hurry!' In a hurry to die, so we later discovered.

The copy of *Hobbies Handbook* we had, which I eventually inherited, was published in 1935. I imagine my father had bought it after my parents were married in 1934, doing what all young newlyweds were expected to do when they set up house together. Mothers did the cooking and produced babies. Fathers went around the house hammering things.

What he decided to do this time some fretworking. This was pretty big in the fifties, judging by the all adverts for the requisite materials, the fretsaw, blades, wood plus instructions with full diagrams. He decided he was going to make some bookends, for the bookshelves we still did not have, for the rows of books we did not have either.

He set himself up in the kitchen, with the door of the coal cellar open to give him more space, and propped up his materials on a wooden stool. The coal cellar was a dark, scary, unlit hole into which every week two men covered with sacks, their faces and arms as black as the night, emptied their bags of coal, carried on their backs round the side of the house from their horse and cart in the road. My mother would be trying to cook, food would be out or being prepared while they pushed past her – and the resultant clouds of horrible coaldust covered everything in the kitchen, and beyond. Why on earth did they have a coal cellar in a kitchen? Percy Dalton has a lot to answer for.

My father started to work, half in the coal cellar, half in the kitchen, attempting to cut out the shapes of two ele-phants from the sheet of plywood supplied, following the instructions. In due course they would be fixed to the ends of some bookshelves, yet to be made, and would be very useful and attractive, according to the illustration.

He was finding it difficult to control the fretsaw, which is a very bendy and unreliable instrument, failing to cut exactly along the required lines, and at the same time hold the wood steady. He was soon shouting and roaring, damning and blasting. My mother had got trapped in the kitchen, unable to escape while the cellar door was open, while we four hovered inside the living room, unable to get into the kitchen till he had finished.

'For Pete's sake!' he yelled, followed by more 'damn-and-blasts'. That was the extent of his swearing, at least in public, or in front of us. Not exactly frightening on paper, but pretty scary in the flesh for the four us, crouching behind the living-room door.

He then called for me to come and hold the end of the wood. I tried my best, but I was never strong. He should have asked my sister Marion, who was stronger than me. I could see that his hands were shaking, and had been since he started his stupid fretwork, showing he had no real control over his saw, but I put it down to his bad temper, getting himself in a state.

The wood suddenly totally split, the part-elephants parted, ruining his whole creation. He threw everything on the floor, then kicked the stool over and then shouted at me, blaming me, saying it was all my fault for not holding the wood steady. He then seemed to collapse, his legs giving way under him.

I stormed off, running upstairs to my bedroom. I got some belongings in a large handkerchief, came downstairs again, stepping over my father who was now sitting up, my mother fussing over him. 'I am never coming back!' I shouted, stand-ing at the back door. 'Yous will never see me again . . .'

The twins, then aged about seven, started crying. Johnny, aged five, looked transfixed, alarmed and scared by what was happening. My mother looked very upset and also on the verge of tears. I stormed out of the back door, slamming it shut. I was probably away for, well, perhaps an hour, at most.

Looking back, that was the moment I realised there was something seriously wrong with my dad. However, it took at least another year and endless tests by experts before finally it was decided that he most likely had multiple sclerosis.

Whatever that was. I don't think the *Daily Express* medical dictionary gave us much information. In fact, no one did back then. The National Health Service, still in its infancy, did not have all the social workers and physiotherapists and support systems they have today.

He carried on working for a year or so, staggering off most days, staggering back, till eventually he was given early retirement on health grounds by 14 MU. In a touching little ceremony at the base, the wing commander in charge of the unit presented him with a horrible, nasty clock, made of ply wood by the look of it.

For a few months, his old chums from work popped in now and again to see how Dave was, which was how he was known, then their visits petered out. He was given a wheel-chair by the hospital, so that was something. Once a week he insisted that I push him up the hill to the Redfern. The wheel-chair was like a tank, hellish to push, and I was embarrassed by him being an invalid, confined to a chair.

We would sit outside the pub for half an hour or so. People

would offer to buy him a drink and bring it out to him. He would smile and chat and wave and be ever so cheerful to anyone who spoke to him or recognised him. Then I would have to push him home again. Once in the house, he would shout and scream and rage against the world.

When he could no longer manage to get upstairs to his own bed, he was moved into our front parlour, the little room reserved for special occasions. The old piano was removed, which the twins had never played, and a divan bed was installed in which he stayed from them on. This was how he remained during all of my secondary school years. In fact, I can hardly remember a time when he was not an invalid, confined to his bed. He was only in his early forties when it all started, a young man really, but in my mind he is always old, always ill, and always in his pyjamas.

My mother brought him meals in bed from then on, which now and again he would throw back at her. 'What do you call this, woman? After all the money I bring into this house. Damn and blast you, woman!'

My sister Marion was the only one who stood up to him, shouting back at him, picking up the food he had thrown on the floor, saying that was it, he was getting nothing else, and if he did that again, if he shouted at our mother like that, he would get no more food again, ever. After an hour of silence, we would hear a tiny pathetic voice. 'Marion. Marion . . .?' By this he meant my mother. She would come in and he would mumble an apology and his meal would be redone for him.

He acquired a passion for salted peanuts, would eat them all the time, dropping most of them so that the hairs on his chest became permanently matted. Washing him was a nightmare, as he hated being washed or helped, struggling and swearing. I have no memory of any social workers or home helpers coming to the house. It all devolved on my mother. Eventually he developed awful bedsores, which made his health worse and his temper more terrifying.

I had to fill in his football pools for him every week, reading out all the fixtures and trying to get him to guess the result of eight games, the so-called Treble Chance. The treble part was because you had three chances – you got three points if a game you had picked ended in a scoring draw, two points for a goalless draw and one point for a home or away win. You had to reach twenty-four points, or as near as possible, then you were in the money.

They had begun in the twenties, the leaders being Littlewoods and Vernons, both based in Liverpool, and the competition between them was intense. In 1935 Littlewoods were spending a fortune on promotion, flying aeroplanes over London with streamers behind announcing 'LITTLEWOODS ABOVE ALL!'

Post-war, football pools were a massive business, with millions putting on bets each week. In 1948, when football started again, the clubs were receiving £4 million a year in gate money – while the football pools were taking in £50 million a year, just from punters trying to guess the results.

The most famous winner was in 1961 when Viv Nicholson won £152,000 on Littlewoods and went on a 'spend, spend, spending' spree. I suppose that would be about £2 million in today's money, so nothing as obscene as some recent big lottery prizes, but in the fifties the whole nation was convinced that a big win on the Treble Chance would set you up for life.

Every Saturday evening at five o'clock I would have to go to his room and tune the radio into *Sports Report*. Then, along with the entire population, we waited for the signature tune, listening in silence, hardly daring to breathe, awaiting the first reading of the football results. The programme began in 1948 with John Webster reading the results then in 1974 James Alexander Gordon took over. By their inflexion, how their voices went up or down, you could guess the result before they got to it. But if I tried to say aloud the possible score, I got screamed at.

The results each week were always the same as far as we were concerned. 'Not a bloomin' sausage,' my father would say, throwing down the copy of his coupon. Not a sausage was really all he had in life from then on.

At the time, I didn't really understand what had happened to him, or feel a great deal of sympathy. I was too preoccupied with school, and my friends, and exams coming up. Apart from Reg, friends rarely came to the house; I was worried they would see my dad, hidden away in the front parlour, or, even worse, hear him shouting.

I don't know what sort of civil service pension he received, but he must have got some sort of disability allowance, after all those years in the RAF and the MU and other government jobs, but I am sure it was minuscule.

10

My Mother

I still don't know to this day how my mother coped, how she managed to pay the rent, household bills, with four young children to feed and clothe. Yet when people asked her, she would say, 'Oh, bags of money, I've got bags of money.'

As far as I know, we did not get any free school meals, if such things existed, for I took dinner money to school. Each Monday there would be pandemonium while my mother rushed round the house, opening old purses, looking under the sofa, to find enough money for our bus fares and dinner money. Each week, Monday caught her by surprise, as if she had never seen it coming, as if this week would not contain a Monday.

She was always a bit scatty, not very well organised, not very neat and tidy, with few domestic skills like sewing, and not much of a cook either. Unlike my Aunt Jean, my father's sister, she could do everything – cook, sew, stitch, make, do, create, paint, as well as holding down a responsible job as a teacher and bringing up two girls.

My mother never complained or criticised people, but, as the years wore on, I think she did resent the fact that the

Davies relations, all of whom we imagined to be well off, did not do more to help in our time of need. They obviously had their own family concerns and problems. The most they seemed to do was have me to stay for holidays, which was great for me, got me out of our house, but they never invited the twins or Johnny. Perhaps it was because I was older, easier to look after.

The only real help we got with my father was once a year he went to some convalescent home near Grange-over-Sands, in the southern part of Lakeland. This was technically to help my mother, give her some respite care, rather than help my father, so some authorities must have been aware of the situation. My father hated it. When my mother visited him in the home he would shout at her, 'Get me the hell out of here!' He didn't seem to be aware that he was there for my mother's benefit not his, to give her a break.

My mother's escape was in books. While we owned no books of our own, apart from those three *Daily Express* volumes, there were always lots of library books in the house. She went every week to Tullie House, where Carlisle's library was then situated, and took out her full quota.

She preferred the novels she had loved before the war, rather than any modern, angry-young-men-type fiction, the sort of gritty northern novels that started to appear in the mid-1950s. She mostly reread authors she had already been through several times, such as Somerset Maugham, Galsworthy, H.G. Wells and Dickens most of all. She went through the whole of Dickens every year. I can still see her standing at the kitchen stove, waiting for the tatties to boil, while holding up *Oliver Twist* or *The Pickwick Papers* and laughing at her favourite scenes, insisting on reading out the good bits to anyone within earshot, whether they wanted to hear or not.

She rarely managed to sit down to read as she always seemed to be standing – at the cooker, at the sink, in the coal cellar, or outside in the washhouse. She stood up to eat, in the kitchen, at the stove, while going back and forward to give us our food at the table, maintaining she would sit down and eat hers later. No wonder she had varicose veins.

We had no fridge, no washing machine, no phone and of course no car, so very often she would shop twice a day, provisioning from meal to meal. I read somewhere that the average housewife in 1951 spent fifty-seven minutes a day on grocery shopping. I bet my mother spent more. She had no sense of direction and would often get lost. We would be left in the house, noses pressed up against the front window, longing for her to come home, worried we would never see her again. I got told off once for having allowed Johnny, when I was supposedly in charge of him, to stand up at the front window, on the windowsill, wearing only a vest, his little willy pressed against the cold window pane. My mother was 'black affronted' – i.e. seriously embarrassed – when she eventually appeared in the street, worrying more about what the neighbours might be thinking of this deprived-looking, abandoned family rather than Johnny's personal discomfort.

She never seemed to make lists of meals for the week, which other mothers apparently did. Most normal mothers, during the war and post-war years, had a strict routine, with the same meals every day of the week – roast on Sunday with roast potatoes and Yorkshire pudding, cold meat and salad on Monday, leftovers minced up the next day, stew on Wednesday, a pie or sausages the next day, fish on Friday, sandwiches or salad on Saturday.

It was not that she didn't care or was not interested – she worried all the time about what she was going to cook for us, asking us what we fancied, as if there was a choice. I don't think we ever had a roast, not of the lamb or pork or beef variety, and a chicken only appeared at Christmas. Mince was her standby, with tatties, which we had several times a week. She also made a lot of chips.

She did buy scrag ends of meat, which was all she could afford. It would be cooked forever, to make it edible, or minced up in her hand mincer, which was a lethal metal instrument, able to mince up even the boniest, scraggiest ends of meat. One of my jobs was to take it to pieces once a week, clean out the gristle and reassemble it.

If you ever got meat for school dinners, that was awful as well, all bony and gristly. You would try to swallow it, and start to feel sick, or slide it out of your mouth and hide it under the table. You couldn't leave it on the plate. There would be no pudding, if you didn't finish your meat, think of the poor people, there is a war on.

All salads were awful, raw grated carrots and thick lettuce leaves and a piece of tomato, plopped on the plate with no artistry or arrangement. Half a boiled egg if you were lucky. Perhaps a slice of Spam. There was no olive oil or balsamic vinegar, no fancy foreign stuff, but we did have Heinz Salad Cream, which you poured on everything, or HP Sauce or tomato ketchup to cover the chips. I hated the taste of salad cream, yet everyone scoffed it, treated it as a delicacy.

We did have olive oil, of course. You got it from the

chemist in a little bottle with a cork stopper and put it in your ear. The drops were meant to soften the wax and debris in your ear so that it would fall out. The thought of eating oil, putting it on your food, was laughable. Who on earth would want to do that? As for garlic, you had to be French to know what to do with that, and anyway it made your breath smell, forever, so who would want that either? Mushrooms were available, and people did get up early and go out to the Solway marshes to pick them, but not for us. They were also seen as funny foreign foods – in this case, the foreigners seemed to be the English.

Anything funny or fancy was considered unmanly. People who fussed over their food, knew the difference between one lettuce and another, preferred one brand of tea to another, must clearly be effeminate. Eating was a task, a routine, something that had to be done, not an experience.

There was one dish my mother did make which we all loved and that was stovies. I think that was the Scottish name for it. It was like a hotpot, or tattie pot, which most northern families lived on. It had some sort of cheap meat in it with a bit of black pudding, dripping, lots of potatoes and onions. It simmered away in the oven for ages and we all loved it.

We ate a lot of bread and dripping, which was very tasty, and also fried bread, even better, and, best of all, French toast. This was a treat when she could spare an egg, into which the bread was dipped before being fried – yum yum. With most foodstuffs rationed till the mid-fifties, it was not just a matter of having money for good food but enough coupons.

The big treat on Sunday morning was to have a fried breakfast, often the only egg we were allowed during the week, plus bacon and fried bread. Every time my mother allowed us a whole egg she would tell us the same old story about a poor family in the Gorbals during the war. The mother would stand outside the tenement, so everyone could hear, and shout at her children who were playing, 'Come and get the top off your dad's egg.' This was the mother showing off that they had eggs that day. She laughed and laughed, every time she repeated it. She also had a similar supposedly funny story about a young woman who had just got engaged who stood at her door, her hand in the air displaying her engagement ring for all to see, who would cry out loudly, 'Has anyone seen my milk-man?' She also loved an appalling song called 'The Laughing Policeman' and rushed to turn up the radio whenever it came on, almost having hysterics, laughing at it. She enjoyed all the subtleties of Dickens, yet laughed at this awful record. I assume it was the memories it brought back.

She did make some good puddings once a week, the cooked ones, not jelly and custard or tinned fruit with Carnation evaporated milk, though we liked those as well. She made what we called steamed puddings, boiled in a bag, full of lard and flour, with some fruit hidden inside, such as apple or rhu-barb, topped off with whatever sweet stuff she had to hand, such as jam or marmalade.

Everybody also had a lot of rice pudding, especially at school meals, and spotted dick and, worst of all, sago, semolina and tapioca. These were traditionally hated by most children, especially girls, who would go 'yuck!' and pretend to be sick. I rather liked all the puddings.

There was no central heating in the house, just a coal fire. My bedroom, and my bed which I shared with Johnny, was normally absolutely freezing. In winter the window frames would be covered with frost – on the inside. I devised a way of getting into my clothes and putting my socks on while still in bed. Otherwise if you stepped out of bed in your bare feet and on to the linoleum, which covered all the floors in the house, you might be there till spring, frozen to the floor.

Behind the open fire, stuck somehow into the wall, was a small boiler which gave hot water for a bath. Yes, we were lucky in our relatively modern council estate, unlike so many people. We had our own indoor bathroom and a lavatory where, if we were lucky, there would be a roll of Izal toilet paper. It was thin, like tracing paper, and scratchy and horrible and felt uncomfortable on your bottom. Almost as bad as when I was in Motherwell visiting my relations in the Buildings where the communal lav was on the landing, opened with a massive iron key. The only way to wipe your bottom was with torn sheets of newspaper, hung up on a nail.

Baths at Caird Avenue were very rare. It took forever to heat enough water and our bathroom was horrible, so unattractive with wet towels lying around. Later, we had a copper boiler installed in the cupboard beside the fireplace, a so-called immersion heater, the water heated by an electric rod, but this was hardly any better and very slow. After one person had a bath, it took about two hours to heat enough for the next one.

In the washhouse outside, my mother hand-washed all our clothes, using a dolly tub, into which hot water was poured, which again took forever, and a scrubbing board, with the help of either a big slab of carbolic soap or some of the new trendy but expensive soap powders such as Rinso, Oxydol, Omo and Persil. Then she put the clothes through a big old mangle to get rid of most of the water and hung the clothes out on the washing line in the back garden.

Monday was wash day for most people and on Monday mornings all mothers prayed for it not to rain. Even if it stayed fairly dry, clothes were still pretty damp and for the rest of the week they would be draped on a clotheshorse round the fire. The constant fug in the living room was a combination of steam and smoke from the coal fire. Not ideal for anyone with asthma.

The walls too were usually festooned with clothes, such as my shirts, once I became a teenager, while the twins had their slips and dresses hanging there. There was a picture rail round most of the walls, from which pictures never hung, used instead for hanging clothes. My sisters, as they got older, used to sit around in their bra and knickers waiting for their frocks to dry on the clotheshorse or picture rail before they went out. I shouted at them to go to their bedroom and not lounge around (un)dressed like that.

As well as the coalmen, other horses and carts went regularly up and down the street, delivering milk, potatoes, vegetables and other goods. My mother was constantly sending me out with a shovel to collect up any horse manure to put on the garden. Our garden was a dump, nothing grew there; my father never attended to it, even when he was well, but my mother had got it in her head that if we only threw on enough horse manure it would miraculously turn into Kew Gardens.

There was a lawn of sorts at the front and I would be forced to cut it with the hand lawnmower, which was rusty and useless, and also trim the front privet hedge. I would moan and moan – 'do I have to?' – then rush at it, making a real hash of it. As the oldest, I was expected to do it, Johnny being too young and the twins being girls and not expected to help with things like the garden.

The twins, when they were young, had long, curly fair hair which looked nice but caused endless tears and tantrums when my mother tried to brush it. She could never get it straight and they would never sit still. Annabelle grew up rather slender and pretty, while Marion was taller and more solid. At school, Marion always protected Annabelle if she got picked on – in fact, Marion was known to beat up girls at the Maggie Sewell and gave awful cheek to any teacher who told Annabelle off.

After my father became a full-time invalid, bedridden at home, I found that two or three of the teachers at the Creighton became especially nice to me, taking me aside, asking how things were at home. I was a bit taken aback by this. I never told them he was ill, so I don't know how they found out. I don't think my mother ever went up to the school. She wouldn't have been able to find her way there anyway. So perhaps there were some sort of social services, keeping an eye on us, through the MU or the civil service.

Despite all this deprivation, with so little money coming into the house, I went to violin lessons. The twins had gone to piano lessons for a few weeks, hence the piano in the parlour, till my father took over the room. It always surprised people when I told them. My family's situation did not appear to suggest the possibility of such middle-class activities.

I started the violin when my father was still at work full time, when I was about ten, and it was all my mother's doing. Her father had played the fiddle, self-taught, and she loved

Scottish tunes and Scottish dancing and was very keen that I should learn music. Though she might have appeared feckless, and un-pushy, when she got something into her head, she would nag on and on, or sigh and look sad, till eventually you did what she wanted.

I was sent to a teacher called Alf Adamson, who had a country dance band that toured the Borders. He also had a full-time job as a driver and delivery man for Ringtons tea. That was all they delivered, door to door, packets of tea. There were lots of products like that, brought door to door. How on earth did they make any profit?

I hated practising, always leaving it to the last minute. I did learn to read music, and enjoyed listening to music, country stuff as well as classical, but I soon realised I had no aptitude. My mother insisted I carry on. I must have gone to violin lessons for about five years in all, for I last appeared in public aged fifteen at the Carlisle and District Music Festival, held every year at the Methodist Hall. I came fourth, out of four, in my section. I think by then, because he had found out my father was an invalid, Mr Adamson was no longer charging my mother – out of sympathy. Can't have been to encourage my talent . . .

I always felt guilty, that I was letting her down, that she had invested so many hopes in me, and presumably quite a bit of money, when she had so little, with nothing to show for it. I also felt ashamed and guilty that I hated going to church with her, especially, oh horrors, if she took my arm. I was of course, the man of the house, now that my father was an invalid.

Warwick Road Presbyterian Church was so dark and dismal and depressing, full of elderly, stiff, uncomfortable people, dressed in elderly, stiff clothes, most of them Scottish, with a dour minister, endless prayers and awful sermons. I quite enjoyed the hymns, though, despite the fact that the congregations were sparse and none of them could sing.

All four of us children had to go to Sunday school in the afternoons, our faces long, our hearts sinking. Traditionally, this was the time when working-class parents had their one moment of the week of sexual bliss, or not. Not in my parents' case, once my father was bedridden.

The Sunday school teacher, a very small, angular spinster, made me learn one psalm a week for a year, which I would have to recite, before starting another. At the end of the year I was presented with a Lord Wharton Bible, which was considered a huge honour. I don't know who Lord Wharton was but presumably a Presbyterian who had left funds. I used to wish he hadn't bothered.

Very often my mother would force me to accompany her again, to evening service. Force is the wrong verb. If I said no, I hate that church, which I did, she would not argue but put on her sad, mournful, soulful face. I would give in. And off we would go, me trying hard to reject her arm in my mine.

Although we said our prayers, and went to church, I don't believe she was particularly religious. My father had no interest at all and never went, even when he was fit. All the same he would not allow me to ride my bike on a Sunday or play football. The whole Scottish ethos was that Sunday was a day on which no work could be done and no pleasure or play of any sort should be enjoyed. That was how they had been brought up. That was what they believed.

'A garden is a lovesome thing, God wot!' she would say,

looking out of the window at our jungle of a back garden, then smile and pause. 'Hunter, what does "God wot" mean?' As if I knew.

She endlessly quoted great chunks of half-remembered poems and phrases from her childhood such as 'They told me, Heraclitus, they told me you were dead' and 'There's a breathless hush in the close tonight'. She could reel off loads of Kipling and all of Robert Burns, whether we asked her to or not.

She was fiercely, proudly Scottish and got upset, huffed and harrumphed at any criticism. When I read out figures saying that Glasgow was the crime capital of the UK, with more razor gangs than anywhere else, she would sniff and say, 'If you believe that, you'll believe anything.' She had once read a line in the *Daily Express* in which someone was quoted as saying that Motherwell (her hometown) was 'a long dreary town'. She never forgave the paper for that.

Like most of her generation, she believed Culloden was some sort of triumph not a massacre, Robert the Bruce did no wrong, the Duke of Cumberland was a butcher and Robert Burns was a paragon of all the virtues. I delighted in telling her once that it had been revealed that Robert Burns had had eleven children out of wedlock. I might have made up the numbers just to annoy her – but the effect was the same. She dismissed it as lies and English propaganda.

She had lots of one-word replies or observations, on the surface banal, meaningless to outsiders, but we knew the depths and subtleties and implications they covered. When she said, 'Help' or 'Oh help' she was not in danger or pain – she was being gently satirical or mocking. It was the equivalent of a raised eyebrow because someone had done or said something not quite decent, like showing naked flesh, making a rude joke on the radio, someone in the street wearing something outlandish. It was a form of non-critical criticism.

It was also a response to someone who was being emotionally over the top, who was gushing or being pretentious. By saying 'Oh help', she could never be accused of being outspoken, rude or critical, but we all knew that in her quiet way she was.

She despised anyone who said they were suffering from their nerves, under stress, though of course she would never say so. The worst was a sniff, followed by, 'Och aye, we could all have a nervous breakdown, if we had the time . . .' I never saw her cry and if the subject came up, because some other woman in the street had been seen sobbing or tearful, she would just shrug her shoulders. 'If I started crying, I would never stop.'

One of her more pointed comments was, 'Anything else while your mouth's warm?' This indicated her patience was being well tested by now, that she was becoming fed up with one of us moaning on – twining, as we said in Carlisle – generally being selfish and a pain, i.e. me.

'Lady Muck' was a put-down for anyone trying to be posh, overdressed, or fancying themselves, though never to their face. It is, of course, a common expression, used everywhere and still around. At one time there was the male equivalent, Lord Muck, but you don't hear that today. I imagine all regions, all languages, all times have their own version of Lady Muck.

On our council estate, it felt that everyone was equal, we

were all in the same boat, no one was worse off than anyone else, so you didn't really feel resentful of others. You knew, without realising it, they were all much the same as us. So anyone trying to come the abdabs, to put on a show, not stopping to chat in the street, changing their front-door knocker to a bell, installing Venetian blinds, wearing a best frock to hang out the washing, was not approved of.

Rationing, and the post-war austerities and penny-pinching, helped to create this feeling of equality. Even if by chance you had a bit more money than anyone else, what could you spend it on, where could you go for a flash, showy time? The consumer boom did not happen till the sixties – and not everywhere, and not to all people, and certainly not in our family.

The prime example in the fifties of Lady Muck was Lady Docker (1906–1983), a figure half-mocked and half-adored by the general newspaper-reading public. In the forties and fifties she delighted the nation by marrying three times, pulling herself up from being a working girl into the aristocracy, or so she thought, when she married Sir Bernard Docker, chairman of Daimler cars. She was always dressed to the nines and being driven in gold-plated cars. In 1952 she was banned from the casino at Monte Carlo for slapping a waiter. In 1954 she paid a regal visit to a coal mine and invited some of the miners back to her yacht, where she gave them champagne and danced the hornpipe for them. 'Who do you think you are – Lady Docker?' For a time, this took over from Lady Muck in the nation's store of mirth and mocking remarks.

A lot of my mother's expressions were Scottish, such as 'Ah kent his faither' – meaning, I knew his father. In other words, how can he/she be much good when I know where they came from? Another put-down.

'You never died a winter yet': I think that was Scottish, because I can hear it being said in a Scottish accent – meaning cheer up, you've lasted so far.

Many of her pet phrases came from the radio or even earlier from the music hall, some with origins unknown, handed down through the generations. 'Tell that to the troops' meant you don't believe them. 'It will all come out in the wash', still used, meaning all will be revealed or explained in due course, usually to someone's detriment. 'A little stiff from Rugby' was her reply to being asked how she felt. It always made her smile, as if she had never said it before.

One thing she never talked about, or could ever bear even to mention, was a dreadful accident that happened to both Marion and Johnny, though at different times. For each of them, especially Marion, it clouded their teenage years, and, in the case of Marion, probably had long-term psychological effects.

I was not present on either occasion, thank God, presumably at school or playing football in the street or staying in Cambuslang. Or have I blanked both episodes from my mind as too horrendous to remember?

My mother had a pan of water on the stove, getting ready to boil even more potatoes, when little Marion, aged about eight, crept up behind. While my mother's attention was elsewhere, Marion knocked over the whole pan of boiling, bubbling, scalding water all over herself. The scream, apparently, could be heard two streets away.

Exactly a year later, the same thing happened again, this

time to Johnny, then about six. Marion would never talk about it, so we never knew what her memories were, or what she had been doing, but Johnny has a memory of picking up a stair rod. We did have a carpet of sorts on our stairs, but the rods were always coming loose and the carpet kept getting fankled. Johnny was running around with this stair rod, waving it in the air, pretending it was a sword. He ran into the kitchen, still waving it – and pulled a pan of boiling water all over himself.

My mother didn't talk about either accident because, I assume, she always felt she was to blame, letting a child anywhere near a stove with water being boiled. But she had four young children, dragging at her apron for attention in a very small kitchen. Perhaps, and I hate even now to suggest it, she had been negligent, absent-minded, possibly with a book in her hand, and didn't see or hear either child approaching.

They each suffered the most awful, nasty, painful third-degree burns, with all the skin on one of their arms coming off completely. My mother, in desperation, had put butter on their arms, which is the last thing you should do (cold water is best). Each time, having put on the butter, she wrapped them in a towel and rushed to the infirmary – which meant taking two buses.

I hate to think what today's social services might have surmised or suspected. Being called twice to the same house for exactly the same sort of accident could well have led them to issue some sort of social work order.

Both Marion and Johnny went through the rest of their lives with one arm disfigured. It never cleared up. It was always totally apparent and horrendous. It did not matter, in theory, too much for a boy, as Johnny grew up tall and strong, worked a lot outside, his arms went brown every summer, but it was tough for a girl once she became a teenager, wanting to wear pretty sleeveless dresses.

Even on the hottest summer day, my mother would suggest to Marion that she should wear a cardigan. Which, of course, added to and fuelled any complex she might already have had. My mother, clearly, could not bear to see the disfigured arm, reminding her of the accident.

I think the trauma – which is a word we never used then – might have been almost as severe for my mother as it was for Marion and Johnny themselves.

All that compulsive reading, always with a Dickens on the go, was presumably a form of escape, a way to hide from the reality of her life, of the situation she found herself in, with a sick husband, accidents to her children. She was not the type ever to show her emotions, which were never revealed in the world in which she had grown up. The idea of being stressed or under pressure or needing therapy would have been laughable. And my mother would certainly have scoffed if we had ever known anyone who was going to a therapist. You battled on, did not share your worries or fears, chin up, keep cheerful, it will all come out in the wash, we never died a winter yet.

I suppose I am a bit like her. I find it hard to reveal or share emotions. I make silly jokes at un-silly times, thinking I am being amusing, entertaining, when really it is my way of coping, escaping, when awful things have happened, which of course they have, in everyone's life. My sister Annabelle is a bit like me. Appalling things have struck her loved ones, yet she has always appeared cheerful, not wishing to discuss it or complain or reveal. On the other hand, her twin sister Marion, when she grew up, turned out to be completely different, saw no shame in going into therapy, more than willing to share her feelings and emotions.

One of the problems my mother had, unlike me, was that she never had a proper, fully trusted, fully loving confidant. My father, even before his illness, appeared unaware of her needs, or emotions, was never there when wanted. She often talked, with a sigh and a weary smile, of having to get up in the night on her own because Johnny was crying, the twins were both sick and I was racked with asthma, the four of us needing attention at the same time. All my father did was pull the blankets over his head.

She had no woman friends, none she was close to, no relations who would rush to help when required. She had no social life, never went out, not when we were growing up, never had holidays. She had three sisters but only one she ever talked about, Maggie, who had emigrated to Canada many years ago. Tea and reading, those were her two pleasures in life – plus, if she was lucky, and in funds, a bar of Cadbury's milk chocolate, dunking each dark square gently into the tea then sucking on it, licking its nectar, her face lighting up.

She did have a very sweet tooth. I once played an awful trick on her. Somehow I had acquired a bottle of some very bitter-tasting liquid, perhaps essence of lemons, or even some chemical from a chemistry set, and I told her it was really sweet, 'Mum, it's like chocolate, you'll love it, here, taste this, Mum.' She looked at it suspiciously before very slowly, hesitantly, taking a sip. Her face was immediately contorted. She began spitting it out, almost in tears, saying her mouth was on fire. The more she spat it out, the worse it seemed to get. I felt so guilty. Why had I been so cruel? I didn't actually know it was as bitter as it was, but even so, I should not have done it. She made a face when she ate normal things like gooseberries, unless there was a ton of sugar on top. So I must have known how she would react.

I don't remember her ever shouting at us, disciplining us in any way, but she could not have been all that soft and feckless. She got us all to bed at the right time every night, no one took any liberties. Her way was to look sad and hurt, if we would not do what she wanted us to do, till we melted, and gave in, feeling sorry for her.

She never wanted to attract attention, for people to be aware of her, or feel sorry for her (the reason she always maintained she had lots of money). Looking again at those photographs of her when young, courting with my father, when she looked fairly fashionable, she was also rather striking, yet she never felt she was attractive, or was interested in her appearance. She was not helped by her own mother, who convinced her when young that she was too tall and ungainly. On train trips, her mother would make her stand up in the carriage for the other passengers to inspect: 'Don't you think she's going to be a giant!' She was not abnormally tall; it was just that as a girl she grew quickly. I never considered her as a big woman, perhaps a bit angular, but she got it into her head while young that she was some sort of freak, who could therefore never look nice or be attractive, so why bother.

When she did put on her best coat or hat, to go somewhere

up town, such as church or the doctor's, always looking perfectly presentable, the moment she got home she would take everything off, put her clothes away, so glad and relieved to get into her old horrible shoes and her stained pinny, feeling comfortable at last.

I have turned out much the same. I do have one good suit, which I avoid wearing, as it does not feel comfy, and I am always scared of spilling food on it. I take it off as soon as I am through the front door, flopping into my horrible shorts and stained T-shirt and sandals.

Describing my mother can make her sound rather pathetic and sad, and with age she did go prematurely lined, which didn't help. In repose, caught unawares, she did look worried and mournful. As we all can. But the real her was bright and witty, in conversation and in letters. I might have been ashamed of her at times, when my smart friends came to the door and she appeared in her awful clothes, like an old bag woman, clutching a mug of tea to her cheek, but on the other hand I did boast to my friends about her reading habits. None of the mothers of my friends, even the grammar school ones, who had middle-class parents, or so I assumed, seemed to read any books, or have knowledge or interest in literature.

I didn't of course properly appreciate or understand the struggles she must have been having at the time, being interested only in myself, because of her constant reassuring, uncomplaining, selfless attitude to life.

There were no major dramas, no early deaths, no abuse, no self-harm, no suicides, no mental breakdowns, no slums, no poverty, no homelessness, no starvation. So, on the face of it, what were the problems? She always managed to pay the rent, to feed and clothe us, keep us clean and on the straight and narrow.

But really, when I think back, she had a hard life. As did millions of other quietly forgotten mothers, who were only trying their best. I think, though, that she did have it worse, at that particular time, than most of the other mothers around us on that council estate. The fifties were a pretty shitty time for my mother.

11

ENTERTAINMENTS

But we were happy then, oh yes. For us children, for almost all of the time, there was so much fun and entertainment, oh yes.

People who write about the fifties today do tend to go on about the rotten food and the crap clothes, the domestic hardships for women and the freezing houses. All perfectly true, but we who were there also remember the freedom, playing out all day long, going in the woods, building dams and dens, being allowed outside for hours with no one bothering us or wondering and worrying where we were.

In both Carlisle and Dumfries, despite being smallish towns, affording us an appearance of urban life, we did have woods and fields around, but of course the biggest freedom and fun to be had was on the streets, on our estate, playing football under the lampposts or endless skipping games. Having empty streets with no motor cars, that was a huge advantage, though we didn't know it at the time.

I know that children, on the whole, say they were happy, which is how most of us choose to remember. It is childhood that is making us happy, rather than our surroundings. It was a golden age, the sun always shone. Most generations have always looked back warmly, believing those days have gone forever – and for the worse. It is their childhood that has gone.

But seriously, truthfully, honestly, the conditions and attitudes of today are different. There are new temptations, distractions, stresses, desires and pressures, so many new gadgets which children feel they must have, while the parents thrust their own fears upon their children, about sex and drink and drugs – problems that seem to arise at an even earlier age with each generation.

Marbles – can you believe I had such super fun for hours playing marbles in the gutter? Seems laughable now. You would get run over by a 4×4 in ten minutes if you tried it now. Off all day playing games in the woods, cowboys and Indians with bows and arrows, gurdling for tiddlers in streams and becks, climbing trees. The police would be called out in half an hour and all the local paedophiles lined up. Making go-carts out of broken-down prams, those old-fashioned sorts, with the big undercarriages and massive wheels, fixed on to biscuit boxes, with a steering wheel – God, some of those were incredible, and so quick. Not be allowed to day, health and safety.

So many of the games were dangerous, the climbing and mock battles, going into empty buildings, clambering up scaffolding on new buildings, hiding in air-raid shelters. We seemed to have cuts and bruises all the time – for which you were always given a dab of iodine, which stung far worse than the cut, then you ran out again.

Even the games girls played could be violent, if you got whacked with one of those massive skipping ropes they tied to a lamppost and then stretched across the street. Once it got faster and faster, it could knock you out if you mistimed it, especially if you were trying to remember the words to all the chants that had to accompany each game.

Football, though, was my first and longest love, playing all day, then under the lampposts in the dark in the evening or in the lotties. It was usually with a tennis ball, for street footballers rarely had a proper leather football – that was only for organised games or school football. Leather balls were expensive and once it rained, they weighed a ton. Cheap plastic balls had not come in. Only the children of Lord and Lady Muck had real leather boots.

The street games would stretch down the whole street, sometimes twenty-a-side, with people joining in, coming and going. There were no cars, of course, to interfere or distract or run us over. We played till the last person wanted to play, even if you were down to one-a-side, or till our mothers finally called us in.

In the lotties, on grass, even though it was all lumpy and bumpy, we had rags or jumpers for goalposts and played complicated games, even if we were just two-a-side. One side would be kicking in, or attacking one set of goals, till a certain point, with the other side defending, then we changed round. There was one game called Worky, short for Workington, whereby if the attacking side scored a bye, i.e. you missed the goal and it went for a goal kick, then you changed round and the other side attacked.

If a game had gone on too long, like all week, then eventually you would hear the cry of 'NEXT GOAL WINS!' coming from the lotties.

I woke up each day looking forward to playing football, my life and pleasure revolved around it, playing at school at playtime, and before and after school, and then in the street at home. I usually kicked a ball on my way to school, or the shops, getting in everyone's way. I was consumed by playing football, like nothing else, probably nothing else since.

The thing about football is that you need very little tackle – just a ball of sorts and some vaguely flat ground. Most of all, anyone can have a go, big or small, weak or strong, gangly or athletic, droopy or dynamic. The most awkward, ungainly-looking kid would often turn out to be a wizard when he got on the ball. No wonder the whole world plays football, from the most affluent country to the most deprived.

I was aware of this even when young. I used to imagine, while kicking a ball on my own, that boys just like me were playing football in the street, in every corner of the planet. I was communing with them. And also communing with all the boys who had ever played football in the past.

If no one else was around, no mother would let them out, or the weather was too grim, I would play on my own. I must have spent hours kicking a tennis ball against our washhouse wall. I would practise returning it with my left and then my right foot. As I was going to be a professional footballer, I needed to be able to use either foot.

When not playing, I cut out and collected photographs from the newspapers of my favourite players. We didn't have a pink 'un or a green 'un printed in Dumfries or Carlisle, the Saturday afternoon edition of the local newspaper, containing all the football news, but often someone from a bigger town, who had the advantage of these wonders, would leave a copy in a bin or on a park bench.

My best fave player for many years was Billy Houliston, which dated from my Dumfries years. He was a bullet-headed centre forward who played for Queen of the South, the Dumfries team. He managed three caps for Scotland, which was unusual for a provincial player. When Scotland played, I would be shaking with nerves, unable to bear it if they got beaten by England, my little heart thumping as I listened to the game on the radio.

Aged fourteen, after all those years playing in the street and the allotments, convinced I was a natural, I joined a proper team, a junior football team, Kingstown Rovers, who were in the Carlisle and District Under-15 league. The manager, the one who picked me, also happened to be our milkman. I suspect he took pity on me, knowing our family situation, when he asked me to sign on. You did, in fact, have to sign a form, which was thrilling, making it feel ever so professional. We had proper strips – red and white quarters, same design as Bristol Rovers, though they are in blue.

I managed to acquire a pair of real boots from the Co-op, which meant we got a divvy. They had proper studs and long white laces which I washed for the first few weeks, then gave up. I bought spare studs in a packet and a tin of dubbin. Our games had proper referees. We had a home pitch at Kingstown, and real nets, and even a dressing room, which was in a chapel hall. Playing away, on the other side of Carlisle, or out in the country, we often had to get changed on the side of the pitch, which was horrible. Playing in the rain is not a problem as all footballers know, at any level. In fact, it enhances the physical elements and closeness to nature, but afterwards, returning to your pile of clothes, they would be totally soaked. I would drag myself home on my bike in sodden clothes, wet and shivering, as well as knackered after being battered by some rural lumps.

I imagined myself as a skilful inside right. That was the term at the time. All football teams had the same eleven named positions and had done so for almost a hundred years: goalie, right back, left back, centre half, right half, left half, right outside, inside right, centre forward, inside left, outside left. They were numbered 1–11, so a number 11 was always an outside left. In professional football, he was often a little weedy bloke, usually Scottish, who ran up and down the wing, did lots of tricks, beat the thick-necked fullback, and finally crossed the ball. He never tackled, never went back to defend, just hugged the touchlines. It meant he was out of the game for ages. Such fancy-dan luxury players have all gone. Now everyone has to be a non-stop workhorse.

While awfully skilful in my head, I did have one problem: I was so weak and weedy that even wearing proper boots, with iron-hard toecaps and rock-hard leather at the ankles, I would kick the ball my hardest – and it rolled about six feet. I just did not have the puff or power to make a killer pass to our centre forward. So my thing became clever short passes, then shouting at the other player for not reading my clever pass.

My love of football has never left me. I played Sunday football till I was fifty, despite two cartilage operations, which was stupid. In the end, I could still play football once a week – but not recover from playing football. Eventually I had to have a new knee. I still miss football, all the time. No other physical, competitive activity has taken its place.

Playing football got rid of so much energy, anguish and bad temper. I never knew I had a temper, till I played football. I consider myself peaceful and placid. I never shout at people in real life, get angry, dislike or hate anyone. But on the pitch when I played football, I was screaming all the time, usually at my own team. Or myself. I realise now it was a brilliant release. Not just a pleasure.

For several years I was a keen Boy Scout. Warwick Road Presbyterian did not have a troop, so, along with Reg, I joined Chapel Street Church of Scotland, the 17th Carlisle Troop. Reg and I remained firm friends, despite the fact that I was at the Creighton. We did most things together – except play football, which he hated – and he included me when he was doing things with his grammar school friends.

We managed to turn the 17th Carlisle into an anti-Boy Scouts scout troop. We mocked and poured scorn, disdaining all those badge-baggers who seemed to dominate all the other troops, who could hardy move for all the badges on their arms, determined to make it as a King's Scout. Reg and I were eventually made patrol leaders, even though we had not one badge between us, apart from our Tenderfoot Badge, which you had to pass to be a Boy Scout. We played Bulldog Drummond in the church hall, did marches and ceremonies, but the best thing, and the reason why we stayed in so long, was the Boy Scout camp. Neither of our families went away on holidays, so going to Edinburgh, as we did one year, and then later to Aberdeen, or just for the odd weekend to Ratlingate, which was a Scout campsite to the west of Carlisle, was a wonderful escape and adventure. Ratlingate seemed miles and miles out in the wild country, for I once walked all the way home, carrying my pack, having spent my bus fare, but I now realise it was just in the suburbs, hardly in the real country. I thought all the Scout leaders were great blokes, lovely men, and later, when I heard people tittering about Scout leaders and what some of them got up to, I could not believe it.

On Saturday morning most kids went to the children's matinee at the local cinema. In our case it was the Lonsdale, the best cinema in town, and we were all members of the ABC Minors. Each week kids whose birthday it was were invited up on stage; we all cheered and they got a present. It was surprising how often the same kids went up week after week. We were shown a cowboy film, a serial or a comedy, and we all screamed and shouted, either in terror or laughter. Slightly older kids, about fifteen or sixteen, were made monitors and were supposed to keep the rowdier element under control, but the more advanced of them used their superior position, and the dark, to canoodle with their girlfriends. Canoodle? Did we use that word? Sounds very stagy. Canoodling was probably what they did in some of the films, not that we liked any soppy films, with kissing and stuff. We wanted the Lone Ranger or Laurel and Hardy.

Members of the ABC Minors had a song we sang each Saturday – and I can remember the words after all these years, which were sung to the tune of 'Blaze Away'. They put the words up on a screen and a blob bounced over each word so you could sing along.

We are the boys and girls well known as Minors of the ABC
And every Saturday we line up
To see the films we like and shout aloud with glee
We love to laugh and have a singsong
Such a happy crowd are we
We're all pals together, the Minors of the ABC.

I assumed at the time that the ABC Minors was special to Carlisle, so how lucky were we, but later on, when I went out into the big wide world, well a bit broader than Carlisle, I discovered everyone of my age in the fifties had been an ABC Minor. Or similar.

It was a badge of belonging, being an ABC Minor, and it is a badge now. The further you get away from your childhood, the more you find bonds between you and others the same age, despite their backgrounds, regions or social class. The fifties has many passwords, secret signs by which we can identify each other. But I suppose all generations do.

When I got a bit older, I would go to the theatre in Carlisle, Her Majesty's, a fine old Victorian traditional theatre, with stalls, balconies and gods high up, where once Charlie Chaplin performed. A touring rep came once a year, the Salisbury Arts, and put on West End plays, usually by J.B. Priestley, which my mother admired and I would sometimes go with her, if she paid.

There were about ten cinemas in Carlisle, and lying awake at night when I can't sleep I often try to remember all their names, and where they were. There was the Lonsdale, the City, Palace, Botchergate, Public Hall, Rex, Regal, Stanley and the Argyl in Harraby. Oh no, I won't sleep tonight. I am sure there were ten . . .

No one had TV, so going to the flicks was the big excitement. People often went twice a week, so the queues were enormous, right round the block. You stood there, in the cold and rain, as the line crawled forward, still with no sight of the cinema, worried that you had invested all this time and would not get in. Some jobsworth in a stained uniform with epaulettes would stick his arm out just as you got to the head of the queue and say, 'That's it, house full.'

Queues were a way of life, for buses, football games, shops, the cinema, almost everything. People were so obedient, never queue-jumping, or else you would soon get told off. I suppose it was a hangover from the war, when we all had to be obedient, if we were going to beat Hitler. Many had been in the services of some sort and were used to doing what they were told.

For many years, Britain was caricatured abroad as being a nation of pathetic, patient, craven queuers, whereas in Europe it was always a scrum, each person for themselves. That is all gone. At my local bus stop people don't queue, they just sit or stand around and then get on in any old order, not worrying about people jumping ahead. It is partly because there are more regular buses, and also no conductors – just press your card, so the bus won't go until we all are on, so what's the hurry? Has the bus system changed our characters or are we no longer a nation that submits to queuing and regimentation?

I joined the junior library at Tullie House, a scary place with beady-eyed librarians with steely specs and grey buns who would chuck you out if you talked or mucked around, but, oh, the excitement of going there and finding a *Just William* or a *Biggles* book. If you found several, and could only take out two, you would secrete one for your friends, or for when you next returned, sticking it in the reference part with the nature books or boring stuff like that, where no normal boy would look. A stern librarian would be watching from her station and bawl you out. I do honestly think that no book since has given me such pure joy as the *Just William* stories.

As exams got more frequent at secondary school, I did plough through most of Dickens and even dragged my weary eyes though Dostoevsky and other so-called classic authors, but dear God, they were so dense and dreary before you got to anything remotely interesting or amusing. But with *Just William*, I was always totally hooked from page one, laughing all the way through. The stories were set in some southern middle-class posh village, and William's parents lived in the sort of house I had never seen, with staff and tennis courts, and yet I so identified completely with him.

Biggles gave me equal enjoyment, though without any of the laughs. With William and Biggles, it was so wonderful, having discovered them, to find there was a whole series of books, which I gobbled up, just as quickly as I could find the next one in the library.

One day, Reg and I decided to write a fan letter to Capt. W.E. Johns, the author of *Biggles*. We thought it was such an amazing, original idea and we told everyone, not realising thousands of boys must be doing the same. We didn't know if he was alive or dead, or if it that was his real name.

Months went by then, to our astonishment, we got a reply.

Reg had actually put his address on the letter, though it was our joint idea, and we had shared the cost of the stamp, so we argued over who owned the letter. We agreed to keep it for a year each. Reg got it first. But he never gave it back to me. The rotter. Said he couldn't find it. It could have been the start of my collecting hobby, which takes up so much of my life today.

In the comics I read, like *The Hotspur* and *Wizard*, there were always public-school stories about a life and people I had never met. When younger, I had loved *The Dandy* and *Beano*, but the appeal there was easier to understand, as it was funny, silly stuff for kids. *The Hotspur* and *Wizard*, along with the *Adventure*, *Rover* and *Champion*, all seemed like grown-up comics, with lots to read and very small print. We swapped with each other or bought our own when we were in funds. 'In funds' – that was the sort of phrase Billy Bunter would have used.

Being Scottish, and having the *Sunday Post* delivered each week, we loved their comic strips, *Oor Wullie* and *The Broons*. At Christmas, if we were lucky, our mother managed to buy one or both of the Christmas annuals.

The biggest source of entertainment for all the nation was the radio. The BBC's first live radio broadcast was in 1920, but it was not till the thirties that most families in the land had a set or access to one. Ours was stuck into the lightbulb socket in the ceiling in the middle of the living room and had to be unplugged when we wanted to insert a lightbulb. The wire got frayed and tangled, so goodness knows how we never set fire to the house.

I loved *Children's Hour*, which had been going since the 1920s. It was from five to six, after we had got home from school and after our tea. It was aimed at boys and girls from five onwards, introduced by 'Uncle Mac' – Derek McCulloch, our favourite uncle. So we were told. There was a series called *Toytown*, starring Larry the Lamb and featuring a character called Mr Grouser the Grocer. I liked *Norman and Henry Bones: The Boy Detectives* and also *Out With Romany*, which was a nature programme about two children being taken on a country walk. I never knew, during all the years I listened to it, that Romany himself was living beside us in Carlisle. His real name was the Reverend George Bramwell Evens and he was a local Methodist minister who wrote a lot of books for children.

We always tuned into the Scottish Home Service, where we also had Kathleen Garscadden, 'Aunty Kathleen' – obviously our favourite aunty. If we entered any competitions we wrote to Queen Margaret Drive in Glasgow. Which I often did – and won myself a silver pencil. There was a very funny Scottish serial called *Tammy Troot*, about a trout, and a long-running series we all listened to as a family called *The McFlannels*, about a Glasgow tenement family. All the surnames were based on materials, such as Mrs McCotton. My favourite Scottish comedian was Jimmy Logan, whose catchphrase was 'Sausages is the boys', one of those dopey sayings you can't believe ever caught on. Stanley Baxter was even cleverer and funnier, as he did lots of different voices, many of them women, all a bit camp, but of course I didn't know what camp meant. Like *Round the Horne* and all their double entendres, we laughed, without quite knowing the joke.

ITMA was probably the most popular wartime programme. My father particularly loved it, laughed all the way through, cheered him up when his favourite characters appeared, such as Mrs Mopp, who always said, 'Can I do you now, sir?' There might have been a suggestive undercurrent to that question, reminiscent of Max Miller and thirties music-hall humour, or George Formby with his little stick of Blackpool rock. During the war, the government kept tight hold of anything not only secret but possibly unwholesome.

ITMA began in 1939 and the title stood for *It's That Man Again*, originally a newspaper reference to Hitler, who was always in the papers, but it was transferred to Tommy Handley, the star of the show. As a primary school kid I never found it as amusing as my parents did. The same stock phrases seem to be repeated all the time, and the same situations, but the nation loved it.

I preferred by far *The Goon Show*, which began later, in 1951, and seemed so much cleverer and more anarchic than *ITMA*. My parents could not see what was funny about it, so of course that was another plus. The sound effects parodied the traditional BBC productions, making footsteps go on forever, or faster and faster. My mother thought the silly voices were just silly, but at school we smart boys in the A stream, and at the grammar school, loved them, competing to repeat the jokes and do the voices of Neddie Seagoon or Bloodnok.

I found Wilfred Pickles, with Mabel at the piano, who went round the country doing corny interviews, a total pain, but he was immensely popular. He had a strong Lancashire accent but, to my ears, he was trying to be affected and posh and came out sounding condescending. *The Billy Cotton Band Show*, which began in 1949, was equally corny, but good fun, with loud, jolly popular music, and always began with Billy himself shouting, 'Wakey-wakey!' Don't these old radio pro-grammes sound pathetic, with their banal catchphrases, yet *The Billy Cotton Band Show* became a highlight of the country's Sunday lunchtime. People of a certain age still think of it when they are sitting down to their roast beef and Yorkshire pud.

The Ted Ray Show was very popular, but I never liked him, as he seemed too slick and pleased with himself. I still listened to it, as my mother enjoyed it. There was a character called Mrs Hoskins, who was always ill and would be moaning to her best friend Ivy about her latest ailment. 'Eee, Ivy, it was agony.' But she loved one of her doctors. 'Young Dr Hardcastle, he's luuuuvly.' Totally banal remarks, but the audience laughed and clapped and listeners went round repeating them. Are all pet phrases, which comedians use, then and now, always totally stupid? Nice to see you, to see you nice. How pointless is that?

Even now, though, after all these years, I can still find myself saying, 'It was agony, Ivy' when something unagonis-ing happens.

I suppose my all-time favourite radio programme as a child and early teenager was *Dick Barton – Special Agent*, which started in 1946 and was on the Home Service each evening. Dick was rather smooth, well bred, well spoken, while his two sidekicks, Jock and Snowy, were Scottish and cockney, and spoke accordingly, just in case you were not sure which was which. I can still hear the music playing, *tarran tarran, tarran tarran*, and the mad rush to get into the house, even if I was in the middle of an exciting game of football. I had to be at the radio at 6.45 each evening, along with every other child in the post-war year.

I can't remember listening to any of the famous wartime

broadcasts, such as Churchill going on about so much being owed to so few, or the King telling us the war was over, but of course they have been repeated so many times since that I can persuade myself that, yes, I was glued to our radio at the time, I remember it well.

I have vague memories of an election where all the kids went out into the streets chanting slogans. 'Vote, vote, vote for Mr Attlee, chuck old Churchill out the door, for we'll buy a penny gun, and shoot him up the lum, for we don't want Churchill any more.' This was in 1945 when we were living in Dumfries. 'Lum' was another word for chimney. We might also have chanted 'shoot him up the bum'. I was only nine and don't recall listening to the result, or taking in that it was the most enormous and unexpected landslide, with Labour getting a majority of 145 seats over the Tories – after all Churchill had done for the nation. We were not a political family, and I never heard politics being discussed. There had been a sudden groundswell in favour of Labour at grassroots level, which the experts appeared unaware of. The theory, now, is that yes the war was won, but the nation didn't want to go back to the old prewar class system, with its inequalities. They wanted a fairer society.

I don't remember the 1950 election either, when Labour were returned but with a slim majority, only to be ousted by the Tories in 1951. I suppose I was too busy playing football, or glued to the radio, listening to Scotland v England, the only time we got live broadcasts, apart from the FA Cup final.

I knew all the names of the Scottish team, in fact the names of most of the famous players of the day, and the clubs, and the strips, and the names of their stadiums, but never took in the names of politicians, apart from the prime ministers. I remember Hugh Dalton as a baddie, possibly because as Chancellor of the Exchequer between 1945 and 1947 he put up the price of beer, which made him very unpopular. Perhaps that was why Labour never got in again in 1951, despite all their marvellous socialistic innovations in health and education. Ordinary people were fed up with yet more belt-tightening, and continual rationing.

TV sets gradually started to appear during the fifties, although our family never had one. The first BBC TV broadcast was in 1936, the year of my birth, from the Alexandra Palace in north London, but during the war, from 1939 to 1946, all TV was suspended – another ruse to fool those Jerries.

It is an urban myth that when TV returned in 1946, the announcer said, 'As I was saying before I was so rudely interrupted.' It was in fact the famous *Daily Mirror* columnist 'Cassandra', aka William Connor, who began his first column after returning from wartime service with those words. What the first BBC TV presenter said, on starting broadcasting again after a six-year gap on 7 June 1946, was, 'Good afternoon everybody. How are you? Do you remember me, Jasmine Bligh?' Jasmine Bligh was one of the original three BBC announcers from their prewar service.

The first time I was aware of TV was on 2 June 1953 for the Queen's coronation. It was the first time that TV came into the lives of most people. Before then, only around half a million homes had TV sets. In 1954, a year later, there were three million. Ten years later, it was thirteen million.

There was just one woman on our estate who had a TV

set, Mrs Porter, who lived in Fraser Grove, opposite Reg's house. She bought it specially for the coronation. The rumour was that she had won some money on the pools. Her family and chosen friends were allowed to sit in her front room and watch it. Close neighbours were allowed to stand at the back of the room. Not-so-close neighbours stood outside in the front garden, looking through the window. The rest of the estate, who were not on such intimate terms, were reduced to standing out on the pavement, staring over the hedge, hoping for a glimpse of our lovely new Queen. Fat chance, as the TV was so small and so blurry and so far away, but goodness the excitement. I played football instead.

But I did clearly remember the big event close to the coronation – Edmund Hillary's conquest of Everest just a few days before, on 29 May 1953. With, of course, plucky little Sherpa Tenzing. We all knew about him, but he was merely a native helper, so got second billing. The following year, on 6 May 1954, Roger Bannister ran the world's first four-minute mile. I didn't see that either, but naturally I was proud to be English, sorry, I mean British, and alive and well at such a clearly stirring, inspiring time for our island nation. So, yes, we were happy then. Mostly, anyway.

12

FRANCE, JOBS AND GIRLS

In my last year at the Creighton, in 1952, aged sixteen, with O-levels coming up, I went on a school trip to France. To improve my French, of course. The strange thing is I always thought I was pretty good at French. As good as the teacher anyway, who was probably about my level – i.e. had an appalling accent and knew very little. Looking through my Creighton reports, I see I got around 50 per cent for French in the first two years, then by the fifth year I was getting 72. Clearly gifted.

It was the main thing that distinguished the Creighton from ordinary sec mods – we did O-levels and we did French, which felt awfully smart. My mother would often say to me, when her neighbour Mrs Forsyth popped in, 'Go on, Hunter, speak some French.' I would refuse of course. We intellectuals were not performing seals.

I don't know how my mother managed to pay for my school trip to France. Did the school help? I have no memory. I was obviously the privileged one as none of my siblings ever went on a school trip, certainly not abroad. My mother had never been abroad, or been in an aeroplane. My father had not been abroad either, but he had been in an aeroplane, as he was always quick to tell us. It had only been a flip round the base when he was in the RAF, but it still counted. He had been up in the air.

I am surprised now that a school like the Creighton, in the far North of England, at a time of post-war austerity, could manage a foreign trip. Makes it sound more like a posh private school. What you don't realise at the time, as a pupil on any sort of overseas school trip, is that it is a jolly for the staff. They want to get away from the dreary round of everyday school teaching – and have, presumably, a subsidised holiday.

We went on the cross-Channel ferry, Dover to Calais, which was exciting enough, but not as much as the social and cultural shock of actually being in France. It smelled different for a start – the whiff of Gauloises, the hint of garlic, the funny smells from the lavatories and bathrooms.

God, their plumbing and lavvies seemed disgusting to our awfully refined tastes and noses. The plumbing in our hotel was a different system from ours at home, and very slow and noisy. The public toilets outside had fierce old biddies sitting in them, glowering at you, telling you off, shouting out because of something you did not know you had done wrong – and then demanding money, or at least forcing you to leave something in a hat. Then once inside the smelly cubicle, all there was was a hole in the ground. Call that a lavatory? We could not believe it. We were caught between shock-horror and sniggering. When we heard that the old harridans were called 'dames pipi' it made us practically wet ourselves again.

French bikes were different, with fatter, red tyres. The

bottles of orange juice, with their fat little bottoms, looked and tasted different. The haircuts and the clothes, especially French school uniforms, were all new to us. The food, of course, was totally exotic.

The French had also suffered through those awful war years, some far more than us, but it didn't seem like it. At home we were still on starvation rations; we suffered endless shortages and when there was food in the shops it was mainly awful, with little choice. By cheese what we mainly meant was Kraft cheese, introduced in the UK from America in 1949, little processed slices, wrapped in packets, which we considered the height of sophistication. Today, being of course genuinely sophisticated, I would not even classify it as cheese. But in France in 1952, the shops and stalls were teeming with a vast array of cheeses, most of them too smelly or scary-looking to even touch, as well as fruits and meats, most of which we had never seen before. Frogs' legs, ugh, that made us sick, just thinking about it. Oysters and mussels and assorted shellfish, you are not getting any of them down my gob.

I suppose the cosmopolitan, southern classes in England were used to much of this French food – possibly cockneys, too, as we were led to believe they swallowed eels for breakfast covered in jelly and other creepy-crawly stuff. But in Carlisle, and I am sure many other provincial towns, when we went out, at home or abroad, which was rare, to a caff of any sort, all we looked for were chips, sausages and fried eggs.

Just going out into the street in France, with your eyes closed, breathing it all in, listening to the sounds, everything felt totally foreign. The very air felt French.

Going back today, France doesn't seem all that French, not

as it did then. Was it the newness of it all, or our youth? For young people going to France today for the first time, I suspect the novelty is far less. We all eat the same stuff, have the same drinks, go to the same sort of shops, use the same mobile phones, wear the same clothes, listen to the same music – and the smelly urinals have all gone. Well, almost. We are all Europeans now. You have to go much further in the world to feel truly abroad these days. Or stay in London. That is probably today the most exotic city in the world.

We stayed at the station hotel in a little town called Abbeville, in northern France, in the Somme *département*. The local girls of our age totally ignored us, making us feel hick and provincial, and of course we could not exchange one word of French with them.

During the stay, we had one day and night in Paris. We took in some of the sights, the Seine and the Eiffel Tower, but then I fell ill with asthma and had to stay all day in my room. It must have been the excitement that brought it on. Or the Gauloise smoke. The French seemed to smoke even more than the Brits, and much stronger, smellier stuff. The French teacher, the one I had always mocked for being useless at French, chose to stay behind in the hotel with me while all the others went off on some cultural expedition. I felt guilty ruining his pleasure, his trip.

I learned very little French during the trip, much less spoke any, and just made silly jokes about pee-pee and French signs like 'Sortie'. What sort of *sortie* did it mean, sir? We spent a lot of time looking for cheap presents to bring home to our parents. For my mother, I bought a toy Eiffel tower in a snow-storm globe, and a very miniature bottle of three-star Cognac for my father. Both were immediately put in our cocktail cabinet where they remained, unshaken, undrunk, forever, but were proof to the neighbours that one of the family had been to France, oh yes.

Back home, in my final year at school, in the fifth form as it was then called, I can't remember doing a lot of revising for my O-levels – but I did an awful lot of other work, in order to earn money. From the age of fourteen, I had had a job – not down the mines, or up chimneys, but it seemed just as knackering. I was a paperboy, lugging a huge bag round our streets, having to get up in winter in the dark and the cold. I had been on a long waiting list before I got the job.

The job was at Clark's, the grocery and newsagent at the top of the hill, beside the Redfern pub, which served our estate. Mr Clark always looked miserable and moany, especially first thing in the morning, marking up the papers, worried that some of the paperboys would be late or non-existent. He wouldn't open up the shop if we arrived early, making us stand out in the frost. He could be seen marking up through the window, his brow furrowed, his face gloomy. I would often go over the road with one or two other boys and climb over the wall of a nursery opposite, and steal apples, scared stiff I would be caught.

I often did sleep in, and my mother would have to shake me awake. Sometimes I would have asthma and literally be unable to get out of bed. When that happened, my mother would wake the twins and persuade one of them to go and do my round for me. Which would mean being eternally grateful, and paying them when I got my wages.

I did that paper round for about four years. It meant I got

to know all the front doors of all the surrounding streets, all the gardens, all the letterboxes, and most of the people. At Christmas time you made a point of hanging about. It always seemed to be the scruffiest, most impoverished family who gave you half a crown as a Christmas box, while the more affluent-looking pretended you did not exist, that the fairies had brought their paper. Perhaps sixpence if you were lucky.

Council estates did have affluent people, with nicer gardens and hedges than most of us, who had certain airs and graces and considered themselves superior folks, which was surprising, as most of them worked at the MU and didn't have any betters jobs than my father, until he was ill.

The most popular papers were the *Daily Express* and the *Daily Mirror*, but quite a few took the *News Chronicle* and the *Daily Herald*. Only one house took the *Telegraph*. I don't remember ever delivering a *Times* or a *Manchester Guardian*.

I then took on an evening paper round as well, which meant delivering to the new estate, still being built behind the lotties. It was a longer walk but was after school so the hours were more civilised. I didn't know the houses over there, or the people, and hardly ever saw them.

After my sixteenth birthday, in January 1952, I dropped the evening paper round and took on a different job at Clark's, in addition to the morning papers – delivering groceries on a bike.

The reason for doing all these jobs was to buy my own bike. My parents could not afford one, and they never gave me any pocket money. I would not have had money otherwise, apart from Christmas presents from our Cambuslang relations.

I bought a green Raleigh Lenton Sports with Sturmey

Archer gears, my heart's desire, a model and a colour with the right drop handlebars and gears that I'd long ogled. I can still smell it now. When it was new and virgin, the tyres and metal and rubber had an aroma of newness, the same as you get with a new car, which is so sweet and strong and overpowering. You clean and polish it all day long, trying to keep its virginity, then you forget, can't be bothered. After a few weeks it smells of roads and traffic and sweaty bums.

I bought it at T.P. Bell's in Abbey Street, where generations of Carlisle teenagers had bought their bikes, paying it up at a rate of 13/11 a week on the never-never. It did seem to take forever, perhaps a year or two. I think the cost was around £20, a huge amount, double what a working man would earn in a week, plus of course the interest that had to be paid. So it must have taken at least fifty weeks to pay it off.

But, oh, the freedom and independence it gave, able to go out into the country, or across town, without needing money for the bus. Being alone, on a bike, you look purposeful, as if you are going somewhere. Unlike walking alone, cycling alone does not suggest you have no friends, no one who will come and do things with you. You are a free spirit. Even more so, if you are a girl.

I used to think that that Raleigh bike, that model, in that colour, was unique to T.P. Bell's, and therefore unique to Carlisle. Never realised that hundreds of thousands of boys all over the country were at the same time lusting after that selfsame bike. Talking one day to John Lennon, it came out that he'd had exactly the same bike. I think his Aunt Mimi bought it for him. I don't remember him ever talking about delivering papers or having any after-school jobs. Spoiled, if you ask me. He did of course live in a semi-detached private house, not on a council estate.

My grocery delivery job paid more than doing the papers, which was how I was able to fund the payments on my bike. The job was mainly on Saturday mornings, when housewives got their week's shopping, which they had ordered earlier. Their orders would be packed up in individual cardboard boxes by one of Mr Clark's shop assistants and I would stack as many as I could on my bike – my shop bike, not my own gleaming Raleigh Lenton Sports.

It was a heavy, ungainly, unwieldy, old-fashioned delivery bike with a massive straw basket at the front. It often fell over while I was loading, so I would have to brush the dirt off any groceries that landed on the pavement, hoping nobody had noticed. Starting off was fine, as Clark's was on a hill, so I whizzed down, the wind blowing my hair, singing away, but coming back afterwards to the shop, struggling up the hill, even with an empty basket, that was agony, Ivy.

The weekly shopping orders would contain HP Sauce, Crosse & Blackwell's salad dressing, Bisto, Heinz beans or spaghetti hoops, Bird's Custard powder, Carnation milk, Rinso, Shredded Wheat, fish or other funny pastes, Oxo cubes, sugar, Spam, perhaps some Rowntree's fruit gums and Spangles for the kiddies. It was mostly tins, packets of non-perishable heavy goods that housewives did not want to lug home. And, of course, almost everyone got at least one loaf. I was so pleased when sliced bread came in. It meant that if the bike fell over, sliced bread, being covered, was not ruined, just bashed. It also seemed lighter.

Can I have made it up that sliced bread came in during the

early fifties? 'The best thing since sliced bread' was a phrase from before the war, after sliced bread had been invented in Iowa in 1928. It came from America, like most good things in our post-war life. But I honestly do remember it being an amazing novelty in Carlisle when Robertsons, our local bakers, started selling sliced bread. It came in heavily greased paper and inside was all white and moist and soft. You could have it thick cut or thin cut. We all thought it was wonderful and gorgeous and tasty. Today, good gracious, we never have white or sliced bread in our house. The very idea.

When I was whizzing down the hill on my bike, with a full basket, I started to find that I had suddenly got an erection. Perhaps it was due to the hard, narrow seat on the bike. Or was I being turned on by the thought of the soft, moist sliced bread? Anyway, it was so embarrassing. I worried that some neighbour would see me, or one of my friends, or, oh horror, a girl, and they would realise what that little lump in my trousers was.

Often when I was delivering the groceries on a Saturday morning, I would walk down the front path and go to the back door, which would be opened by a housewife, still in her dressing gown or even a skimpy nightdress, clutching her bosom.

'Where shall I put it, Mrs Graham?' I would ask, sniggering in my head, but turning slightly red.

'Oh, Hunter, that is so kind. Now where do I want it? Oh, just come in for a moment, let me think, put it over there ...'

So I would go into the kitchen, find a space and put down her box of groceries. Then pause for a moment, in case she wanted me to do anything else.

Obviously, never for one moment did I actually imagine that an older woman, say in her twenties, would have any sexual interest in a skinny, weedy, teenage boy. It was just fantasy. Which, of course, almost every teenage boy has. Probably a few housewives as well, so we now know.

I can't remember when I first started getting erections. Later than other boys, judging by the boasts of certain lads at school during PE. From about the age of thirteen there was one who would stand in the showers holding his cock between his legs, so you would just see his pubic hairs, then he would walk round, pretending to be a girl, asking if anyone fancied him. I was alarmed and appalled, having no pubic hairs, or any cock worthy of the name.

One day I bunked off a maths lesson and with a few boys from my year sneaked down to the River Eden. We lay down in the long grass and, before I realised it, we were having a masturbation session. One of the bigger, more advanced boys, Vinny, grabbed me and began manipulating, quite roughly, so it rather hurt. Then they all cheered. He might well have shouted out the names of film stars and pin-ups of the day, like Brigitte Bardot. That's what John Lennon used to shout out when he was leading similar sessions at his school.

At school dinners, Vinny was always boasting about his cum. When the pudding arrived, often spotted dick with custard, he would tell the whole table that his spunk was thicker and more plentiful than all of the custard we had been given.

There were so-called dirty books passed round the school, such as Hank Janson, and copies of *Health and Efficiency* with photos of naked women, all unreal, with no pubic hair, as if I knew what a real woman looked like, shot artily in black and white with clever lighting.

Having a hard-on, jack, throbber, came on so suddenly and was so weird. Where had it come from, why was it so hard? Was there a bone there? If so, how had I missed it? I did get out my ruler and measure it, which was more difficult than you might think, for where do you start, right at the root, wherever that is, or just the bit that shows? It was not to compete and compare, for you don't know what is normal, normal is only what you are, though at the same time you wonder if you are normal. I suppose it was to measure it regularly to see if it was still growing, still expanding. Having a ruler down the side of your sock was very handy, for I am sure I was still in short trousers at fifteen when all this kerfuffle with my body and mind started.

At home, pleasuring myself, I had no material to work on. I would peer out into the street from my bedroom window, the curtains half-pulled, hoping that a female, young or old, fat or ugly, any woman really, would walk along the pavement outside and I would imagine her naked. Just the way her dress folded between her legs when she walked, that would be enough.

Afterwards I would feel so ashamed and guilty – and also sore with all the violent effort. I did believe it was shameful and disgusting, that there was something wrong or perverted about me. God would not like it. I also half-believed it was bad for you, that you would go blind, which is what Baden-Powell had indicated in *Scouting for Boys*. He warned all boys not to take part in these sorts of disgusting practices.

Aged about fifteen or sixteen, I did start getting invited to girls' parties, usually girls I hardly knew, perhaps girls at our sister school, the Margaret Sewell, around the same ages as my sisters. They also seemed to live miles the other side of town on another council estate, so it was handy having my bike.

One day I was invited to a posh house in Stanwix, thanks to Reg and other friends at the grammar school. The high school girl who had invited us, who was my age and had been at Stanwix primary with me, had a younger sister aged fourteen who was also at the party.

I got off with her, at least when the lights went off I made a grab for her and started snogging. I eventually managed to get my hand up her legs, and into her knickers. What a fright I got, so I withdrew my hand quickly. I felt ashamed, taking advantage of a girl two years younger. I told no one, not even to boast at school.

Lads did it all the time, of course, most of it fantasy, boasting about what they had managed. 'Did you fin' her?' was what you asked someone who had been out with a girl? 'Did you get a sticky finger?'

In Liverpool the expression was fish and finger pie, which appears in 'Penny Lane', though no one outside Merseyside understood it at the time. I would look revolted by such crude and vulgar conversation.

'What number did you get to?' That was another question. Number one meant a kiss, two meant feeling her breasts, three was feeling her minge, four was when she tossed you off, five was all the way. No one I ever knew throughout my school years ever got beyond three – and even that was very rare.

Who would have imagined that teenagers today would be sending photos of their genitals to each other, or of various positions and pursuits and practices, of things like blow jobs, which I had never heard of in the 1950s, and would not have believed, even I had been told. How sheltered we were. But do we want it back? Or do we envy the fun and freedom of today? Discuss.

Despite all these jobs I was doing, and going to the occasional party, I did not feel particularly nervous about my O-levels. The night before my French exam I even went out with Reg when he called for me. They were doing different exam boards at the grammar school. I knew I should have stayed in for last-minute swotting, but I felt blithely confident.

In 1952, when I took my General Certificate of Education at O-level, to give the full title, it was a relatively new exam, though I was not aware of that. It had been introduced in 1951, replacing the old School Certificate, which was a harder exam, by the sound of it, in that you had to pass six subjects, including maths and English, before you were said to have 'passed' your School Cert, or matriculated as it was often called.

When O-levels came in, you were given a pass or fail for each subject, so you usually had some success to boast about, as opposed to a blanket failure. Pupils tended to take more subjects, which was one reason for changing the system, to make pupils have a broader range.

These days the examination system seems to change all the time, and is endlessly confusing, and must drive teachers mad, but the O-level system I took lasted a long time, till 1988, when GCSE – General Certificate of Secondary Education – exams were introduced. The names of the exams people sat are one of the ways of telling someone's age. If they let slip they passed their School Cert, you knew that they must be pretty old. It's like girls' names. If they are called Margaret or Dorothy, they were probably born just prewar. Ivy or Jean, they were the generation before. Sue and Sarah and Caroline, probably post-war babies.

I sat nine subjects for my O-levels – English literature, English language, French, history, geography, maths, general science, RE and technical drawing. I passed seven. One of the two I failed was tech drawing. Which I knew I would, being hopeless at it and not interested.

But, oh my God, I also failed French. So much for that school trip to France. Naturally, I blamed that useless teacher.

Seven O-levels was pretty good, though. It was what most of my friends at grammar school had achieved – in fact, more than most of them. But I was livid about French, which they had all passed. Oh well, I suppose it wouldn't matter in the end. When I left school at the end of the academic year, and started looking for a job, I was sure French would not be vital.

I had no idea what I might do, and had never properly thought about it. I supposed some sort of white-collar office job, perhaps junior clerk. Perhaps a level up from my father. The jobs to which the cleverest, hardest-working, neatest Creighton boys aspired were vaguely technical, such as draughtsman, drawing plans, measuring and marking, perhaps apprentice surveyor. The thought of any of that made me shudder. Imagine doing drawing, all day, every day.

On my final report at the Creighton School, I see I was marked as number one in the class – the first time I had been so high. There had always been at least two others well ahead of me in every year till then. Back in the third year, I had been as low as thirteenth in the class, out of forty. So I had improved or advanced, or perhaps it was because many of the others had lost interest, given up, or left after the fourth year. I never understood why so many boys at the Creighton who had appeared just as good as me in the early years, and often much quicker and brighter, suddenly started to fade, lose all ambition or hopes or just interest. Perhaps it was lack of encouragement, either from their family or teachers, or maybe something inside them was lacking. I could not believe it was due to any innate stupidity.

In the early years I had assumed my relative modest success in schoolwork, feeling so many were ahead of me, was down to arriving from Scotland and having to get to grips with a different life and system. I had overcome that, so I told myself.

But what was I going to do now?

13

GRAMMAR CAD

And then I found myself at the grammar school. I have no memory of applying, or being interviewed. I had never heard of any boys going on from the Creighton to the grammar in the past, and I am sure I would have done. I had assumed such a system did not exist. Till it just seemed to happen.

I can't believe anyone at the grammar school said, 'Let's look at some of those eleven-plus failures, the ones who didn't make it to the grammar school five years ago, surely one or two of them can't be totally useless, there might be some half-decent chaps we could run our eye over.'

Nor can I imagine that any of the Creighton masters badgered the grammar school head and said, 'Hey, come on now, don't be snotty, we have some good lads this year, give them a chance.' I should imagine none of the Creighton staff knew any of the grammar school masters, and vice versa.

Obviously my parents could not have done the pushing. They had no idea how things worked in England, least of all the education system. My dad was an invalid in bed, feeling well pissed off with everything, not surprisingly, and, as for my mother, most things in Carlisle were still a mystery to her.

I can only assume that it was somebody on some education committee in Carlisle or some official who suggested that possibly it was about time the city attempted to implement one of the aims of the 1944 Butler Education Act. This was the notion that the eleven-plus would not be a once-and-for-all demarcation line, there would be a chance later on to move between schools, for the brightest or keenest students each year, should they show enough interest, motivation and capability. In Carlisle, this was clearly demonstrable with its three-tier system and a proportion of boys at the Creighton and girls at the Margaret Sewell achieving O-levels each year. It should already have happened or been attempted everywhere, but it had been overlooked or forgotten. Very few schools around England ever managed to do it.

In 1952, three of us were chosen – Brian Cooke, Alistair McFadden and me. I imagine they were as surprised as I was to be told at the end of our last term at the Creighton that we were being promoted to glory, transported to join the gods.

Carlisle Grammar School was only a few hundred yards away along the same road, but the cultural and social and educational differences were going to be enormous. With its distinguished history and traditions, and its ivy-covered buildings, it would be like moving from a prefab to a stately home.

I can vaguely remember some discussion at the end of my last term at the Creighton, after we had been told we were going to the grammar school, about whether we would all be going into what was called the 'fifth remove'. This was where those grammar school boys who had not done so well in their O-levels, but who wanted to go into the sixth form, had to repeat a year, retake exams. But we three Creightonians had all done well, got seven O-levels apiece.

The dreaded French, though, that was going to be something of a problem. During that long summer holiday, before I started at the grammar, or even visited it, one of the French masters, knowing I had failed French, contacted me to say he was going to arrange an exchange for me. It would help me with my oral, when I resat my French O-level.

One day we got a letter from the French master, Mr Watson, known as Jules, to say that my exchange would be arriving to stay with us for ten days. I hadn't really understood what an exchange was, that it would mean a total stranger would be living with us – in our awful council house, with our awful coal-dusty kitchen, useless bathroom, no heating, horrible wet towels scattered around the house, invalid father. And they would have to share the bedroom with me and Johnny – perhaps all in the same bed. Oh God, what have I agreed to? It will be so embarrassing and shameful.

My mother had no worries. She was sure she could borrow a single bed. She loved people staying, on the rare occasions they did. She had bags of room, she said, just as she always maintained she had bags of money, bags of food. None of it true, of course, but her spirit was always willing. I felt ashamed of being ashamed of our house, when she clearly wasn't.

We then got a telegram, as of course we had no phone, informing us that the exchange would be arriving at a certain time at Carlisle railway station. It was signed Adeline. Oh help. My exchange was going to be a girl. The thought of looking after a French boy was bad enough, but how would we cope with a strange French girl?

The song 'Sweet Adeline' was a popular prewar tune, which my mother knew – and she immediately began singing it: 'Sweet Adeline, you're the flower of my heart. For you I pine, my Clementine . . .'

'Dear God, woman, give us a break!' I was soon shouting at her.

I went to Carlisle station at the time given to pick her up – and she turned out to be a boy, just a year or so older than me, called Jean-Claude Adeline. His father had sent the telegram and just signed it with his surname.

He had fairish hair and wore an obviously French sports jacket, sort of black and white tweedy with little knotty lumps, the sort I had never seen before, certainly not in the windows at Burton's. He seemed older and more mature than me, but didn't say much, as his English was even worse than my French. Like me, he had to retake an exam, in his case English, in order to get into what sounded like some sort of hotel school, or cookery college, so his parents had signed him up for a random exchange. He didn't say much, as I took him home on the bus, but seemed pleasant and affable.

To my total amazement, he was rather charmed by our house. He was interested in our living arrangements, our decor, my mother and her stories, and even the food. My invalid father lying in his bed was on his best behaviour. Jean-Claude seemed very sympathetic. He appeared pleased to be here, in our house, so much so that I felt he must be really desperate to improve his English.

I had been working like mad for the few weeks before he

came, doing extra papers and deliveries, determined to have enough money to take him out of the house as quickly as possible. So, after a couple of days showing him the delights of Carlisle, I dragged him off to Scotland, going on the bus, for which I paid, to stay with my Cambuslang relatives, which of course was free. I wanted to show them off to Jean-Claude, that we did have quite well-off relations, as their houses were smarter and more affluent than ours. He hit it off with one of my cousins, Sheena, who took him to see her friends, perhaps even held hands with him.

A few weeks later, it was my turn. I went off to France to stay with Jean-Claude and his family at Chaumont-en-Vexin, in Oise. I can remember his address exactly, yet I have never been back since or had any contact. His father was an affluent farmer, or so it seemed, with a large house and lots of acres. I had my own bedroom and was given a glass of wine at meals. I loved the breakfast, which I usually ate alone in their large farmhouse kitchen. Most people in the house were up early and off working on the farm. His mother gave me croissants, which I had never had before, and real coffee, not Camp, served in cups the size and shape of soup bowls. His mother did sup her coffee as if it were soup, which I thought very weird.

While I was there, a hunt – *la chasse* – was held on the estate. Lots of other local farmers arrived for the day. I followed behind the beaters, being told to stand and wait at certain places, not knowing what was going on. But we did get to sit down and a huge spread was laid out and everyone stuffed themselves with wine and hams and cheese.

Jean-Claude also took me to a party in a nearby house,

local families, with quite a few teenagers, girls and boys. They danced a funny way, none of the quicksteps and valetas we did at our church youth club dances. They were mad on '*le bebop*', which seemed to be their version of jazz. They also loved sloppy romantic ballads such as 'La Mer', which I quite liked as well. I even got Jean-Claude to teach me all the words – managing to pronounce most of them without too much of a Carlisle accent.

None of the girls would speak to me, dance with me, or even look at me. I was left to my own devices, a little roast-beefy wallflower, while he bebopped. I couldn't really understand this. When I had taken Jean-Claude around Carlisle and up to Glasgow, my friends and relations had all made a big fuss of him, making him the centre of attention. But in France, as a foreign visitor, I did not exist. His parents were kind enough, though neither spoke English. I was mainly ignored. In a big farmhouse, on a big estate, they probably hardly registered I was staying with them.

Thinking back, we were rather in awe of French culture throughout the 1950s. They had arty films made by directors like Truffaut and Jean-Luc Godard. I remember queuing at the City Picture House to see *La Ronde*. We thought all French films were intellectual and sophisticated, compared with the silly, corny English films, with Will Hay or George Formby, and even the Ealing comedies which were thought to be good at the time. French films had sexy stars, such as Bardot and Jean-Paul Belmondo.

They also had all those philosophers and intellectuals like Sartre and Simone de Beauvoir who wore fashionable black and looked ever so, well, philosophical. And writers like

Albert Camus. We had no English authors who were remotely contemporary. Nobody later than Dickens seemed to exist. Not to mention all that wine and food, South of France sun and romance. I think we Brits felt rather inferior by comparison, while they seemed to us arrogant and superior. And they were.

You didn't hear then the French being worried about the influence of the English language, replacing so many of their words, or English fashions and pop music dominating French culture. If anything, they thought our culture was pretty pathetic. No wonder the girls wouldn't dance with me. That was my considered wisdom, after two brief visits, unable to speak the language.

In the autumn term of 1952, aged sixteen, I presented myself at the main entrance of Carlisle Grammar School. This in itself was an enormous privilege. Only the sixth-formers were allowed to use the front entrance. Even those in the fifth remove, who had been at the school just as long, were relegated to a rear entrance.

That main entrance was not as ivy-covered as I had imagined from afar, passing on the other side of the street for the last five years. Nor was the actual building all that ancient, more mock-Gothic Victorian, built in 1885.

But the school itself was tremendously old, much older than Eton. It dated back to AD 685 when St Cuthbert, Bishop of Lindisfarne, visited Carlisle and founded both a school and a church. For the next 900 years, the school continued in the grounds of the cathedral, occupying buildings on West Walls, some of which are part of the diocesan offices to this day. It was in 1883 that Carlisle Grammar School moved to its new handsome building on Strand Road.

It modelled itself on the public school system, as did all our ancient grammar schools in towns all over the country. Some did charge fees, if they had a preparatory department – which CGS did until just before I arrived. One of the friends I had made through Reg was Mike Thornhill, the son of a dentist. He had been at the prep department before he entered the grammar school itself. I was most impressed. I had never met anyone who had been educated privately.

Most towns in England, even of a modest size, had an ancient grammar school, used by the local quality, such as solicitors and tradespeople, charging small fees, but there were also scholarships and free places for less well-off children, as most of these old grammar schools had charitable funds. William Wordsworth went to Hawkshead, a small, remote grammar school in Lakeland, yet every year it sent pupils to Cambridge. One of them, Wordsworth's big brother Richard, ended up as master of Trinity College.

I don't think any Old Carliols – as our ex-pupils were known – became as famous as the Wordsworths, but over the centuries, according to the noticeboard in the hall, many pupils had won open scholarships to both Oxford and Cambridge and some gone on to be bishops and MPs.

In the 1950s, the school still considered itself on the level of a public school. The headmaster, V.J. Dunstan, a classics scholar, was a member of the Headmasters' Conference, which was the association for public school heads. He floated around the entrance hall in his gown, a rather eccentric, abstracted figure, often followed by his wife who would be shouting things at him. They seemed to have accommodation some-where in the school.

Not long ago, I noticed a 1913 poster for sale at Sotheby's in an auction of football memorabilia. It was entitled 'Football Colours of Our Public Schools'. It showed ninety-six football caps from ninety-six different public schools, including Eton, Harrow, St Paul's, Winchester. And, blow me, there on the top line was a football cap marked 'CGS 1912–13' and below it the name Carlisle. The colours were black and yellow, the same school colours that were there when I arrived. So it was true, we had been considered a public school at one time.

The staff all wore gowns, most were Oxbridge graduates, the forms had Latin names. There was even a tuck shop, as in *Billy Bunter*. There had been a cadet corps, but that had recently gone.

I went straight into the sixth form, not lingering and loiter-ing in the fifth remove for a year, which had been threatened. It was called Lower VI Alpha Modern. This meant you were doing arts subjects. There was a science sixth and also a classics sixth, though that was quite small. Lower VI Alpha Modern contained twenty-three pupils.

I was to do A-levels in English, history and geography. We also all did a general science course, encouraged by the education authorities, as the government did not want too much specialisation by sixth-formers, divorcing arts students from the sciences, and scientists from the arts. Was this due to C.P. Snow going on about the 'two cultures'? I have just looked it up and he gave his famous lecture in Cambridge in 1959, warning that if science became too separated from the humanities we would never solve the world's problems. Or something like that. This worry was doubtless in the air some years before Snow started wittering on. Most theories are, before someone pins it down and becomes associated with it.

Apart from my three A-levels, and general science, I was doing French O-level again, resitting it, hence the exchange. But then I found there was another exam hurdle to be overcome, which I had not expected. In the 1950s, to get into a half-decent university, so I was informed, and study for an arts degree, you had to have O-level Latin. None of us from the Creighton had ever studied Latin. I don't think we were asked our opinion. Latin just appeared on our timetable. I presume they decided we could all cope, which is why we had been allowed to go straight into the sixth form. But I was not so sure. How could we fit it all in?

I had always considered Brian and Alistair swots, neat bastards, not like me. They would knuckle down to all their studies, do what they were told, follow the rules and guidelines. I never considered myself academic in any way, it was all a drag; my object was to get away with as little as possible, without being stroppy or bolshie or drawing attention to myself.

We found ourselves down for Latin with Mr Hodges, who took the three of us from the Creighton in his own time, when he had a free period, starting us from scratch. We did not sit in a proper classroom, as they were all being used, but crouched in a little cubbyhole storeroom miles up at the top of the old building. Mr Hodges, who had a little walrus moustache like Captain Mainwaring, realised we would never be as good at Latin as others in the sixth form who had been studying it for five years. So he worked out that we had to learn the basics, quickly, then memorise all the set texts, which was mainly Tacitus. The set texts provided half your marks, so if you could memorise as much as possible, even without understanding a lot of it, you had a chance of scraping through the exam. The theory was good, but as you were only aiming to attempt little more than half the syllabus, it was easy to come a cropper.

Mr Hodges was incredibly kind and helpful and patient, as was Mr Watson, the French teacher, and also Gerry Lightfoot, one of the English teachers. But I felt most of the other teachers had no interest in me. They didn't know who the three new boys in their classes were, our personalities and skills, such as they were, and nothing of course of our school career so far, whereas they had known everyone else in our class from the age of eleven. One or two clearly felt we were a lesser breed, coming from a lesser school, so how could we be much good?

The main English teacher, Adrian Barnes, always seemed to me so superior, disdainful, giving a sort of sarcastic, sideways sneer, when I attempted any answers or gave him my pathetic essays. Perhaps I imagined it all. Reg and all my other friends who had been at the school from the first year loved Barnes, admired his brain and his cleverness and attitude, said how nice he was, once you got to know him. He did strike me as clever, too clever, as if he thought he should be an Oxbridge tutor, not a grammar school teacher, especially of boys who had not even had the benefit of a grammar school education.

Socially and culturally, I never felt at all out of it. I was accepted straight away by all the boys in the sixth form, was on their wavelength, but I sensed Brian and Alistair might perhaps have felt a bit on the fringes. It was mainly due to my long-term friendship with Reg. That gave me an entrée, which had made me part of his group while I was still at the Creighton. Many of them had been at Stanwix with me, which was considered the best, most middle-class primary school.

Reg was the star, the one everyone admired, not because he was the cleverest academically but because he was clearly the most original, most talented, who was witty and could write amusingly. He edited the *Sixth Form Debating Society Magazine* which sounded official, but it was a homemade, duplicated and stapled few sheets, with drawings and stories and jokes, like an early *Private Eye*. There was an official school magazine, *The Carliol*, edited by one of the teachers, but this was incredibly boring and banal, even though it was professionally printed and glossily produced. Reg had even got the school secretary to duplicate the sheets in the office, at the school's expense, on the office Cyclostyle, one of those monster machines with stencils, a handle and ink flying all over the place. Your hands got black just looking at it. I don't think the staff twigged many of the references or hidden obscenities. We all thought it was marvellous, so subversive and funny — for a school in 1952. I never contributed any articles. I just admired it. I didn't think I could ever write as well or as amusingly as Reg.

The cleverest boy was Dicky Wilson, who knew everything, understood everything, from politics to science and economics, all things I knew nothing about, and could speak several foreign languages, when I couldn't even pass one. Some of them he had taught himself. During that first year in the sixth, while still only seventeen, Dicky won a scholarship to Queen's College, Oxford. Despite being a superstar for his cleverness, he was popular, well liked, didn't think he was anything special, not a show-off, aloof or arrogant – unlike a couple of boys in the classics sixth, who considered themselves the chosen ones, clearly heading for Oxbridge.

Lower down the school, the all-star legends, as in all boys' schools, were of course the sports stars – the captain of the first XV rugby team, or the cricket XI, natural athletes who had been heroes all through their school years. Everyone wanted to be them and, naturally, they seemed to get the girls. This had been evident at Creighton as well.

But in the grammar sixth form I began to sense a change. The arty set, led by Reg, who were interested in artistic things, music and drama, writing poetry and satire, they had their own following and were if anything more admired than the heavies, the jocks, the rugger buggers.

I find it hard to believe now, but during my two years in the sixth form I did become really keen on classical music. Reg and I went on our bikes twice to the Edinburgh Festival, attended classical concerts, watching famous violinists, like Yehudi Menuhin and Isaac Stern. We even queued up for *Hamlet*. There was another boy in our group, Brian Donaldson, who had family in Edinburgh, so we all stayed with them. Reg and I shared a bed.

We planned to go down to London together for the Proms, but at the last minute Reg couldn't make it, nor could anyone else. I went off on my own, all the way to London, hitchhiking down. I booked into a youth hostel and every morning went off to the Albert Hall and queued all day for tickets for the concerts. Was that really me? Did I really enjoy it? I don't recognise me at all. At least I could read music, so all my years of learning, or failing to learn, the violin had not been wasted.

And I did love watching and hearing all the great violinists doing it properly, playing the famous violin concertos by Beethoven, Dvorak, Tchaikovsky, Mendelssohn, Sibelius, all of which I knew, the best bits anyway. Sibelius was my fave.

I also learned to play chess and took part in plays. Both of these were relatively short phases. Led by Reg and some of the Stanwix-based sixth-formers, we started our own drama group, rehearsing in the Miles MacInnes Hall in Stanwix. I was useless. Couldn't act for toffee. But when you are in a group, you all take part in whatever is the new craze, until it becomes the old craze.

Perhaps the most surprising thing that happened during the sixth form was that I started to play rugby. At the Creighton, I had been excused games from the first year, standing around with the drips and the useless. When I first began at the grammar school I decided it was a chance to change. I could be a new me. There would be new people, new masters, who didn't know me. They didn't know I was a weakling who didn't play games. I could be anything I wanted.

So I decided to play rugby. Although I was in with the arty set, we were not anti-sport. Games were compulsory, so we all had to do them, but deciding to do them properly became a new game, a new obsession, like classical music. Giving it a go, I suppose. It was easy for Reg to throw himself into rugby, being very tall and fearless, if without much skill. And for the others in our group, like Mike, all of them huge. Harder for me, being a weed.

I worked out that if a small, weedy player tackled a big player, when the big player fell to the ground he would do more damage to himself than the small player, having further to fall and being heavier. And it worked. I became a demon tackler. By the end of my first year in the sixth I had made the school's second XV.

On my report at the end of the year, it didn't give places or percentages, just grades. I see I got an A in history, B in geography, B in English. 'Steady improvement' is what they mainly wrote. In Latin, I got an AB. 'Has made sound progress', so Mr Hodges wrote, giving his initials as R.G.H.

The report stated, under out-of-school activities, that I was a member of the debating society, the gramophone club and the school orchestra. The summing-up comments at the bottom of the report were not as pleasing; in fact, they were rather worrying. 'He is working steadily but he must give serious attention to certain shortcomings,' wrote the form master, whose name I can't read. The headmaster, Mr Dunstan, wrote: 'B+ He will need to make a big effort next term.'

I don't remember ever talking to the headmaster, so what did he know? I put it down to prejudice.

French was not listed on that report – for the simple reason that at the end of my first year in the lower sixth, at Christmas time, I had retaken the exam – and passed it. Oh rapture. The second year would be more testing. As well as three A-level exams in the summer, hanging over me and coming up at Christmas time was my Latin O-level. Would there be any time for personal pleasures and amusements?

14

WOMEN AND WORK

I think I must have lied about some of those activities, such as the debating society, or greatly exaggerated them, and been affected and pretentious when I was going to plays and classical concerts and playing chess. I'm sure my main concerns were more on the lines of wine, women and song. Okay, not the last one, as I can't sing. Nor wine, now I think about it, as I never drank wine during my school years. As for women, we didn't have them either in the 1950s, only in our dreams. But you can be concerned about certain things without ever participating in them.

Drinking was a concern, or at least a challenge, for any teenagers at the time, as supermarkets and shops did not sell booze and pubs would chuck you out if they suspected you were not eighteen. I turned seventeen in 1953, but I still looked about thirteen. At least I had moved into long trousers, which I thought I would never manage. All my friends, like Reg and Mike, had been in long 'uns for ages, but I don't think I went into them till I was fourteen. In photos of me in France with the school, aged fifteen, I am wearing long trousers, but I can't have been in them for long.

The agony of getting a drink in Carlisle as a teenager was made worse than most places because of the State Management Scheme. This was a unique situation begun in 1916 to control and limit mass drunkenness during the First World War among the Gretna munitions workers, most of whom used to come into Carlisle and wreck the place. According to Lloyd George, more harm was done to the war effort by the drinking than all of the German submarines. So what the government did was nationalise all the pubs and breweries in the local area, bringing them under state control. It was supposed to be just for the duration of war, but it carried on, for decades, right throughout my lifetime in Carlisle, and did not end till 1973. Lots of new pubs were built, in a distinctive style, now praised by architects, and they hired an excellent chief architect, Harry Redfern. The local pub where my father drank, the Redfern, was named after him. The pubs were mostly cheerless but the big attraction was that the drink was relatively cheap. It was all their own State Management brand, from the beers to the whisky.

Reg and I couldn't go to the Redfern, as the neighbours would see us, or to any of the popular pubs in the centre of the town near the grammar school, so what we did, during our learning-to-drink period, was go to a pub almost out in the country, where we knew nobody. Our favourite was the Near Boot, which had a bowling green. We would sit outside and the biggest, oldest-looking among us, such as Mike, would go in and order three halves, bring them out and we would sit on a bench watching the bowling, and sup. Or pretend to.

I instantly hated the taste of beer. It was so bitter. You could get bitter or mild, but the mild seemed just as bitter. I used to force it down, hoping a taste for it would eventually come. Why? Slavishly following the others, feeling it was what men did, and surely I would be a man soon. Also the notion of being drunk was something, like having sex with a woman, to which we all aspired without knowing what it was like or whether it would be any good or worth doing.

I usually stuck to cider, though even then half a pint was enough for me. Now and again, if we were flush, we ordered a half and half, which meant half a beer and a small whisky. The State Management's whisky, Border Blend, was excellent, so all real men said. Whisky did seem to make the beer go down better. But I never had enough beer or whisky to make me feel the slightest bit drunk. Whatever drunk was.

But I always did seem to have a girlfriend, from about the age of sixteen onwards, someone I could boast I was going out with, someone I had once taken home from a dance, or danced with twice, or exchanged meaningful glances with, even though she might not have been aware that she was now my girlfriend.

There was a Girl Guide I caught sight of at some church parade, Jenny Hogg, and I thought she was stunning. I thought the name Jenny was wonderful, my favourite girl's name, and used to say it to myself. I didn't worry about the Hogg bit. It was a common local surname anyway, so I didn't think of a pig. I walked her home from the next church parade and that was all that happened. No hand-holding, never mind any kissing. I don't think she said a word, almost as if she was unaware I was walking her home, but for weeks my little heart gave an extra beat whenever I saw her across a crowded bus queue at the town hall.

Reg did not like dancing, being big and clumsy and not well coordinated, so I used to go to most dances on my own, fancying myself as a dancer, or at least having no inhibitions about embarrassing myself. There were local hops on the new Belah estate beside us, or church dances across town at the Wigton Road Methodist Hall. At local or church hops you danced to records, with some awful creep in a bow tie announcing the next dance, such as a valeta or Dinky two-step. If it was a Dashing White Sergeant, he would take us through the movements.

In the excuse-me dances, you would make a dash for the girl you fancied, who in theory was not supposed to reject you. But they could turn away, pretend not to see you, or suddenly have to go the lavvy.

In the waltzes and slow foxtrots, you would try to get as close as possible, especially if the lights were being dimmed. You would attempt to insert your knee between her legs, which was harder than it sounds when there was a stiffened petticoat under her skirt. The girls used to steep their petti-coats in the bath in some sort of salts to make them stiff and stick out when they twirled around, but if they used too much it felt as if they were wearing armour. You would push harder, only to be told, 'Gerroff!'

The old joke that goes 'Is that a gun in your pocket or are you just pleased to see me?' was based on the truth. There were young girls, totally innocent in every sense, who would be genuinely surprised by your erection. They simply did not know what it was, suspecting a pencil or a ruler left over from doing your homework.

Now and again you would convince yourself you were on

to a winner, when a girl you really liked the look of agreed to the last dance, and, yes, she said you could take her home. You would wait outside the girls' cloakroom, already on heat, but when she reappeared she was with a friend, always uglier and boring. All three of you would walk home, with often the two girls linking arms, making you feel a right wally. And of course they always lived on a council estate at the far end of town.

What you were hoping for was to get a girl on her own, then kiss her up against a hedge near her house, hoping to get your hand somewhere on the region of her upper body, perhaps even undo the upper button on her school winter coat.

Once I was in the upper sixth, I upgraded to some of the better dance halls, such as the County Ballroom or eventually the really posh one, when I got a bit older, the Crown and Mitre. They had proper, live orchestras. But the problem was that you were competing with farmers' sons who had come into town for the night, or boys who were at St Bees, the local public school. They would stand at the side and jangle their keys, indicating they had a car, so naturally they got all the talent.

I did try the tougher dance halls, like the Cameo, full of working-class, council-house girls, from the same background. Aged fifteen or sixteen, they would already be out working, in a shop or packing crackers at Carr's. But I began to find I had lost contact with such girls, unable to relate to them or them to me. I think they thought I was a grammar cad, which of course I had become.

At school we talked constantly about sex, about girls we fancied – but I never for one moment imagined that girls might be much the same. If only I had known. They seemed a different species, interested in different things, and we were programmed to pursue them and doomed to fantasise about what we might do to them.

There were boys who boasted they had bought a johnny, were really going to get it this time, she was up for it. Did we say up for it? Perhaps not. That sounds modern. A goer – I think we were all hoping to meet a goer. From whom we would probably have run a mile.

There were endless stories, mostly lifted from cartoons and jokes on the radio, about going into a chemist's and feeling so embarrassed about asking in a whisper for a johnny – and finding your mum was standing beside you. Vinny, that rather advanced boy at the Creighton, used to carry a condom in his wallet, unused by the look of it, keeping it ready for his next conquest, so he boasted. We all knew it had not been used and never would be. I think the sell-by date was about 1944.

Nobody we ever knew had sex – yet it must have been happening, out there, if only once a year, tops. This was because around once a year there would be a girl from the high school who would suddenly disappear for a few months, not be seen locally, or at school, and rumours would spread that she had fallen, been caught, was in the family way, up the duff, had a bun in the oven, nudge nudge. The poor lass would have gone off to a mother and baby home, miles away, probably near Newcastle, had her baby, then handed it over to be adopted, never to see it again. Which is what had happened to young women for centuries, not able to bring up a child on their own, having no money, no support, feeling they had brought shame not just on themselves but their whole family, who could never of course admit publicly what had occurred. Now and again, the boy did marry the girl. For some it worked out. For others it did not.

Today, it is so different. Unmarried mothers get help, money, housing, support and there is no shame at all. In fact, young women often decide to have a baby as a personal choice, despite their age and economic position. I happen to think this is an advance. The system might get abused from time to time, the state taken advantage of, but it is so much better than the old days.

Although we heard now and again of a girl getting pregnant, we never heard about gays, lesbians, paedophiles. And in Carlisle, we never came across any Jews, blacks, anyone remotely foreign, apart from the odd cockney left over from the war. No real foreigner would ever come and live in Carlisle, unless they were Scottish. The UK was an insular island in the 1950s, but in Carlisle we seemed cut off from not just the mainstream but all the tributaries as well.

Going up street on a Saturday you would see all the little kids being dragged around by their mams – the girls and boys with incredibly blonde hair and blue eyes, though later, when grown-up, the blonde hair mostly disappeared. The local lineage, with all that Anglo-Saxon plus Norse and Viking blood, carries on today, as Carlisle, unlike most English towns, has had little immigration.

There were Catholics in Carlisle, of course, for there was a Catholic secondary school, descendants of the Irish who had come to work on the railways or the coal mines on the west coast, but I didn't actually know any.

The word 'gay' was not used in its modern sense, though

we did by the time of the upper sixth form hear stories of men called homos, down south. It was during 1953 that they started prosecuting Lord Montagu of Beaulieu. He was accused of under-age sex with a fourteen-year-old Boy Scout. He pleaded innocence and was not convicted. Then in 1954 he was sentenced to twelve months in prison for a gross offence with an adult, an RAF serviceman, which took place on his own estate. The whole country was agog, the first such post-war incident that had entered national consciousness, but it was mainly whispered about, especially in front of the children.

What exactly did they do? That's what we all wondered. A cock up your bum? Surely that was a joke, who would want to do that? In the showers, after PE, when we were all naked, someone would say, 'Backs to the wall – here comes Monty.' Then we would all pretend to be afraid that we were about to be buggered, still having little idea what it meant.

The Buggery Act had been in force since 1533, so it was probably a joke that sniggery schoolboys had been making for centuries. But one result of the Montagu case was that the Wolfenden committee was set up, though it was not for another ten years that consenting adults could do what they liked in private.

By the time of the upper sixth, there was a chance of a better class of girl, from our sister school, the high school, but I didn't have a lot of luck. We didn't mix for lessons, or take part in joint events, such as school plays, which is what I gather happened elsewhere if the local boys' grammar school had a sister high school nearby. It delighted me to learn many years later that Diane Abbott, the black Labour MP, was at the sister school in Harrow to the boys' grammar which Michael Portillo, later a Tory MP, attended; both were born in 1953. The two schools did plays and films, in which they performed together and became friends. So unlikely, but so sweet.

The nearest we got to, er, intercourse was playing the girls' school at hockey. It was a scratch match, as we did not officially play hockey, just rugby, but of course everyone wanted to play against the girls. It took place on their pitch and there was a large turnout of cheering girls. We liked to think it was for us, but they were cheering on their own first XI hockey stars, on which the younger girls had mad crushes.

There was one high school girl, daughter of a solicitor, who suddenly arrived at our house one day. I saw her coming down the path, about to knock at the front door, so I hid behind the sofa and told my mother on no account to answer the door. She did, of course, pleased by all visitors, even total strangers. She gave a great smile. 'No, Hunter is not in at the moment, but come in, come in, have a cup tea . . .'

Fortunately, the girl, Joan Atkinson, declined to come in, but she gave my mother a written invitation for me to come to a party at her house. I could not work out how she had got my address and tracked me down. When I went to the party I told her how sorry I was that I'd missed her when she'd called round.

There was a meeting place for sixth-formers, boys and girls, in the middle of the town, called the Garret Club. It was in a disused building in one of the old medieval lanes, now long since demolished to become a shopping precinct.

I think the council owned it, or the education authorities. Grammar school and high school sixth-formers used it for meetings, debates, cultural events, table tennis and social evenings.

By the upper sixth form, you had met every member of the opposite sex you were ever likely to meet, ever, probably in your whole life, if you didn't move away from Carlisle, which of course most people didn't. Even though you might not know them, in the sense of going out with them, or even speaking to them, you still knew of them, had had them pointed out. The pool of talent, from which breeding might eventually come, had become pretty familiar, apart from those who hid themselves away and swotted, never coming into the light.

One of the ones I had never spoken to was called Margaret Forster. Her best friend was also called Margaret, Margaret Crosthwaite, both with short dark hair, both said to be clever. I had seen them after school a few times, standing around outside Thurnham's bookshop. I'd heard that Margaret Crosthwaite supposedly had a boyfriend from our school, but nothing about the other Margaret. Her reputation suggested she was something of a bluestocking, very studious, said to be fierce and forthright, not known for appearing at social events.

One evening she was at the Garret Club, the first time I had seen her there. Someone wound up the gramophone, put on some records, and couples were starting to dance. I went across and asked her if she would honour me with the next foxtrot. Or it could have been a Dinky two-step.

'Certainly not,' she said. 'I don't dance.' So that was it.

Given the bum's rush before I had even managed a second sentence. Oh well. So I asked someone else to dance with me, who did agree. Very soon after that, she left. Back to her books, I shouldn't wonder.

During that first term in the upper sixth, I did in fact manage an academic achievement. At Christmas that year, December 1953, I passed my O-level Latin, along with Brian and Alistair, also from the Creighton. Not bad, getting Latin from scratch in just eighteen months, while studying so many other things. I can scarcely believe it, even now.

Apart from my three A-levels, I was still doing general science, though this was a farce really. We knew it would not count, either way, towards university entrance. And the poor old master was a bit of a farce as well – Mr Done, known as Flash Done, supposedly a brilliant Cambridge scholar in his day, excellent scientist, but he just could not control our class. I was taken aback and rather appalled by how cruel and unkind our class could be to him. Throughout my five years at the Creighton, we had never terrorised or given cheek to any teachers – we were terrified of them, if anything, even the ones we considered pretty hopeless.

Flash Done took us in the school library, gathered round a large circular table. We all sat with our knees under the table, then at agreed moments, when his back was turned, we all lifted up the table with our knees and moved it a few feet. Then another few feet. He would eventually turn round to find we had moved right across the room.

'Not me, sir, I haven't moved the table, sir – look, sir, my knees have not moved.'

'Nor me, sir, you say it's moved, not us, sir.'

'Must be a poltergeist, sir. Perhaps Mrs Dunstan is holding a séance next door.'

'I did see her floating down the corridor, sir . . .'

Mrs Dunstan was the headmaster's wife and was reputed to be rather dopey and off with the fairies.

'Stop this nonsense!' said Mr Done. 'Come on, I know who it was. Own up.'

Then he would bend down to see whose knees were propping up the table, and therefore responsible for moving it.

The moment he bent down, we all, as one, moved the table back again – this time over him. He would end up right under the table, being kicked and pushed by twenty legs – all, of course, accidentally.

'Sorry, sir, didn't see you there, sir, are you all right, sir?'

He was supposed to be teaching us the history of science, when he eventually restored any order, but even then we would give silly answers, mispronouncing names, but keeping a straight face, just to amuse everyone else.

'Copper Knickers, sir! He said Copper Knickers. It's not Copper Knickers, is it?'

'No, it's Copernicus. Now sit down, boy.'

We did a bit on the history of geology as well and everyone insisted on pronouncing coomb, meaning a hollow on a hill or valley, as quim, which means something different, another sort of hollow. Everyone would roar and laugh, mock the person who had got it wrong.

Mr Done was small and thin with a bald dome, specs and a worried countenance. I went along with the ragging, yet felt guilty for joining in, making his life miserable. Yet we were supposed to be grammar school sixth-formers, the cream of the school.

There was one teacher we would never play up – Mr Banks, the deputy headmaster. His job was to deliver whacks. He was the heavy you were sent to for disciplinary purposes who beat you with a strap. Mr Banks was huge and thickset and said to have been at one time Carlisle United's goalkeeper. He also happened to be our geography teacher – and the only teacher at the grammar I thought was useless. He didn't give lessons, didn't explain, didn't ask for any questions; all he did was dictate to us and we had to write it down. He had a supply of exercise books in which he had written out class notes, probably decades ago when he had first started teaching A-level geography. It must have been as boring for him as it was for us, year after year, ploughing through the same old dreary notes.

At the end of my last term at the grammar, the spring term of 1954, I got an AB for English, an A for history and an A for geography. I was a bit disappointed by the English mark. Adrian Barnes had written in the margin: 'Creditable industry but his standard of attainment was not high.' Cheeky sod.

During that term I did get one A for an English essay, but this was from the other English teacher, Gerry Lightfoot. I was helped on that essay by my dear mother, but of course never revealed it to anyone. I had been stuck and asked her for an idea, an example of something. Can't remember what of. All those years reading Dickens must have paid off.

A few weeks before I sat my A-levels, I found myself on a charabanc going across to Durham. I might have made up the charabanc, it could have been the train, but the school had arranged for around a dozen of us to go together, all at the same time, for interviews at various colleges of Durham University.

I don't remember filling in application forms for any university, but I must have done. I did once have to go into my dad's room and ask him what I should put down as his occupation, which troubled him greatly, causing a lot of damning and blasting.

'You can see my occupation, God damn it. When I get out of this bed, I will show you what an occupation is. Hand me that stick. Marion! Marion! I'm getting up, where is my bloomin' stick, damn and blast, after all the money I have brought into this damn house ...'

In the end, in the column for father's occupation, I put down 'Civil Servant (Retired)'.

Applying to Durham had been totally decided and organised by the school. None of our parents had been to university, not even the apparently posh ones living at Stanwix, though presumably Mike's dad, being a dentist, must have attended some sort of college. But the fathers of all my other friends, as far as I knew, were more or less white-collar workers. Ian Johnstone's dad worked in a bank. Dicky Wilson's dad worked at 14 MU, as did Reg's, as had mine. I assume all of them had left school at fifteen or sixteen.

Dicky had already got into Oxford, while Reg and Mike were going to stay on for a third year in the sixth, whatever happened in their A-levels, in order to try the Oxbridge entrance exams. But for most of the rest of us in the upper sixth, the school had guided us to places where they thought we might get in and where they had contacts, having sent pupils in the past. They knew how universities worked. Our parents didn't.

They had apparently been sending a lot recently to Durham, which was about our nearest university, geographically, though it was right across the country, over in the Northeast. It was a small northern city with a cathedral, so it didn't seem as if it would be a massive cultural upheaval, compared with trying for some Big City University, like Birmingham, or even scarier London.

My interview was with a Dr Thomson in his overcrowded suite of rooms in Durham Castle, the home of University College. When I entered, there was opera music blaring out loudly and he asked me if I liked opera. I stupidly said, 'Oh yes, I am very fond of *Rigoletto*.' I had recently been taken to a performance in Glasgow, while visiting my Uncle Jim and Aunt Linda. I found it totally boring, stiff and false. We then spent most of the interview talking about opera. I thought that is it. I will never get in.

Some weeks later, when the A-level results came out, I went down to school to pick them up. I found I had passed all three, with a B in each of them. Then I received a letter saying I was being accepted to read for an honours degree at Durham, followed by a letter from the City of Carlisle Education Office, signed L. Charnley, Director of Education, informing me was I was being given a 'Major Award', which would be F + £210. I have it in front of me, and I still don't know what the 'F' stood for, but it meant that all my tuition fees would be paid direct by them. I would get an annual maintenance grant in three equal portions, plus travelling expenses back and forward to university if they exceeded £7 per annum. I would also get a vacation allowance.

I was in the money! I could not take it all in. All I knew was that everything, whatever everything might turn out to consist of, was going to be paid for. Despite having an invalid father, and no income coming into the house, I was going to go to university.

We all went from school and waited for the pubs to open. I had half a shandy and compared notes with everyone else about how they had done and where we would all be going next year. To everyone's amazement, Reg had failed one of his A-levels, German. It was a stupid one to have taken and he had always moaned about it. He didn't know what to do now. Sitting for Oxford seemed pointless, as they would not be impressed by his A-level results. He didn't know whether to resit his German at Christmas, then do his national service, get it over with, or try Oxbridge all the same. Mike had got his A-levels and was still going to stay on to try for Oxbridge entrance.

Ian Johnstone, another of my Stanwix friends, had also passed and was coming to Durham, but to a different college. Brian Cooke, one of the two others who had come from the Creighton with me, was going to the same college at Durham. Alistair McFadden, had also passed and was going, I think, to Sheffield or Birmingham.

So, all three of us from the Creighton had got into university in two years, at the first attempt. In fact, the other two went on to get PhDs. Brian even became a professor. So much for a second-class school for eleven-plus failures. I will always feel grateful to the Creighton, taking me in when we arrived from Scotland, and preparing me for O-levels. Then, of course, to the grammar school, especially for teaching me Latin in such a short time.

During the long school holidays of 1954 – or should I say vacation, as I was about to go up to university (not 'uni', for no one used that annoying abbreviation in the fifties) – I got a summons to go and visit the minister of Warwick Road Presbyterian Church. Oh no, I groaned, not him, that boring bloke.

He was the dour Scotsman I thought was a total pain, just like his church, where I had been dragged along for years by my mother. I was to call at his manse one evening and was given the address.

I expected an old Victorian detached residence, but it was a dull semi in Stanwix. He chuntered on about how well I had done, getting into Durham, a credit to his congregation, blah blah. Then he handed me an envelope – in which there was £10. I was overwhelmed. I immediately took back all the awful things I had said and thought about him. Apparently, some member of the congregation had left money to give to people like me, a young member of the church, who had got into university. He hadn't given it out for some time – because, of course, so few went to university.

Ten pounds in 1954 is around £200 today, so it was a great present, enabling me in theory, when I got to Durham, to buy loads of books. Or, more likely, countless shandies and entrances to student hops.

I went past that church just a few months ago. It is at the top of Warwick Road, a prime location in the middle of the city. It closed as a church a few years back. Opposite it, the

Lonsdale cinema has also gone, Carlisle's major cinema, where I attended the ABC Minors and the Beatles once played. The church is now an antiques emporium. Where I used to listen to the dreary sermons you can now buy vintage clothes, postcards, books, toys. Downstairs, where I went to Sunday school, there is now a very pleasant coffee bar. Much more useful.

I also recently went back to my old schools. The two secondary schools I attended, the Creighton and the grammar school, had amalgamated, along with the girls' school, the Margaret Sewell, and become a comprehensive in 1968. They still use the same buildings. The main part of the old grammar school, which I was so thrilled to enter in 1952, is now the school's sixth form and has 350 pupils. We had about sixty.

There were black leather armchairs in the corridors, with pupils lolling around in them. Mr Banks would have brought out his whacking strap for that.

It's sad in a way that the old grammar school is no more, the name wiped out after all these centuries, but, on the other hand, I am all for the comprehensive system. Too many lives were stunted by that awful, divisive eleven-plus exam.

15

UP AT DURHAM

With some of the money from the church I bought a trunk, in which I packed all my stuff for the term ahead. It felt like *Tom Brown's School Days*, having one's own trunk, on which I pasted a huge label saying E.H. Davies, University College, The Castle, Durham. No postcodes in those days. I thought I should put my official name, as that was the one on my grant letter from Carlisle education department.

I then went down to the railway station, paid some money, and a British Railways truck came to our front door and took the trunk away. It then got transported to Durham where it was dumped on the ground floor of the Castle Keep. It was a good system, and not too expensive. Presumably the middle classes, who had their own car, took trunks and their loved ones all the way to university.

I did not have many clothes and only a couple of pairs of underpants, rather tatty. For many years I never wore any, not knowing they existed, or my mother had never been told about them. Have I made that up? Vests, I had loads of vests, as grandmothers and aunts sent them for Christmas. I also took my father's overcoat and his shirts and collars, the ones you put on with a stud at the front and back and were hell to wear as they stuck into your Adam's apple. He was clearly never going to need his clothes again. The ambitions of male teenagers in the early fifties was to be old enough, i.e. eighteen, and to look and dress like your dad, proving you were now grown-up.

I went on the train with several others from school, three of them going to the same college as me, while one of them, Ian, my friend from Stanwix, was going to St Chad's and another to St Cuthbert's.

My trunk was there when I arrived, among dozens of other trunks which had landed from all parts of the country. I found my room number on a list and got someone to help me up to the room I was allocated. Then I helped him with his trunk. My room was miles up, on the top floor of the Keep, along endless stone corridors, all cold, and then up cold stone staircases. You entered through double doors, made of ancient oak, an outer and inner door. I learned later that if you closed the outer door, it meant your 'oak was up' and you did not want to be disturbed because you were studying hard. Or similarly busy.

It turned out to contain two rooms, a large sitting room, plus a separate bedroom. Lucky me, I thought, having all this, after all my life sharing a room with my brother. I went in and found a figure in spectacles sitting at the window looking out across Durham towards the railway station, from whence I had just come. He had a notebook and a stopwatch and was busy writing down train times and details. Oh my God, I had not realised I had a roommate, Hugh from Peterborough. I had been stuck with a trainspotter with whom I would have to share a study and a bedroom for the next year. Bringing

My paternal grandfather, Edward Davies (1866–1938), an engineer who owned his own house in Hamilton Road, Cambuslang, near Glasgow. He played the fiddle and wrote the odd article for the *Airdrie & Coatbridge Gazette*.

My maternal grandmother, born Mary Black, married James Brechin, a railway engine driver. They lived in a council flat on the Bellshill Road, Motherwell.

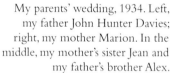

My parents' wedding, 1934. Left, my father John Hunter Davies; right, my mother Marion. In the middle, my mother's sister Jean and my father's brother Alex.

My father in the Royal Air Force (back row, third from the left), circa 1930, possibly in Perth.

My mother with me in Johnstone, Renfrewshire, where I was born, 1936.

Davies family gathering in Cambuslang, 1936. I am on my grandmother's lap. My father John is third from the left on the back row; my mother is second from the right, on the back row. Uncle Jim, the 'literary one', on the far left, worked as a rent collector and wrote a biblical play in the Scots dialect.

Studio photograph from 1940. How on earth did they afford that? Me, aged four, and my twin sisters, Marion and Annabelle.

Me, on the left, struggling with asthma and an itchy suit; with Marion and Annabelle and my brother Johnny, in Dumfries, 1944.

Here I am (aged eight) in Motherwell, with very attractive buck teeth and my cousin Sylvia.

The 17th Carlisle Church of Scotland Boy Scouts, 1950. I am on the back row, fourth from the left. Reg Hill is seventh from the left. We specialised in not passing any badges.

Creighton School fifth formers, 1951. I am on the front row, fourth from the right; Brian Cooke is second on the left; Alistair McFaden third from the left. All three of us became the 'Chosen Ones', who went on to Carlisle Grammar School.

In France with the Creighton School, 1951. I am on the right. The trip didn't actually improve my French language skills.

Carlisle Grammar School hockey team, 1954. We were about to play the girls' high school, and hoping to score. I am on the front row, second from the right. Brian Cooke is at the left end of the front row and Ian Johnstone at the end on the right. Reg Hill is at the very back. Mike Thornhill is also at the back, second from the right.

Durham graduate, 1957. Daisy Edis, the photographer, managed to give me a perfect complexion. So worth every penny (predecimal).

A polyphoto strip of me as an ace reporter on the staff of the *Manchester Evening Chronicle*, 1958.

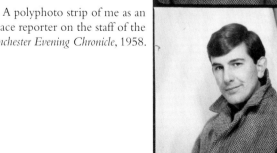

Telephone: BLackfriars 1234
Telegrams: Chronicle, Manchester

London: TERminus 1234
Telegrams: Kemnews, London

Evening Chronicle

London Office: Kemsley House, W.C.1

KEMSLEY HOUSE, MANCHESTER 4
(P.O. BOX 290)

RW/SC   July 29, 1958.

Mr. Edward Hunter Davies,
28, Caird Avenue,
Carlisle.

Dear Mr. Davies,

Many thanks for your letter of July 28.

We appreciate the difficulty in starting
with us on the date I suggested in my previous
letter, but it does not present any major problem
at all. Instead of joining us in the middle of
August, we suggest you take up your duties at 9 a.m.
on Monday, September 1, which will be much more
convenient than starting in the preceding mid-week.
Perhaps you would confirm this arrangement.

I shall, in fact, be away on holiday
at that date, but perhaps you would report to my
deputy, Mr. Harold Mellor, under whose jurisdiction
you will work pending my return.

I would like to take this opportunity of
welcoming you to the staff and to wish you every
success and happiness in your activities.

Yours faithfully,

(R.Walker)
News Editor.

A letter from the news editor of the *Manchester Evening Chronicle*, 1958, welcoming me to the staff. My wages were to be £14 a week, more than my father got in his working life.

Off to Cyprus

TODAY HUNTER DAVIES, Evening Chronicle Staff Reporter, flies to Cyprus to find out on the spot how Lancashire and Cheshire boys are faring on the trouble-torn island.

What is life like for the men of the Lancashire Fusiliers?

How are they facing

HUNTER DAVIES

up to the immense difficulties of their task? His dispatches will give the full facts.

Davies is taking with him a sheaf of messages from wives, sweethearts and mothers of the boys in Cyprus. He will hand these over personally, and bring back messages from the troops.

Evening Chronicle

A small piece in the *Manchester Evening Chronicle* telling the dear readers of my epic trip to cover the situation in Cyprus.

I became a war reporter in 1958 – for two weeks anyway. With the Lancashire Fusiliers in Cyprus, handing out letters to the lads.

Bashing away at my typewriter on the *Sunday Times*, which I joined in 1960.

Margaret Forster (aged thirteen), in 1951, at the Carlisle and County High School. She protested at the school having a day off, due to our local Carlisle United playing the mighty Arsenal FC.

On holiday in 1959 with Margaret, who was by then at Oxford University.

My wedding on 11 June 1960 to Margaret, in Oxford, to which no family or guests were invited.

girls back, if I ever struck lucky, was going to be awkward, not to say embarrassing. Would he keep notes, write down the times?

University College, Durham was situated in Durham Castle, although it also had other buildings around Palace Green. It was the first of the Durham colleges, founded in 1832, which made Durham the third oldest university in the whole of England, after Oxford and Cambridge. A long time after. All the same, it felt suitably ancient and traditional, located in a building dating back to Norman times. It had courtyards and a grand hall, towers and galleries, with college servants and a High Table butler, and was totally residential, aping the Oxbridge pattern, not that I had been to either Oxford or Cambridge. We had a bedder to make our beds and clean our room, a motherly local woman with a very strong Geordie accent which I could not understand.

You had a subject tutor you saw each week for whom you wrote essays, and also a moral tutor you saw once a term when he invited you to his rooms for a sherry party. I had never had sherry before, except the horrible sweet British stuff that my mother sometimes bought at Christmas and kept in our cocktail cabinet till it turned to sugar.

There was a college buttery, beside the Great Hall, where you could buy bread and milk and eggs and basic essentials as well as college sherry – bottles bearing the college's coat of arms, awfully smart. Best of all, you did not have to pay cash. You could put it on your battels, sign for it and settle up at the end of term.

The servants addressed us as 'mister' and the tutors referred to us as gentlemen. So unlike our dear life back on the council estate.

We were all members of the JCR – the junior common room – which meant the undergraduate body of the college. The common room itself was a rather nice large sitting room with sofas and chairs, the morning newspapers, a record player and suggestions book, where clever clogs would write long if rather silly things.

Having unpacked my trunk on that first day, said a few words to Hugh, in between trains, I came down to look for the common room. I went in slowly, looking around, not sure if I had the right place. As a newcomer, you kept quiet, let the second and third years make all the jokes, read the papers first, decide what music would be played. If you fell foul of some rule or tradition, you'd be penalised for your transgression and have to pay a sconce, which often meant drinking a bottle of wine while upside down or some such juvenile jape.

There were regular JCR meetings, run totally by the undergraduate body, with the Senior Man in charge and the JCR secretary making notes. It seemed so formal, with gentlemen begging to differ, making points of order, moving on to item number three on the agenda. I had never come across this sort of committee-like organisation before, yet it was all being run by students like me, lads only a year or so older, as opposed to dons or proper grown-ups. Several of the students did seem incredibly grown-up to me. And of course many were, having done their national service first, seen the world. There was also a handful of public school boys who were so fluent, so well spoken, so clever. They just seemed to stand up and out it all came. Was it a trick – how had they learned it?

I thought it was rather wonderful and quaint, if rather elitist and pretentious. I didn't know at the time, having no experience of Oxford or Cambridge, that this sort of residential collegiate life was a straight pinch from Oxbridge.

I discovered many years later that one of the best-known, most amusing, most successful nineteenth-century books about Oxford undergraduate life, *The Adventures of Mr Verdant Green* by Cuthbert Bede, was in fact written by a Durham student, not an Oxford student. His real name was Edward Bradley (1827–1889), a clergyman and novelist who had been at Castle in the 1840s. The clue was in his pseudonym – Cuthbert after St Cuthbert and Bede after the Venerable Bede, two of Durham's best-known icons. (Cuthbert's shrine is still in the cathedral, as are the bones of Bede.)

In 1954 when I arrived at Durham, there were nine colleges in all: University College (known as Castle), Hatfield, St Cuthbert's, St John's, St Chad's and Bede – all for men – then there were three for women, St Mary's, St Hild's and St Aidan's. The total student population of the Durham colleges was 1,500 – all of them residential. We were officially Durham Colleges in the University of Durham, because the university also contained King's College, Newcastle. (A few years later, Newcastle became an independent university in its own right.) We had nothing to do with Newcastle. That was a much larger urban, redbrick, modern, city centre college, somewhere miles to the north. We considered ourselves a cut above them, classier all round.

We were told, and believed, that our perfect situation and residential system was the ideal, how a varsity should look and feel. We were on a peninsula in the middle of an ancient city, with the River Wear making a loop all the way round, cutting us off inside it. The cathedral and castle, most of the colleges and ancient university buildings, were clustered in the centre of the peninsula, around Palace Green, a large open, grass space in the middle on which you were not supposed to walk. University policemen, known as bulldogs, could fine you for walking on it.

Those who felt intimidated by it all, or reacted against it, considering it unreal and phoney, went around saying that Durham was an ivory tower, cut off from the real world. I felt proud and privileged and fortunate to be there, but rather over-whelmed. Despite having friends with me from Carlisle, and the fact that there were two or three Old Carliols in the years above, I seemed to be on my own most of the time and a bit lost. Everyone seemed cleverer and more confident. I wondered how long it would take to understand how it all worked . . .

You had to wear gowns for all lectures, when seeing your tutor and for formal dinner in the Great Hall in the evening. All meals were in the same hall, and the first years all sat together. The High Table was at the top of the room, where the dons sat together and were served by their own uniformed butler called Eddie, who tended to mince about, make catty remarks, was very funny and camp. He was the first homo-sexual I'd ever become aware of.

My main feeling in those early weeks was one of elation, anticipation and hope. I felt for the first time in my life that I was starting something new – at the same time as everyone else was starting something new. In Dumfries, I had seemed out of it, arriving from England. At the Creighton, I had just arrived from Scotland. At the grammar school, I had always felt an outsider. Now I felt on equal terms with all the others, beginning a new life, all together.

When eventually I got to know the people in my year, most were very much like me – from northern grammar schools, in Tyneside, Yorkshire and Lancashire, most of them with regional accents. As I had. There were some from the Midlands and London, but mostly they seemed to be northerners.

Unlike mine, their family backgrounds were mainly lower middle class; their parents owned their own houses. But everyone I knew was first generation university. The public school boys had stood at the JCR meeting, but there were very few of them. One had been at Winchester and one at Fettes in Scotland. Today, around half are privately educated, or the sons and daughters of professional parents, all of them graduates themselves. I wonder if the council house comprehensive kids feel out of it. In 1954 I was never really aware of any class divisions. The differences between us were mainly regional.

There was, however, one significant group of people with chips on their shoulders. These were the people who had failed to get into Oxford or Cambridge. At their schools they had been academic high-flyers, tipped to sail through A-levels and get an Oxbridge scholarship, but, at the final hurdle, they had not made it. For whatever reason. Possibly some lacked the supposed or perceived spark needed to stand out in an Oxbridge interview, or the confidence and fluency that a better public school would have given them. One or two maintained they had got into Oxbridge, but had opted for Durham instead because they'd been offered a scholarship. I never knew there was such a thing, but the college did turn out to have organ scholars and classics scholars who seemed to have higher status.

For the first few weeks, some of the Oxbridge rejects did mope around with a slightly disgruntled yet superior air, as if they were too good for this place. I couldn't understand it. Having not tried Oxbridge, or applied to anywhere else, I felt Durham was totally wonderful and marvellous. Whether Durham would feel that about me remained to be discovered.

When my first grant cheque came through, I paid it into the local Midland Bank and opened an account. It was a Midland Bank cheque, so I presumed it had to be paid in there. My parents never had a cheque book or used a bank. With the money I bought a maroon college blazer and a maroon-and-white college scarf from Gray's, the college outfitters on the Bailey. That was what you did, what all new students did. I also bought a suit, the first in my life. It was in charcoal grey from Burton's, the height of chic.

I longed to have a duffel coat, the third item of clothing that every fifties student needed to acquire, but my funds did not run to this. Instead, I used to borrow one on special occasions – i.e. taking a girl out – from Edmund Vardy-Binks, who lived below me in the Keep. He had a very thick, expensive duffel, hardly worn, so I was doing him a favour really, giving it an airing. Often I just took it, without telling him. Edmund Vardy-Binks – now I look at his name, he does sound a bit posh, but I don't remember him appearing so.

To save money I posted my dirty clothes home every week to my mother to wash. As if she didn't have enough to do. When she sent me back the clean and ironed clothes, she always enclosed a large slice of her homemade gingerbread. I don't remember her ever visiting me at Durham, not till the very end, or my sisters and brother. Was I ashamed? I hope not. I don't think any other students had parental visits either – yet I bet most parents would have liked to have been invited. I don't think parents were as involved as they are today. They had no idea what university was like. It was all a foreign country.

I did have one family visitor, out of the blue, who just turned up at the Castle gatehouse, asked the porter for my room and was shown up. This was my Uncle Jim from Cambuslang, the one who had written the Scottish dialect play. He took me out for a Chinese meal and drank Drambuie all the way through.

In my first term, I went for a trial for the college football team, but they were all so much better than me, then the rugby XV and they were total hulks, so I joined the boat club. They were desperate for new members, advertising for absolute beginners.

At that age you always think there must be something you will be really good at, that you will discover a hitherto unknown natural talent lurking inside, just waiting for you to find it. The thing about university, starting off from scratch, is that you can give new things a go, then move on, without being embarrassed or anyone ever really noticing.

The boat club was full of hearties, ever-so-public-school types, but I had heard that the boat club dinner at the end of term was a total piss-up, so it was worth joining. I was too small to row, so I was told, too weak and useless, so I was made a cox. I felt a bit insulted by this. I might have been weak and weedy, but I wasn't titchy. Coxing turned out to be quite good fun, sitting at the back of the boat, making sure we got through the bridges, shouting orders at four lumps.

I quite liked getting up early in the morning, while everyone was still asleep, going down to the college boathouse before breakfast. It felt healthy, clean living, virtuous. It was rather a smart, classy boathouse, with our college coat of arms on top. You left a pair of old rubbish shoes inside the boathouse which you put on when you carried the boat out, to avoid any mud and wet, and then put them on after you had finished. I liked the ritual, feeling I really was in some elite, special club. Our boat took part in one of the novice races at the Durham Regatta, which was an enjoyable event, but we got hammered.

I then took up sculling, which was more satisfying. You could go on the river at any time, no need to worry about any crew, on a whim, then glide off into emptiness, skimming across the water, lost in thought. Except I wasn't. I was busy imaging people on the river bank admiring this lone sculler, gliding along. More like splashing along. More like crawling along. I wasn't much good at that either. But the point was to try out new things, new self-images. I still could not believe I was getting it all for free.

But the boat club dinner was a great success. I turned out to be good at the getting drunk part. I even managed to throw an orange through a medieval stained-glass window in the Great Hall. I am not sure if it broke, but I hid under the table, hoping no one had seen. I somehow got myself back up the stairs of the Keep to our room, waking up Hugh. I was then very sick. Fortunately I managed to get the window open in time, so my vomit decorated the battlements rather than our sitting room.

My subject was history and I was in the first year honours class, considered to be an honour in itself, as there were those who were following an apparently slightly easier degree course, in General Arts.

Almost from the beginning, I was either bored rigid or had no idea what was going on. The history was mainly either Roman or medieval, whereas at school I had enjoyed modern history, i.e. nineteenth century, about the railways, trade unions, the Industrial Revolution. Now it was all dreary documents in Latin or medieval English. The Roman history professor was Eric Birley, well known in his field, who did at least radiate a bit of excitement for his subject, but the medieval man, Offler, seemed as dead as his subject. I had him as my tutor for a while and he spent more time filling and puffing at his smelly pipe than talking, and when he did, through clouds of smoke, it was all a mumble.

Even worse, all those doing first year history had to do a course in economics. This time I was totally lost. The theories and systems, words and notions, all seemed to be nonsensical – or totally obvious, common sense dressed up in a pretend scientific language.

Lectures were not compulsory, so I started missing a few where I decided I was understanding nothing, or was dozing off. You had to do a weekly essay, see your tutor, read it out and have it discussed. My history tutor for a while was a Dr Gerald Harris, a member of our college, whom I quite liked. But he left to take up a history lectureship at Oxford. I suspect a lot of the tutors felt like a lot of the students – that, really, they should have been at Oxbridge.

I didn't reveal my feelings of boredom and incomprehension to anyone, just accepted this would be what it was like; you had to get through it, stick at it, somehow, as I did with Latin at school, and it would turn out okay. But at the same time, I had begun to suspect I was there on false pretences. I was not the academic type. I didn't like studying, always trying to get away with as little as possible. In one way I think university is often wasted on the young. Aged eighteen to twenty-one, I had no interest in studying, ignored the unique opportunities afforded by having no responsibilities, no need to earn money or worry about others. A few decades later that all changed. I even once spent a whole year walking and studying Hadrian's Wall. Writing non-fiction books is studying, which I now do and love all the time.

Yet all around, there seemed to be so many swots, going straight back to their rooms, into their books, down to their essays. They seemed to me totally joyless. I am sure they, in turn, considered me trivial and a waster.

There were two Africans in my history group, the first black people I had ever seen. They were from Sierra Leone and had been at Fourah Bay College, founded in 1827, the oldest university in West Africa, which had had a connection with Durham since 1876. They never saw fresh air, never drank, never played, never spoke, made the most of every moment to study. An example to us all, I suppose, but not, alas, to me.

I blame Nobby, for leading me astray. In the silent, empty afternoons, I would eventually drag myself to my room and sit at my desk, staring out of the window, supposedly reading a book on medieval strip farming, my mind miles away, while Hugh my roommate was busy at his desk writing up some geography field excursion.

Nobby would appear in the room, having ignored the 'oak up' that Hugh had insisted on, and start singing 'Let's go to the Buffs, oh baby, let's go to the Buffs'.

Now I look up the date of that great song by Danny and the Juniors, 'At the Hop', I see it did not make number one till 1957, so Nobby could not have been singing that tune in 1954–55. But he did come in crooning his blandishments, his enticements, his sweet nothings in my ear.

And so we would go down the stairs of the Keep, across the empty courtyard, through the gatehouse, where presumably Cicely the porter spotted us, as she spotted everyone, and went tut tut. Then left across a deserted Palace Green, down Saddler Street and into the Buffs – the Buffalo Head public house. It would be empty in the early afternoon, as even the hardened local drinkers would not be there at that hour. We preferred it to the Union bar, playing shove ha'penny and spinning out a half glass of Mackeson for the rest of the afternoon. Not exactly a drug den or an orgy, but it did feel awfully wicked, wasting away an afternoon. Shove ha'penny was new to me, and so was Mackeson stout, a sweeter alternative to Guinness.

Obviously it was not Nobby's fault. I was more than willing to be distracted. Nobby was the same year as me but reading for a General Arts degree, which was considered a doddle, at least by him, compared with an honours course. He did strike me as clever, and would obviously survive in life on his wits.

I probably wasted a whole term mucking around with

Nobby, till I grew bored, deciding there was a more amusing, enjoyable way of wasting my time, using my energies.

I had no luck with girls in the first term. As a fresher, you think you will – after all, there will be new girls, and all the freshers' parties and balls and events, but the second and third year students get there first. They know all the ropes, read all the signs, pounce first and pick up the best. Many would even come up a day early to do some scouting, help the innocent newcomers find their feet, har har.

Durham was like Oxford and Cambridge and most British universities in the fifties in that there were not enough women to go round. Not even for sharing. The proportion was around five men to one woman. And, of course, the few women who had got in were very hard-working and practically locked up every evening in their college like nuns.

Around Durham, just a few miles away, were a couple of girls' teacher training colleges, Neville's Cross and Wynyard Hall. I was told they were usually easier meat, stuck out on their own in the country, and some might even be up for it. So I suppose at Durham we were luckier than some places. At Oxford, I was told the ratio was ten to one. Having to compete with the gilded youth from the best public schools, what chance would a spotty fellow from Carlisle have?

The two training colleges had regular Saturday night hops and a charabanc would be laid on for all the single, unattached Durham chaps, departing from Palace Green. It didn't seem strange at the time, just obvious logistics, but it was rather artificial and soulless, heavy-handed match-making, if not marriage-making – being bussed in for a specific purpose, like factory farming. Lots of relationships were started, and eventually consummated in marriage, but mostly you were eying the girls and watching the clock, worried that you would miss the charabanc going back to Palace Green and be stuck in the God awful wilds of rural Durham.

What you hoped to do, if you managed a few dances with someone half-reasonable, who seemed half-interested in you, was invite her back for afternoon tea at the Castle on Sunday afternoon. This was a decent ploy, for university undergrads were considered a notch up from teacher training students, and getting into the Castle itself was a big attraction.

So you would buy crumpets from a bread shop in the middle of Durham, perhaps steal some jam from the table at breakfast, straighten the bedclothes, open the bedroom window to let out the pong, tidy the desk and prepare your lair, making it all as attractive as possible. The most vital thing, of course, was to get Hugh out of the way, bribe or threaten him, encourage him to go off and see something exciting at the railway station – surely there were train numbers he had not spotted? On no account come back till chucking-out time at six, which was when all women had to leave the premises.

I would borrow Edmund Vardy-Binks' duffle coat – not even telling him I had taken it – then hang around the porter's lodge till the latest object of my lust eventually trotted up, in her best frock, heavily lacquered hair and stiffest petticoat.

Then what happened? Not a lot. I would usually suggest a walk first of all, along the river, over Prebends Bridge, then back to the Castle and up to our rooms high up in the Keep. There was a sort of kitchen on the landing where I heated up the crumpets and made tea, taking them back to my room and the waiting, expectant female, passing on the way some lewd fellows who would give the thumbs-up sign, lots of winks, nudges and other vulgarities.

Probably an hour of idle chat about films, pop songs of the day – did you like Pat Boone or Guy Mitchell? – the usual crap you had to get through, before possibly, hopefully, managing to manoeuvre her on to the bed, supposedly where she would be more comfortable, take the weight off her lacquered hair. Then there was a frantic final five minutes of wrestling, pushing and shoving to get your hand somewhere, anywhere, if only into the pockets of her belted raincoat. Eee, dear, as my mother used to say.

It must have been so frustrating for the girl as well, though we hardly thought of their feelings, just our own, furious at her for being a tease, as we saw it, and the waste of time and energy, not to mention the crumpets. It was worse, of course, if during the wrestling you had shot your load in your pants. The fury, the shame, the humiliation and the annoyance. I could not send them home to my mother, but would have to wash them myself.

I usually managed to have a girl round to tea most Sunday afternoons, which didn't go unnoticed by everyone else in the Keep. I would pretend how exhausted I was afterwards, keeping them happy.

I went to a hop, somewhere, every Saturday night. There were college hops, training college dances, hops at the town hall and also at the County, Durham's smartest hotel. I would put on my best charcoal grey suit, my best white shirt and attach to it my best Van Heusen collar. I did not send these collars home to be washed as my mother was never any good at starching and ironing. I would use them several times, turning them inside out when too grubby, then splash out and send them to the laundry to be properly starched. Laundry was picked up each week at the porter's lodge and then returned in your cubbyhole.

One of the problems with the County dances, unlike the college or training college hops, was that you were competing with the other young men of the town. Hard to believe it now, but young miners had a surprising amount of money in the 1950s, if they were doing shiftwork. And they were fit and cocky, proud to be miners, a job for life, just as it had been their father's job for life, a job no one expected ever to end.

The County and the town hall were also frequented by sixth form girls from the local Durham High School, a posh local school for girls. I got lucky and picked up a girl who had a silly nickname, like Kipper, or Fishface, or Cod, who I went out with for a few weeks. She was very bossy and organised, told me what to do, where to be, what we would be doing next. I began to feel a bit trapped. That was one advantage of the long vacations. You could use them to extricate yourself from difficult or delicate relationships.

During the first term, I did get another unexpected visitor, apart from my Uncle Jim. It was Reggie, Reg Hill, formerly Toddles, my best friend from Carlisle. He stayed for the night, sleeping on our floor, and then went next morning for an interview at Hatfield. This was our rival college, full of hearties and rugger buggers. He'd got an interview to come up the next year, as he was convinced he was not going to make it to Oxford after all. If all else failed, he would just have to go off and do his national service. He seemed pretty fed up.

But not as much as I was. At the end of my first year, when the results came out, I found I had been chucked out of the honours school. Next year I was going to be demoted to General Arts.

Nobby had also made a mess of his exams, but he was straight out, as he was already on the lowest tier of human undergraduate life. He wasn't at all put out. He went off to join the police force. Last I heard, which was many years ago now, he was a chief superintendent.

When I came home for the long vac, it was all round Carlisle, among the grammar school and high school types. Have you heard, Hunter has failed his exams, women and booze, serves him right, silly prat, I bet his mother will be very upset.

I did not dare reveal the truth to her. She had invested such hopes in me, allowed me to stay on at school in the sixth form, then go to university, when another mother in her situation might well have insisted I went out to work, to bring some money into the family. She had paid for me to go to France, twice, trips my brother and sisters had not enjoyed. She had advanced me money when I was broke. And done all my washing, lavished loads of gingerbread on me.

I didn't exactly lie to her, or use the words 'failure' and 'exams'. Just indicated I was doing a slightly different course the following year. But not to worry. I was still going back, to study for my degree.

But I knew I might not get a degree. If I mucked up again, at the end of my second year, I would definitely be out this time.

16

JOBS FOR THE BOYS

I had a good grant, and train fares to Durham, but I still needed to work in the holidays, as all students did. I didn't want to stay at home, especially in the long vacations, but travel, anywhere, just travel. We didn't have gap years in the fifties. A gap month was the best you could hope for, if you had saved enough money.

Another reason for not hanging around too long at home was that my bed was occupied. While I had been away, someone had moved in. My half of the bed, beside my younger brother Johnny, had someone else sleeping in it. Not long after I started at Durham, someone from some sort of social services in Carlisle asked my mother if she could take in a boy temporarily, from a children's home. He had reached sixteen, was about to start a job, as a driver's mate, but had nowhere to live. He was too old for the children's home, and had no money to rent anything, and they didn't want him to be homeless.

My mother met him, felt sorry for him, thought, well, I have a spare half-bed, now that Hunter is away, can't let it go vacant when there is someone in need, so she said yes. I don't think she was doing it for the money, though presumably there was a small payment. It was mainly that she felt sympathy for the orphaned, homeless lad.

She forgot to tell me. So when I came home a bit earlier than I originally intended, I climbed into my bed and found two bodies already there. He was called Tony McMynn, a tall, gangling, ever-so-cheerful, good-natured lad. Once he started his job, he was not always there, as he worked on long-distance lorries, but everybody in the family liked him and he loved my mother.

I demanded my own half of the bed when he was there, and he slept on a mattress on the floor, but he moved back in with Johnny when I returned to Durham, or was away somewhere. He stayed for about a year, but even when he got married, and had his own children, he regularly came to visit us, bringing my mother a present. My mother loved him. 'Poor Tony,' she would go around saying. 'I feel sorry for Tony.'

That first Christmas vacation as a student, I got a job with the Post Office. I did it several Christmases, the most popular job with all students. It was always a bit of a skive, a laugh, you met all your friends, and it didn't last long. The Post Office would engage hundreds of casual labourers four weeks before Christmas, and hire lots of extra vans and lorries. This happened all over the country, not just in Carlisle.

I was usually on one of the parcel lorries, much better than door-to-door deliveries where you had to walk a lot. There was a regular postman in charge of three or four students and he knew all the tricks. We would rush round, get it all done in an hour or so. Instead of going back to the depot, we'd either sit in caffs or go to a pub or even home.

The first day at the Junction Road sorting office, when

you got allocated your jobs and rounds, it was a like a school reunion. All the boys and girls just down from their first term at varsity would turn up wearing their college scarves, sometimes even their blazers. People were proud of wherever they were studying, wanting to show off their university colours and badges. Nowadays, I think you would be laughed at if you ponced around your hometown in any sort of student scarf.

I always wore my maroon-and-white Castle scarf – well, it was winter, and winters in Carlisle were always freezing. It seemed the normal, unselfconscious thing to do. I think it took me another year to realise how naff and pathetic it was to wear any sort of college gear.

One Christmas on the post I got an awful shock. I walked into Junction Road and came face to face with my mother. Oh Lord, the shame. She was in her usual old and ill-fitting clothes and 'bauchles', a Scottish term for any old shoes, fit only for the dustbin, which you wore in the garden or following a horse and cart down the street to pick up the horse shit. She had assumed she would be trailing round in the rain delivering post, so obviously wasn't going to wear her best designer shoes.

When they discovered what a slow walker she was, with no sense of direction, they moved her inside, sorting the post. She had to sit in front of large cubbyholes, read the address and plop the envelopes into the appropriate slot. Fat chance. She scarcely knew her own address.

She loved it, getting out of the house, earning some money for a few hours a day. And she loved meeting people. Her biggest disappointment whenever she went anywhere, on the bus to town, on the train to Motherwell, in a queue at the shops, was if nobody spoke to her. She was desperate for a chat, for temporary intimacy and friendship, dying to know everything about everybody, desperate to share. A bit like me.

Getting a few weeks at Christmas with the Post Office was easy, but finding something in the long vacations was hard. I so envied those friends who had parents with contacts, who could fit them up with something cushy. Ian Johnstone's father was the bank manager of Martins Bank in Stanwix. One summer he managed to get Ian a job as a luggage handler at Carlisle airport. I didn't know we had an airport, assuming it was a mythical creation, like Atlantis, or a Cumbrian joke, like the World's Biggest Liar story about a whole village made out of giant turnips. It kept the villagers dry and warm and they ate the insides when they got hungry.

The airport did exist, left over from the war. At regular intervals since then, there have been exciting plans for service flights. Jets to London and Europe get announced in the *Cumberland News*, but never seem to take off. In the 1950s, there was for a time one flight a day to the Isle of Man. Mostly the handful of passengers did not even bring luggage. So what a doddle that was, being a luggage handler. Lucky beggar, Ian.

As soon as I was home for the summer, I trailed round knocking at factory doors, as, of course, our family knew nobody. I did get myself a job at Niven's, a timber merchant on Dalston Road. I was a labourer, moving wood around. I had to lie down when I came home.

Another time I got an even harder job working for the council. They were building a new council estate at Morton. I think they gave me a job as a hodman out of wickedness, seeing me stripped off, with no muscles whatsoever. A hod is a triangular wooden box on a pole in which you place six bricks and then climb on a ladder, up the scaffolding, to where the building work has reached. The hod carrier's job is to supply the bricklayer with a constant supply of bricks, as his time is money and he is not to be kept idle. I could only ever carry two bricks at a time, so I had to climb the ladder three times as often and got shouted at all the time by the brickies.

The interesting part of the job was breaktime, when we had our bait and sat and talked to the other building workers. We perched on wooden benches under a huge tarpaulin that had been put up in a corner of the site. A very old, doddery man, one of the retired labourers, who seemed to live there, kept a large boiler constantly filled with hot water. He would be screamed and sworn at if we rushed in for our break and the water wasn't ready.

The older bricklayers seemed so intelligent and wise to me – and their jobs so skilful. I used to stand and admire how cleverly and quickly they could put up walls, go round corners, create windows.

I tried to keep it quiet that I was a student – and obviously did not wear my Castle scarf on the building site. I didn't speak unless spoken to, not wanting to stand out in any way, though I quickly realised that my accent had already begun to change, was not quite the same as theirs. But of course they soon found out, and considered me very young, naive and unworldly. All true of course. One of the brickies was always telling me about his wife's fanny, how last night he had put his hand on her hairy minge, then given her one. I never quite knew how to react to that, or how to set my facial reaction. They all seemed to have nicknames, like Pineapple Balls, or Chunky Cock.

I became friendly with a young labourer, probably aged

twenty, two years older than me, who had a teddy boy haircut. He was also a hodman, doing the same job as me, but he was in it for life, not just the summer vacation. It seemed unfair he was getting the same money as me, yet I was only passing through. He didn't seem resentful of me. I don't think he understood what university was.

One day after work he invited me to his digs. It turned out he had a wife and baby, living in two rooms in a horrible damp and dirty terrace house on Corporation Road, near the castle – a slum dwelling that was later cleared for the new bypass road. I tried to ask him if he was looking for something else, a better-paid job to provide for his family. He wasn't bothered, he replied cheerfully. Not being bothered is a common and automatic reaction in Carlisle. It was and is not done to show emotion, reveal weakness, vulnerability.

A lot of the older brickies were clearly intelligent, thoughtful, knowledgeable, and could easily have gone to university, if they had been born at a different time. Yet there was me, given it all on a plate, and I had gone and mucked it up by messing around in my first year.

I did manage to acquire a new girlfriend, Anne, during my spell as a labourer, though the two things were not connected. I don't think they would have been rushing at the sight of my fine torso. I picked her up at a Crown and Mitre dance while in my natty charcoal grey suit, wearing my college tie, looking quite presentable. I didn't take her home, as she lived miles out in the country and she was being collected and driven home by her dad.

But we arranged to go to the pictures a couple of times,

walked out, had the usual idle chat. She was working in some smart office as a high-class secretary, very well dressed, fashionable and sophisticated for Carlisle, or so it seemed to me. She had only arrived fairly recently in the area, her father having become manager of Binns, Carlisle's smartest department store. She seemed totally out of my league, not the sort of girl, I mean proper woman, I had ever been out with.

I assumed I was a passing amusement for her, a temporary chum while she got to know a new city – then, blow me, she invited me to spend the night with her. That was what she said. At her house. With her. All those fantasies of housewives inviting me in when I was delivering their groceries could be coming true.

I boasted to everyone, told my mother and sisters, and they could not believe it either. House guest, I said. Did you not invite young men as house guests when you were growing up in Motherwell? I made my mother wash my only pair of pyjamas – though hopefully I would not need them – and find me a toothbrush that was not totally worn and filthy. I cycled to her house on the Saturday evening, as arranged, out on the coast, near Burgh.

I was worried I would be all sweaty with the cycling, and didn't want to pong, so I took a spare shirt and put it on when I got near her house. Her parents were there, and all four of us had dinner. Proper cutlery and wine glasses, but of course I was now used to that at Durham. Then we all sat and watched TV. Possibly *Dixon of Dock Green*, or some awful comedians like Bob Monkhouse or Charlie Drake. As we did not have a TV in our house, that would normally have been a bit of a treat, but I had not come all that way, with clean pyjamas, just to watch some boring TV shows. Then when the TV was switched off we all went upstairs at the same time. I was shown to my bedroom. Anne gave me a quick peck on the cheek, and that was it.

I slept badly, imagining footsteps down the corridor and a gentle tap on my bedroom door, the swish of a negligee, but it never came. When I got up in the morning, they had all gone to work. Cornflakes and coffee had been left out for me. I ate them then got on my bike and cycled slowly back to Carlisle. I never saw Anne again.

The best holiday job I had during my student days was as a Ribble bus conductor. This was the most coveted, best-paid job possible. I was on the waiting list for ages.

Ribble buses were all over Cumberland, Westmorland and Lancashire, part of the landscape with their familiar red livery, part of everyday life, for they had been going since 1919. Their headquarters were in Frenchwood Avenue, Preston, where I had to report to start my induction course. It was a three-day, residential, intensive-training scheme. I thought it was a joke at first, a wind-up. What is there to learn about being a bus conductor?

It was, of course, more complicated than I had imagined. You had to keep an eye on each fare stage, alter the fiendish mechanism on your ticket machine accordingly, charge the right price, give out the right ticket – and then the right change from your large black bag. You had to know all the fares, where you were, and ring the bell when someone wanted off. The uniform was black serge, rather shiny trousers and jacket, plus a cap.

At the end of the course, there was a passing-out parade.

Can I have made that up? No, I have a clear memory of us all standing in line as our ticket machines were inspected, and then being congratulated.

Back in Carlisle, you worked shifts, some early, some late, and some split shifts which were the most difficult of all. Often you had one or two hours between, not long enough to do anything else, so you sat in the bus station canteen and ate fry-ups. The food was subsidised, and very cheap.

The worst time was to be on a city centre route during Glasgow Fair week. The town stopped, completely blocked. The best shift was out in the country. Half the time the bus was empty so you could just stand on the deck and stare at the countryside. Not sit. There were inspectors lurking everywhere and you could be for it. I can still remember the names of remote fare stages, such as Brow Nelson on the road out to Dalston. There was no visible habitation around, but decades ago the Ribble authorities must have picked the name for its fare stages. You altered your machine accordingly when you had passed each one.

Bagging up at the end of the day, that was always a worry. The cash in your moneybag had to correspond to the total recorded on your clever ticket machine. If you were missing some, you had to pay it, out of your wages. Mistakes were easily made, people cheated, or slipped in some foreign coins when it was a crowded bus. So what you did, as the old sweats soon explained to me, was fiddle it so that you built up a small surplus on every shift, regardless. That way you were covered. When someone gave you their money, and you knew they were getting off at the next stop, you would take your time whizzing your machine. The moment they were jumping off the bus platform, you then issued a ticket from your machine, a blank ticket, pocketing the money.

The Ribble bus company is no more. It ceased operation in 1989, submerged into Stagecoach, but now it has a cult following, loved by transport enthusiasts and collectors.

For many years afterwards, I used to dream I was still a bus conductor. At certain times of the day I could see myself finishing the morning shift, in that smelly, greasy, crowded staff canteen, counting up the money in my black leather bag.

I did not know what I was going to do in life, when the time came to get a proper job, as opposed to temporary employment as a student. I wondered if all jobs would be much the same, stuck on shifts, endless routines, fierce inspectors about to jump on you, or bad-tempered foremen shouting at you, putting in the hours till breaktime. I assumed all jobs, however glamorous from the outside, must have their own drudgeries. It was quite comforting to think that if all else failed, nothing turned up, I could get a job on the Ribble. I was qualified. I had the passing-out certificate to prove it.

One day, while working as a bus conductor, I was on the Dalston Road run and realised that Margaret Forster, the girl in the high school sixth form, had got on my bus. She was going home presumably, to wherever she lived. I was on the top deck when she got on, but I spotted her carrying a load of books and then sitting down. I could see her before she saw me, as I worked my way down the rows of passengers on the lower deck. When I reached her, she held out her fare. I pushed her hand away. 'Don't bother, pet,' I said. 'It's on the house today.'

I moved on quickly, giving out tickets and taking money from the other passengers, planning to come back later and smirk, when she recognised me, and bask in her gratitude. The bus was busy, so I did not have time to go back and chat to her till we were near her stop. Before she got off, she came up to me and gave me her fare, watching me carefully while I put her money in my bag.

'I'm letting you off,' I said. 'You don't have to pay.'

'I do not want to be let off my fare,' she said.

And she got off the bus, leaving me standing on the platform, watching her disappear. I swung my moneybag, trying to appear not bothered, but decidedly discomfited.

Back at Durham, I did often think about her, but realised she was out of my league, on a different intellectual and moral plane. From all accounts, she was going to do brilliantly in her A-level exams, or in fact any exams she might ever sit. Unlike me.

During my second year at Durham, everyone in my year at Castle had to move out to Lumley Castle. So much for boasting about how wholly residential our college was. We were, in one sense, in that we all lived in college, but for one year everyone at University College had to move twelve miles away to Lumley Castle near Chester-le-Street. It was another ancient castle, dating from the fourteenth century, which our college had taken over, as we had run out of accommodation space in Durham itself. It was run like a mini version of the main college, with a Lumley JCR and Senior Man, a resident master, Dr Prouse, who was an old boy of the college. There was a Great Hall where we had breakfast and dinners, but we all travelled each day on a coach into Durham City. If you missed the free bus, either there or back, you had to trail into Chester-le-Street and pay to go on the normal bus.

The food was better in the Lumley Great Hall and the maids who served us were younger and more attractive. High up in the attics of the castle, there was an enormous, timbered and panelled room where we played indoor football, bashing a ball against ancient panels. That would not have been allowed in Durham Castle.

I have never been back to Lumley Castle since that year, 1955, but I have caught sight of it on TV. I don't follow cricket but the towers of Lumley are usually in the background when Durham CCC play at home at Chester-le-Street. Durham was not a first-class county in the fifties; in fact, I had no idea there was a cricket club, yet it dates back to 1882. It was not until 1991 that they were admitted into the first-class county game, but they went on to win the County Championship and host Test matches. I rush to the telly, hoping for close-ups, to see if I can spot my old room.

Lumley Castle is now a hotel, last time I looked it up. Durham students no longer need to traipse out there, as there are so many new colleges and buildings in and around Durham itself. Today there must be getting on for almost 20,000 students at Durham – compared with just 1,500 in my day. At least half of them women. Lucky so-and-sos.

Being stuck out at Lumley did have one good effect. I must have done some work for once. My General Arts degree course was a combination of ancient history, Roman history and geography. It was probably easier, for I sailed through my exams at the end of the second year.

So my undergraduate days did not come to a premature end, as I'd once feared they might. And I am sure my mother had feared it as well.

17

TEENAGERS ARRIVE

During my third year at Durham, 1956–57, some new and exciting and different things happened out there in the world at large. And also in my life.

Firstly, teenagers were invented. Yup, and I was there. This is obviously a silly, stupid, unprovable, impossible, factually incorrect thing to say, but really, where I was standing at the time, or hanging about moaning, there was a definite cultural and social and economic change that took place, around that time, around that place, where we were living in the so-called Western civilised world.

For thousands of years, whenever humans had reached the age of thirteen, and then somehow struggled on to the age of nineteen, they were technically teenagers, whether or not they described themselves as such, or somehow felt any different. There must have been the bolshie few, the groups and gangs who felt separated or different, and there must have those experiencing what we now call adolescence, with various traumas and worries about their identity and/or spots, but presumably they were ignored, told to get up out of bed, or out of the cave, and get on with it. For the vast majority of humankind, until the 1950s, you were a child, then you were an adult. That was it. No definable, describable, recognised gap in between.

The notion of teenagers as a definite stage, with a definite identity, surfaced in the post-war years and, naturally, was first spotted in the USA. *Life* magazine in 1944 ran an article called 'Teen-age Girls: they live in a wonderful world of their own'. The hyphen between 'teen' and 'age' was soon dropped, making it one word. They were wealthier over there, staying on at school much longer, more indulged. They might not have been allowed anywhere near the liquor store till much older than us in the UK, but they did have access to their family telephone and car. Lucky blighters.

At this early stage it was mainly a fashion thing, the bobbysoxers, wearing the same sorts of teenage clothes, painting their nails, talking on the phone all day to each other and then hopping into the backs of their enormous cars with their boyfriends. In the UK, ordinary families did not have cars till the very late fifties, and there wasn't enough room on the back seat to manage to take your bike clips off, far less your long trousers.

The arrival of teenagers alerted the post-war American manufacturing sector, which began producing clothes, films, TV programmes, aimed specifically at the teenage market, both boys and girls. We were all unaware of this, stuck in boring old austerity-ridden, ration-booked, war-torn, war-exhausted Blighty.

My expectations, in the post-war years, was to grow up and look and dress and act just like my dad, as everyone else of my age expected. That was why I wore his coat and his shirts in

1954 when I went to Durham. I even stole his Brylcreem and plastered it on, but couldn't get my hair to lie flat.

When the teddy boys came in, around 1955, with their mock exaggeration of so-called Edwardian clothes, sporting drainpipe trousers and slicked-back hair, it heralded the first vaguely teenage male fashion I was aware of. I don't remember them being associated with rock'n'roll or any sort of music, not in the beginning. They were often in gangs, with razors and chains. They caused riots in London and Brighton. Even in Carlisle, where they hung around the town hall, you avoided them, unless you were looking for trouble.

But their styles caught on with ordinary teenage boys, especially the trousers. I did try to get my hair to go up in a quiff, and attempted a DA – a duck's arse – at the back, but I never seemed able to manage it. I blamed my head. It was the wrong size.

At school I had spent a lot of time looking at my hair in the mirror, trying to do something with it, if only pour on buckets of water last thing before I went out, hoping to make it behave. In the end, I stuck to a side parting, hair brushed to one side as my mother had first brushed it when I went to primary school. I also spent ages, as all boys did, trying to get my trousers as narrow as possible. I even paid for a little woman in the street who did sewing to take them in. Girls would often carry their skimpy party or dancing clothes in a plain paper bag, knowing their mothers would never let them out if they saw them.

But it was pop music that finally did it, forming teenagers into an identifiable cultural and social group, different from those who had gone before. Most of our popular music until the mid-fifties was sub-American. Awful English crooners sang soppy songs in a mid-Atlantic accent, wearing shiny suits, telling us we were a wonderful audience. And I loved them all, oh yes. While mocking Pat Boone and Guy Mitchell, I knew their songs and sang along with them. Frank Sinatra was a cut above them; his songs had better words and orchestration.

Our home-grown pop singers, such as Dickie Valentine, David Whitfield, Frankie Vaughan, Ronnie Hilton, Alma Cogan, Jimmy Young were pale, pallid imitations of the Americans, but we still listened to them.

In my third year at Durham I was amazed one day to find that Dickie Valentine was appearing at the Union. This was a very dignified, ancient building on Palace Green, where serious debates took place and students who were really little old men intrigued and plotted to be president or secretary. This event was in the Union coffee bar. Someone had somehow got Dickie Valentine to turn up and answer questions from students. I think he must have been appearing locally, or in Newcastle, and his agent thought it might be good PR. His answers were all banal; he was smaller than I had imagined, but I remember thinking his hair was really good.

Most students felt rather superior to the Guy Mitchells and Dickie Valentines and other popular singers, the sort enjoyed by shop girls. Being convinced of their own higher taste, they preferred listening to jazz. In the JCR at Castle, there was a good selection of jazz records and I did enjoy listening to Dave Brubeck, Humphrey Lyttelton, Ken Colyer, Chris Barber and others. The MJQ – Modern Jazz Quartet – they were what the intellectuals really loved, in their black polo-neck pullies. No bubble-gum pop music ballads or corny novelty songs such

216

as 'She Wears Red Feathers and a Huly-Huly Skirt', very big in 1953, were played in the JCR. Personally, I was willing to listen to most forms of music.

The first defining signs of the arrival of a new and exciting form of popular music, rock'n'roll, which seemed to be aimed directly at teenagers, came in April 1954 when Bill Haley & His Comets produced 'Rock Around the Clock'. It took a year for most people in the UK to notice it, when it became the theme tune for the film *Blackboard Jungle*. People started jiving in the aisles and then tearing up seats – even in Carlisle, according to my sisters.

Jiving was frowned upon in the classier dance halls, such as the Crown and Mitre in Carlisle, and often banned. Then came a strange crossover, hybrid period. Jiving had not quite achieved mass acceptance, but it was allowed, sometimes, in different parts of the dance hall. So there would be kids jiving away at one end, turning themselves round and round, their skirts flying, their beehives and DAs bouncing, while at the other end people were still sedately doing the valeta or the waltzes.

I was surprised when I first saw a photograph of Bill Haley. He was not a teenager for start, aged thirty at least, and was fleshy and flabby with a silly quiff at the front. Hardly a sex symbol, so why were girls screaming? Nothing at all like Elvis, who turned out to be the biggest and most exciting new singer of the fifties. Perhaps of all time. By May 1956, his 'Heartbreak Hotel' was top of the charts in fourteen different countries.

I went out with a girl from St Hild's for a time; she came from Liverpool and knew all the words and tunes of Elvis's latest hits. She wanted me to come and visit her in Liverpool, and meet her parents, but I got out of that. But she did teach me all the words of 'Blue Suede Shoes' – and explain that Carl Perkins had sung it first.

In the UK, the single biggest influence on our home-grown popular music was the arrival of skiffle. In January 1956 Lonnie Donegan's 'Rock Island Line' became a surprise hit and spawned hundreds if not thousands of skiffle groups all over the country. On Merseyside, so we discovered later, there were about ten million skiffle groups being formed, so they all claimed later.

The attraction of skiffle was that you did not need to be at all musical. You didn't have to play an instrument, or even have an instrument. There was room in a skiffle group for people rubbing a thimble up and down your mother's washboard, or plucking a string attached to a large tea chest, the sort that Lipton's threw out.

Going home to Carlisle in the hols in 1956, I joined in one evening with an impromptu skiffle group who were playing in the pitch-dark beside the suspension bridge. All I did was rub a washboard, which is harder than you might think, and tough on your knuckles. We did it for a few evenings, planned to find somewhere proper to rehearse, but nothing came of it.

Back in Durham, in my third year, I went to pubs to find that skiffle groups had taken over all the back rooms, and were packed out. I thought they were all wonderful, exciting and full of energy, however rough, preferable to the phoneys in blue shiny suits.

There was one group called The Blue Devils, who had just won some local skiffle competition and were calling themselves the 'Northeastern Skiffle Champions'. I decided to book them for an engagement, along with two of my friends. One was my new roommate, John Davies. We had decided to share a room for our third year, back in Durham again, and we were fortunate to get excellent rooms in what was called Hall Stairs. This was right in the heart of the Castle, up a broad wooden, ancient staircase behind the Great Hall. It was above the college library, so handy for studying, har har, with a large bay window overlooking the college courtyard. You could see everything going on, who was bringing girls in through the porter's lodge, or sneaking them out.

John was a scientist reading chemistry, and came from Newcastle, lived in a private semi, and his father was an electrician who worked at Kemsley House in Newcastle. We didn't have a lot in common, but had become friends at Lumley. We went drinking together, but not of course to excess, not like in my early, silly first year.

My other new friend was Michael Bateman, not a Durham student, but an Oxford graduate who had recently arrived in Durham, working on the local paper, the *Durham Advertiser*. He had been given the task of writing about university affairs, which was how I had met him.

The three of us clubbed together, tracked down The Blue Devils and offered them money to perform in Durham at the Wearmouth Bridge, a large pub with a big upstairs room. We talked the pub into letting us have the function room for free, explaining that we would be bringing in so many students that they would make a fortune on the drinks. I can't remember how much we paid The Blue Devils, but we worked out we would easily cover their fee by charging for entrance. We printed tickets, with rather arty blue type, designed by

Michael, who was very good at drawing. The evening was a huge success. We filled the room and made quite a bit of money. I still have one of the tickets to this day, with all our names on.

A lot of students, over the decades since, have discovered or created careers for themselves by organising student hops, student discos, then going on to bigger things. It never occurred to me at the time that anyone could ever make a job out of what we had done. It was for our own amusement, to see if it could be done. We never did it again. Moving on to other things, other amusements.

But I did for the first time begin to wonder during my third year what I might do when I graduated. I realised my CV was practically empty – drinking and shove ha'penny were not going to impress any potential employers. Sports-wise, I had not made any proper team, nor did I have any badges or decorations on my blazer to prove I had represented the college. When you made the boat club proper, you earned the right to have crossed oars embroidered on your college badge. If you ran for the college or played rugby, you could add UCAC or UCRUFC. If you were actually capped by the university, you were awarded what was called a Palatinate, the Durham term for a Blue, which entitled you to a fancy purple tie and scarf. They were our heroes. And even though the Durham colleges in the 1950s were so small, the sporting standard was high, with many playing for county or national teams. (Later on, Durham even produced some England stars like Will Carling and Nasser Hussain, who became England rugby and cricket captains.)

What was I going to do to get something on my CV, show I had not totally wasted my time? Clearly, my degree in General Arts, if I got it, was not going to have them panting.

In desperation, I joined something called the Durham Colleges Fine Arts Society, despite having no interest or talent for art. They were pleading for members so I joined and even became secretary. I managed to get a well-known art person, Mervyn Levy, to come and address our society. The president of the society and I entertained him to drinks beforehand and then took him to supper afterwards at the Three Tuns. So I did get something out of it. The point of being an officer of an official student society was that you got funds from the Students' Representative Council – SCR – some of which you could use to spend on yourselves.

John Davies, my roommate, had somehow got himself a job to put on his CV – advertising manager of *Palatinate*, the student newspaper. After a term, he decided to give it up, because of all the lab work he had to do, which took up a lot of time as the science labs were some way out of Durham. I hadn't quite taken in what he did, what the job entailed, but I found myself saying, 'Hold on, John, don't hand in your notice, I'll take it on. Just inform them you are handing it on to someone else, they won't care, probably not even notice.' And so I became advertising manager of *Palatinate*.

My job was to go round the shops in the town that students patronised and try to sell them three-inch adverts, single column, for whatever money we could get out of them. The shops and services included the House of Andrews, which sold books; Gray and Sons, which was the university outfitters in

Saddler Street; the SPCK Bookshop; Daisy Edis, who was photographer to the university; and, of course, the Buffalo Head. After the ads appeared, I had to go round with the invoice and collect the money.

We sold very few ads, so the income was minimal. Durham was not a place with any major or well-off local businesses interested in appealing to students. With only 1,500 students in Durham, the circulation of *Palatinate* was commensurately small, just 500. We didn't have the pulling power of Oxbridge or the redbrick universities, all of which were much bigger. The paper survived on its cover price, which was 6d., and a grant from the SRC. However, we liked to think we were operating as a proper business enterprise, paying our way, with proper professional-looking journalistic content and production.

One day, after I had been doing the job for a few months, I took the latest batch of ads I had managed to gather into the editorial offices – which was the editor's room in Hatfield. The paper had been in the hands of Hatfield people ever since I had arrived in Durham – friends from the same college handing it on to each other, which was and probably is how most student societies operate.

I had never thought of writing or offering anything to the paper, even though I read every issue, all the way through, impressed that mere students were producing a proper-looking newspaper of six to eight pages. I had assumed that you needed to be gifted, have some sort of skill to write, even for a student newspaper, and be really good at English. Somebody like Reg Hill at school clearly had that talent, and wrote such amusing stuff. I felt inhibited from even trying. In fact, the idea had never entered my head. When very young, at primary school and at Sunday school, I had entered little writing competitions, and did once win that BBC pencil, but they had all been at my mother's prompting, and she helped me write them.

I had been into the editor's room a few times, and met the other people from Hatfield who were running the paper. I always dutifully handed over my list of ads, which they accepted with hardly a grunt, didn't speak to me, and then I exited humbly. Selling a handful of adverts was considered way down the scale of importance, compared with actually writing for the pages. But over the months, any initial awe I had felt in their presence began to fade. I began to realise they were not all that bright or talented but really pretty ordinary. Just like me, in fact.

On this particular day, as I was dropping off my ads, I heard them saying there was a hole in a page, something had fallen through, where can we get something to fill it, preferably funny?

'Let me fill the hole,' I heard myself saying.

They looked at me, disbelieving. They glanced at each other, looked at the gap in the page, looked at the clock and said okay then, they could give me one hour. I rushed back to Hall Stairs, licked my little pencil, for I did not have a typewriter at the time, nor could I type. I wrote a piece about a day in the life of a boat club hearty, a first person piece, as if he was writing it – about getting drunk and vomiting, full of bad spelling and stupid public school comments and slang, based on the Castle boat club members I had come across and the boat club dinner I had attended.

The editor liked it and it was rushed down to Bailes, the

printers. God knows how they managed to read my handwriting, which has always been rubbish, but they were accustomed to working from handwritten copy. I was so proud to see my words and name in print. Readers seemed to like it, so I was asked to do another one for the next edition. This time I did a science student, based on my friend John, continually trudging back and forward to the science labs. With even worse spelling, like Just William's. I always found bad spelling funny. Then I did a don, a moral tutor, getting pissed at his own sherry party. I also did a theology student, but avoided bad language, vomiting and any sexual undertones. Didn't want to upset them – or the authorities.

We had loads of theology students and clerics at Durham and they were a powerful presence. Two of the colleges, St Chad's and St John's, specialised in theology, preparing people for the Church, and their principals were always reverends. At Castle, we also had quite a few students reading theology or planning to go into the Church after graduating.

Durham, historically, had always provided lots of clerics, ever since the early nineteenth century. With its famous cathedral and prominent bishop – number three or four in the Church of England hierarchy – it has provided several Archbishops of Canterbury, notably Michael Ramsey, who was Bishop of Durham in my day, and then more recently Justin Welby. For about a month in my second year, when I was sobering up, I did go to a couple of DICCU – Durham Inter-Collegiate Christian Union – meetings, hoping for some sort of spiritual light, as a couple of Castle students I was quite friendly with did seem to take comfort and confidence from believing – but I couldn't hack it.

I kept up my first person piss-taking *Palatinate* column for a whole term, covering all the archetypes, all in the same format. I called the series 'A Life in the Day Of'. I thought it was witty, reversing the old clichéd phrase.

I also started writing other columns and articles for the paper. Very soon I found that *Palatinate* was taking over my life. All I seemed to be doing was constantly thinking of topics and stories, jokes and columns, making endless lists and notes, laughing to myself, at my own amazing wit. When I was supposed to be writing an essay in our room, I would say to John, 'Hey, John, listen to this, don't you think this is really good?' I would watch his solemn scientific Geordie face for any crease or semblance of a smile.

For the first time in my life I thought, I can do this, this suits me. I had discovered that you don't have to be clever or talented to write stuff, you just do it, don't talk about it, get it written, amuse yourself and hope it will amuse others. After various cul-de-sacs, blind alleys, roundabouts, dead ends, skiffle groups, art appreciation, not forgetting shove ha'penny at the Buffalo, I had finally stumbled on something I really, really enjoyed doing.

18

MARGARET

During that same final year, the other momentous event in my long-legged life so far also happened by chance – in a cinema queue, back in Carlisle during the long summer vacation of 1956. In June or possibly July. How awful that I can't now remember the exact day of the week or month. I was coming through the town one evening, on the way home, when I passed the City Picture House. This was right in the heart of the city, near the Old Town Hall, one of Carlisle's many cinemas, where at one time worked a character known throughout the town.

There were three 'characters' in Carlisle in the 1950s, people nobody really knew, not even their proper names, but they stood out in some way. One was a dodgy, scruffy, slavering bloke known as Paddy Mason. He was a potter – a Carlisle term that covered rag-and-bone men or tramps, presumably because they had originally sold pots door to door. He was said to pester children, but was considered harmless, staggering around either Caldewgate or the centre of town most days.

Then there was a man, name unknown, but everyone knew his voice. He stood in English Street, on the corner of

Bank Street, and sold the local paper from a little booth. You could hear him streets away shouting the same thing – 'NOT MANY LEFT! NOT MANY LEFT!' – over and over, all day long, from the moment his first papers arrived. Yet he clearly had loads left.

Then there was the woman at the City Picture House, a mystery woman who worked in the box office, sitting there with her Pre-Raphaelite hair and long red flowing velvet cloak. She never chatted, gave anything anyway, and when her shift finished she could be seen haughtily walking up Stanwix Bank, her red cloak swishing, to wherever she lived, presumably somewhere off the Scotland Road. There was endless gossip about her – that she was a woman whose loved one had been killed in the war, and since then she had vowed to talk to no one ever again. All small towns, small communities, have characters who are known, but not known.

So in passing the City Picture House that evening, I glanced towards the entrance to see if the Lady in Red was on duty. I couldn't see much as the queue was enormous, as usual, stretching for miles down the pavement and up an alleyway. I suddenly realised that at the top of the queue were four friends of mine, two boys and two girls. One of the boys, Ian Johnstone, was now at Durham with me, though at a different college, and the other, Mike Thornhill, was at Balliol, Oxford. They were with two high school girls, the two Margarets, Forster and Crosthwaite.

Reg Hill, who was usually with the others, was not there. He had retaken his German A-level and eventually got into Oxford – to St Catherine's Society (it did not become a college till 1962). But they could not take him for two years, so he had decided to go off and do his national service, get it out of the way. That evening he was probably on guard duty in some isolated army barracks in East Anglia, poor sod.

I could see that the front of the queue was at least beginning to move. Like a worm, the queue did a little jerk, concertina-ing itself, then slithering forward again, before getting ready for a last dash to the box office. They would all be inside in a moment, gone from sight, from my life.

I had not planned to go to the cinema, did not even know what was showing, but I found myself pushing in beside them. People in the enormous queue behind groaned, objecting to me pushing in, having no idea where I had come from. 'Thanks for keeping my place,' I said to Mike and Ian loudly, pretending I had just gone off somewhere, but had always been in the queue.

They, of course, didn't know where I had come from, or why, and were rather confused and also a bit annoyed by my sudden appearance. They reluctantly budged up and I went in with them, chattering inanely to all four of them, without any replies or any encouragement. They were clearly a four-some, two boys and two girls, on an arranged evening out, yet here was someone barging in. They managed to get four seats together. I could only manage a seat in the row behind them. From time to time I leaned over and made funny or silly remarks about the film we were watching.

Afterwards we all stood outside in English Street, talking about the film. I didn't really know if they were two couples, each a boy with his girlfriend, an 'item' as we might call them today, though I had not heard of anything romantic going on between them. Or was it just social, school friends, who had known each other for years? As we all had.

I kept up an inane rattle of chat, and it became clear they were about to make their respective ways home, and expected me to do the same, and as quickly as possible, leaving them to say their own farewells. I hung on, ignoring their snubs. When it was clear they were going their separate ways home, not as couples, I found myself asking Margaret Forster if I could walk home with her. Twice in the recent past I had been given the bum's rush when trying to be chatty and friendly with her – in the Garret Club and on the Ribble bus. This time, to my astonishment, she agreed. I am not sure she actually said, 'Yes, how lovely,' but she didn't say, 'No, go away, you drip.' I took her silence as an affirmative.

She had very short hair, cut almost like a boy's, much shorter than when I had seen her on the bus, not that I ever take in hairstyles or what people are wearing.

I had no idea where she lived, about her family, what sort of house they had, or where we were heading. I was too busy keeping up the bright chatter, walking in a dream, no idea what I was saying or where I was going.

I realised she was at the end of her second year in the sixth form, so must recently have done her A-levels, and must be waiting for her results, so I did at least manage to ask her about that. She said she was probably going to apply to Oxbridge, but she was worried that she had failed her A-level Latin. I was impressed by that, doing A-level Latin. She said it was a mistake, she was useless at Latin. I found that hard to believe, that she was useless at anything, not from all I had been told about her.

She had heard about me failing my history honours exam – and had heard it was to do with my dissolute life. I didn't know whether to deny this or boast that, yes, I was a helluva fellow. She said she had first seen me when I had played hockey for the grammar school against the high school. She was in the crowd of girls watching that day. Another girl had pointed me out, she explained, making clear she had not been personally much interested. But my heart gave a little nervous flutter all the same, that she had even remembered the incident.

I told her how I had seen her about two years ago in a school play at the high school, when she had played the main part in *The Snow Queen*. Me and Reg and Mike had all gone, just to sit in the back and mock, but it had been rather good, surprisingly.

I boasted how I had been to the Edinburgh Festival and also down to London to the Proms, on my own, thus show-ing what a true culture vulture I was. I dragged in my years learning the violin, playing and performing in the school orchestra. I told her I loved Sibelius. 'What has he written?' she asked, as if assuming he was a novelist. So she wasn't quite the cultural brainbox I had been led to believe, which was a small relief.

We somehow started talking about football and I discov-ered that back in 1951, when Carlisle United drew Arsenal at home in the FA Cup, while she was still in the second year at the high school, she had been the girl who had organised a petition to the headmistress, protesting about being given a half-day off school. At the time, it was a famous local story. She had maintained that lessons were much more important than any stupid football match, at least they were to her.

We eventually reached Longsowerby, at the far end of the

town, on a council estate I had never visited before. Her house was at 180 Richardson Street, opposite the main gate of the cemetery. It was dark, so I couldn't see much, but her house was obviously a council house, though a lot neater than ours, with a trim hedge and a tidy garden.

I did not attempt a kiss, just said goodnight at her front gate, thanks for the walk, thanks for the chats, could I see her again? She said yes, so we made an arrangement.

I walked all the way home to St Ann's Hill in a daze, a stupor, wandering in a dream. Talking to her had been so exciting, invigorating, stimulating. It had seemed endless, with so many strands and threads, jumps and bumps, that I could not wait to see her again to continue talking. I had never met or talked to or imagined a girl like her before.

I felt so lucky to have finally met her, but realised it was probably to do with the fact that she was post-exams. That was the reason she had weakened and let me walk home with her, the relief and release of getting her A-levels over with, till the next hurdle. She had momentarily dropped her guard. That's what most other people thought when they heard I had walked her home – and was going to see her again.

I found out nothing about her personally or about her family during that first walk. That began to come out after a few more walks. But apparently, in my idle chat on that first walk, I had given the impression I must be from a higher-class home. I had mentioned going to violin lessons, my mother reading Dickens, describing our years in Dumfries in a house called Nancyville where I rode my bike down the corridors. I could well have been showing off, just a little bit.

*

Her father worked at the Metal Box factory as a fitter, setting off each day on his bike. She had an older brother, Gordon, who had been in the RAF doing his national service and was now working in a photographic shop, and a younger sister, Pauline, who was in the fifth year at the high school. They had not long been in Richardson Street, having moved there from another council estate, Raffles, where she had been born at 44 Orton Road. This had been a model council estate when first built in the 1930s, but had become rough and run down in recent years and was looked upon as the worst estate in Carlisle. Longsowerby was considered a step up, and they had an indoor lavatory for the first time.

We went on so many walks, almost every evening, plus longer expeditions at the weekends. Meeting Margaret also meant I got to know Cumberland for the first time. She knew it so well, coming from a proper Cumbrian family, who had lived there for generations, unlike mine who knew nothing about Carlisle and its immediate area, nor had they ever taken us anywhere. Her surname, Forster, is a common Cumbrian name, especially around the Borders. It appears in Walter Scott's 'Lochinvar' – 'Forsters, Fenwicks, and Musgraves, they rode and they ran'.

I had not even been to the Lake District, but Margaret had been everywhere, either with her dad on the bus to Keswick, on the train to the seaside, or long bike rides on her own into the countryside. She loved Silloth, twenty miles away out on the Solway coast, and had such happy memories of being taken there on the train when she was younger. I never knew Silloth existed, yet it had been part of local culture and mythology for a hundred years, Carlisle's favourite seaside family resort. I grew to love it as well, as Margaret took me on outings, walking along the front, round the green, looking at the docks, walking down the coast to Skinburness, round Grune Point, all the time having a bit of a blow. That was how most Carlisle families described going to Silloth – 'a bit of a blow' meant the wind practically took you off your feet and transported you across the sea to Scotland.

I loved touching her, not just talking to her. I mean in the pure and chaste sense, which mostly meant holding hands. Her skin was so soft and smooth, slightly tanned. Like me, she easily got brown with the first hint of the sun. She glowed with health, didn't have spots or rashes, unlike me. Not long after I met her, I imagined her as an old woman, that she would age beautifully, with a wonderful brown, rosy complexion and thick white hair. A bit daft, not to say premature, as we had hardly been going out more than a few weeks.

She had bare legs most of the time, which made me shiver should I chance to touch them, and always wore flat shoes, often simple ballet pumps. She hated high heels and vowed she would never wear them. She also never wore make-up, which I approved of. I always hated make-up, the smell of perfume and creams. My mother hardly used make-up, but she would often dab horrible-smelling powder on her face with an elderly sponge if she going out somewhere, or smear on Pond's cold cream, for no reason I could see.

My sisters, of course, once they became teenagers, were always trying out make-ups and lipsticks, new hairstyles, buying the latest flouncy skirts and lurid tops. Margaret was totally unlike them; in fact, she was unlike every other girl in Carlisle I had ever gone out with. While most other girls of her age were growing their hair long, piling it up high, trying to manage a beehive by backcombing it to death and smothering it in lacquer, she had cut her dark brown hair short and simple, like Audrey Hepburn.

She often wore a black polo-neck, which made her look like someone from a French film, very Left Bank and bohemian. She sometimes wore trousers, which girls did not do at the time. Not jeans, because they had not come in, but tailored slacks, I suppose they must have been called. Her style was understated, but utterly distinctive. Just as she was. I could not take my eyes off her, or my mind.

On 4 August, just a month after we met, she announced that her parents were going away for a night to visit relations in Scotland, taking Pauline with them.

I asked idly where they were going in Scotland, and to my surprise it turned out they were heading to Motherwell, to visit Margaret's aunt – her mother's sister – in the same road, Bellshill Road, where my grandmother lived, staying in the same tenement block where one of my own aunts had lived. I discovered I had played with her cousins, the Wallaces, on the Bing. I might well have played with Margaret as a little girl, or at least seen her, when she too was visiting her Motherwell relations. So, what a coincidence! We had met, or almost, in another, earlier Scottish life. It seemed a sign, a portent.

While her parents were going to be in Scotland, the house would be empty, as Gordon was also away. But of course there was no suggestion that this would be a chance for me to stay the night with her, perish the very idea. But what it did provide was a chance for us to stay out together really late, without bothering about what time we had to come back.

We got a bus to Keswick, arrived in marvellously unexpected sunshine, walked round Derwentwater and then sat watching the sun set lying on the grass near Friar's Crag. Perhaps hand in hand, but nothing more, half falling asleep, only coming to when we realised we had missed the last bus back to Carlisle, some thirty miles away. Oh God, what were we going to do now?

Margaret set off walking, and I trudged behind. Despite all those vacation jobs doing physical labouring, I certainly wasn't fit or much of a walker. More of a trudger. Whereas Margaret could walk forever.

Once well away from the town and any habitation, it was pitch-black. I had no idea where we were, and was getting more and more knackered. I suggested a rest, moaned I was tired, so we sat down beside a hedge. I tried to get her to lie down, and put my arm round her – when suddenly there was a loud yell. An old tramp jumped out of the hedge, shouting and screaming at us. He had been asleep under the hedge and we had inadvertently disturbed him.

We got back to her house at about five in the morning. I lay on the sofa in her front parlour for an hour, trying to keep awake and get some energy back, until it was time to stagger to the bus stop for the early bus into town, where I caught the St Ann's Hill bus at the town hall. My mother never asked me where I had been, or noticed how late I had come home. I was a student, after all, practically an adult.

It was quite a while before I was invited officially into her home. After we had been out somewhere, on a walk, or to the pictures, her mother Lily got into the habit of now and again inviting me in. We sat in the front parlour together and then her mother brought me milky Camp coffee and a Carr's Sports chocolate biscuit, yum yum. Her dad, Arthur, coming in from the pub on a Saturday evening, might give me a grunt, but otherwise he ignored me.

He seemed not to approve of me, or was just naturally grumpy. He apparently thought I looked foreign, with my thick, black hair, and didn't really like students either. Margaret was staying on to try for Oxbridge but she thought her dad would really have liked her to have left school at sixteen, as her older brother had done, and got herself a decent local job, even if it was only packing crackers at Carr's biscuit works.

When her A-level results came out she had got Latin after all, just scraping through, and could now drop it forever. But her results in English and history seemed unbelievable, 95 per cent in each, so the headmistress, Miss Cotterell, had told her. You heard of people getting those sorts of amazingly high marks in science subjects or maths, but nobody got them in any arts subject.

There were teachers at her school who had been encouraging her acting, saying she should now try for RADA. Others suggested that, as she was good at art, she should go to art college. But most said she must try Oxbridge entrance, for the honour of the school. Where had they come from, all these talents? Nobody in her background had ever been remotely academic or artistic.

So what was she doing with me? That was what our Carlisle

friends thought. It won't last, you'll see. They are too unalike. Which is what I believed as well.

She sat the open scholarship exams for both Cambridge and Oxford. At Cambridge, she found she was on the same exams and interview round as another girl of her age, also called Margaret, Margaret Drabble, who was at some Quaker boarding school in York. In between waiting for interviews, Margaret Drabble took her to a Friends Meeting House.

Both Margarets got awards at Somerville, Oxford – and their names appeared in the same list in the *Manchester Guardian* on 21 December 1956, one after the other, in alphabetical order: 'M. Drabble, Mount School, York, English. M. Forster, Carlisle and County High School for Girls, History.' They also both got awards at Cambridge, and M. Drabble chose the Cambridge one, so they never met again, not till many years later.

At the high school in Carlisle, Margaret's name went up on the honours board in the school hall. Not many girls at the high school had won such an award before.

To celebrate, her father, to everyone's surprise, pulled out his wallet and gave her a ten-bob note. I suggested we should spend it by going out into the country for a slap-up meal at a posh place called Fantails in Wetheral. It was raining when I picked her up, so I had the cheek to ask Arthur, as I was now calling him instead of Mr Forster, though he never quite approved, if I could borrow his umbrella. Then off we went on the bus, me in my best charcoal grey suit and Margaret in her best frock.

I studied the menu, realised it was more expensive than I had imagined, so steered Margaret towards the cheapest item, an omelette, which I hate. Even so, the bill came to more than I had on me, including Arthur's ten bob. I let Margaret go outside and went to settle up, trying to explain to the pompous owner that really, I had money at home, but, so sorry, just not quite enough on me at this moment. He was very unfriendly and suspicious and I feared I might have to do the washing-up. He took all the money I had and made me give a written agreement that I would return first thing in the morning and give him the two shillings still owing, the bastard.

I then joined Margaret on the step outside the restaurant where it was still raining. I opened up Arthur's umbrella, gave it a few twirls to look nonchalant. I realised I was being watched by two local farm lads clearly thinking, who is that twat with the brolly? The handle suddenly came off and Arthur's brolly collapsed, falling down the steps.

We had to walk home, as I had no money left for the bus. Next morning I came out on my bike to pay the rotten sod his two bob. When I'm rich, I told myself, I'll buy Fantails and sack him. Bastard.

While I was back at Durham, Margaret went off for six months to France as an au pair. Oxford had remarked on her lousy French – which was as bad as mine, though her accent was much better – and suggested that while she waited to come up to Oxford she did something to improve it. So she got a job as an au pair in Bordeaux. We wrote to each other all the time, but already it seemed she was moving away, having new experiences I did not share. But once she was back, and I was home in Carlisle for the Christmas vacation, we continued to be inseparable.

All the same, we were beginning to have lots of heated, silly, petty but furious rows. They were often to do with me being late, or getting the arrangements mucked up, or both. We usually met up at Burton's corner when we were going out, then set off on a long walk. I would arrive late, panting, saying I thought we had agreed to meet at the City Picture House, which of course was not true. My idea of being prompt, such as when catching a train, is to jump on it when it is leaving the platform. Margaret's idea of prompt is being there half an hour early.

We used to argue about who said what, who had agreed this, then we argued about who had started it all, going back over the conversation till we were shouting at each other, with one walking off in a huff. Luckily, by the time we had parted for the evening, we had made up, or at least were walking together again, if in silence.

I was slow at understanding things she had said, or explained, partly because I never listened properly, or so she maintained. More likely I am just slow on the uptake. I like to get things straight, to interrupt and ask questions, which annoyed her when she had made it perfectly clear. I maintained she was too quick for her own good, that she was saying she understood something when she couldn't possibly. She was almost always right, able to know or predict what was coming, before I or anyone else had finished what they were saying.

Sometimes, of course, she got it wrong, but then she would quickly lie, turn it round, make it my fault not hers. Her lying was amazing, making things up on the spot, giving plausible explanations and answers. If she got caught out in the fib, she would laugh and say, 'So what, I lied – surely you realised?'

Her reactions were often unexpected. I could never predict what she would say or think or feel. I suppose it was the reason she had done so well at the Oxbridge interviews – being fluent, quick, quirky, decisive in her responses.

She did not think it was much of a skill, more of a trick, to be able to take an unusual position or thought and defend it, a verbal game she knew Oxford dons loved. How did she learn all this? Where did it come from? Her father Arthur, I suppose. He was a contrary bugger, went his own way, could not be flattered or impressed; but he lacked the gift of the gab or the mental dexterity of Margaret. She did not consider herself brainy, not in the intellectual sense, just good at understanding and quick at being decisive. I learned that many girls in her school were quite scared of her, probably some of the teachers as well. She could be too direct, too outspoken.

I did sulk now and again, get hurt if she called me stupid, or if she refused to discuss a topic any more, saying she was bored, we had discussed it enough. It was exhausting, but somehow exciting and stimulating. The only time I ever got really upset was when she said, 'This is not going to work. I will just make you miserable; you'd better leave me now.'

'Don't be stupid,' I would say. 'You are just saying it so I can say, "Don't be stupid, it *will* work."' And she would reply, 'No, it won't, I won't make you happy. Anyway, I am never getting married and I never want to have children, so off you go now, go on.'

I wanted to cry when she said this, but pretended to laugh,

be amused by her adolescent posturing. I was never sure if she was testing me, or herself; I wondered if she really was a pessimist at heart, about the world in general, about people and emotions, about us, or just saying it. It was not at all like me, being a cheerful little soul, thinking good things will happen, it will all work out, don't worry. She did seem to worry a lot, which she denied, saying she was merely a realist. By imagining the worst, so she said, it made it easier to cope when something did happen.

We seemed to be opposites, in so many ways. Like poles repel, unlike poles attract. That might be true in electromagnetism, so I learned at school, but was it the same for people? I think on the whole it does apply. There is an attraction in opposites.

Despite being optimistic about most things, I was also at the same time restless, impatient to get on to the next thing, having new ideas, living ahead in my head, wanting things to happen, now, I can't wait. She was more accepting, realistic, clear-headed. She would sigh and groan at my optimism – but I sensed she liked me being that way. And we would have a hug.

On most of our long walks, I was hardly aware of where we were, in a dream, still talking all the time. Often we were lost, deliberately going ways and routes we didn't know, then having to find our way back. She would never ask anyone directions, and stopped me doing so. It was as if she considered it a weakness, having to depend on others. I like asking, listening, even if I then ignore their directions or advice.

We were once miles away up the River Eden, heading towards Rockcliffe and the Solway marshes, arguing about something or other, with me getting sulky and moody. We found we were walking down a country lane behind two boys aged about ten, one very tall, who reminded me of Reg, and one small, i.e. like me. They were not aware we were behind, but as we caught up with them, it was clear they had been having words and one was sulking, just like me. 'Oh well, if that's your attitude, Keith,' said the smaller one, furiously, storming off, leaving the other behind.

It made us smile; our own little tiff was forgotten. It then went into our lexicon, our own private glossary of banal words and phrases, which had a meaning and memory only for us. 'If that's your attitude, Keith,' one of us would say to the other at fraught moments.

Then we would smile. And hold hands. Ahhhhh . . .

19

HOLD THE FRONT PAGE

I was twenty-one on 7 January 1957. I remember it well, for I was there, but also the cost – did I moan about the cost. Can't of course remember now exactly what it did cost, but I recall regretting that I had decided to pay for everything and be Big Mick. That was one of my mother's expressions, when someone foolishly shows off in some way, usually by being unnecessarily generous.

I could not expect my parents to pay for my twenty-first, which seems to be normal today, or feed my friends at home. A pound of mince and a bag of tatties can only go so far. I worked extra hours and long shifts for the Post Office over the Christmas hols in order to pay for a slap-up do, whatever sort of do I might decide to splash out on.

The revolution in food has been one of the biggest changes in my lifetime in what we now call Cumbria. (In 1974, Cumberland and Westmorland, plus a bit of Lancs and a bit of Yorks, became the new super-county of Cumbria.) In fact, in the nation as a whole, the transformation in eating – at home and in restaurants – has been dramatic, across all classes, all regions.

I never ate out as a child, never visited hotels or restaurants till I went to Durham, but then nobody I knew did – the main reason being that there was nowhere to go. I am straining hard to remember the names of any restaurants in Carlisle in the fifties, apart from Fantails, which was out in the country at Wetheral. In the city, there were chip shops, like Brucianas, where you queued in a side alley and bought chips, mushy peas, pies. And there were some dusty, old-fashioned teashops, where ladies in from the country went after they had done their shopping and sat in the window with pots of tea and had scones and cakes. All such teashops and cafés closed at five o'clock, as did all the shops. At five o'clock each day, they signed a suicide pact, gave up the ghost, died a sudden death. The centre of Carlisle then became a morgue, till morning.

The only place you could go and eat after six o'clock was one of the hotels. Even the crummiest commercial hotel had a dining room. The best hotels, like the Crown and Mitre, County and Central, had nicer dining rooms, with oak-panelled walls, but the food was very much the same in all of them.

Waiters in those days, in so-called smart provincial hotels, wore soup-stained dinner jackets, dribbled at the mouth, staggered about and, if you arrived at one minute to two for lunch, they wouldn't let you in. As for the food, well that was mainly soup, tired watery cod and vegetables boiled until they screamed for mercy before being dumped on the table in silver dishes, their original features obliterated.

With the choice of venue for a slap-up do so limited, some-where I could mark this auspicious, coming-of-age occasion, I decided to book my twenty-first dinner at the County Hotel.

This was on the viaduct. Not quite as posh as the Crown and Mitre but still intimidating. I invited Margaret, my best friend Reg and his girlfriend Pat, Mike Thornhill and Margaret Crosthwaite. I paid for everything, gritting my teeth. I then went mad and told my second-best friends, the ones I could not afford to invite to dinner, that I would buy them a drink beforehand at the Friars pub, which was where the loucher grammar school masters and upper sixth-formers used to go. Anything you like, I announced to them, it's on me this first round. All but one chose a half of bitter. His name, which I am not going to mention as it still rankles, asked for a whisky. The bloody cheek. He knew how I'd had to scrimp and save my money all over the Christmas holidays, yet he went and ordered the most expensive drink. I never spoke to him again.

The meal, of course, was appalling, horrible soup, then chicken, followed by ice cream, a set meal, which was the cheapest available. I was in a sulk all evening. Margaret was furious with me.

Oh, if only I had become twenty-one just ten years later. It was in the 1960s that things began to look up, food-wise. Chinese and Italian restaurants began to arrive in Carlisle and, out in the countryside, gourmet dining started at Sharrow Bay on Ullswater. It was first opened in 1948 by Francis Coulson, arriving from Euston with saucepans on his back, later joined by his partner Brian Sack, but it was in the sixties that it became nationally famous. Miller Howe on Windermere came a bit later, in 1971, but together these two wonderful hotels with their marvellous food attracted the local and then the national quality for the next few decades, spawning many imitations. Eating out in Cumbria had become fun.

Now, it often seems as if the national passion has become not just for eating food but looking at it – photographing it, doing books about it, advertising it, watching it on TV. The technical magic of TV has turned food and cookery into a form of soft porn. Not that I have ever watched a food programme. Or read the books. I grind my teeth in jealousy when I see cookery books dominating the bestseller lists. Restaurant critics and chefs becoming celebrities – how on earth did that happen? Why do we not have celeb plumbers or electricians?

Even if there had been a wider choice in 1957, with better food, more and varied types of restaurants, I would probably still have gone for the cheapest option. But it would have been a lot better.

Any road up, I did it. I managed to turn my coming of age into a modest occasion, for Carlisle, for someone turning twenty-one from the St Ann's estate in 1957. I treated my friends, splashed out, tried to be generous. And sulked privately at the cost. Perhaps not so privately. It did seem to amuse them, my silent resentment.

Back at Durham, in the spring term of 1957, I was made editor of *Palatinate*. I had moved on to be features editor, writing even more columns and pieces, and at last got promoted to glory. Rapture. I don't honestly think I have ever enjoyed any sort of job or position quite as much.

The thing about a student newspaper, amateur and chaotic though it may be, is that you have no real worries about circulation and advertising, no suits or lawyers hovering over you, no readers complaining or rivals bettering you, yet it is still real, a proper newspaper, only in miniature. You also don't get pigeonholed, the people who work on it get to do everything, write for all sections, do the headlines, sub copy, report sport, write leaders, compose jokes, compile readers' letters, lay out the pages, write posters, then go out in the street or to colleges and sell copies on publication day.

It was in those days steam printing and archaic production methods dating back to Caxton, with acres of galleys coming back from the printers which had to be read and corrected, then taken back to Bailes. The galleys were cut up and stuck on blank pages, headlines written in, hoping they would fit. You had to learn the basics of typography, type styles and sizes, all in a new language. Photographs were turned in blocks – lumps of solid metal. We could only afford two or three blocks per issue, so I devised a system of having certain blocks cut in half. If, say, there was a new president of the Union, I would have his photo made into a block, then cut it in two, right down his face. In the caption I would say, 'Sorry, girls, you will have to wait for the next issue to see all of him.' How we giggled, laying out the pages.

As editor, I found myself writing more and more, naturally putting in my own stuff, but using pseudonyms. I wrote a column called 'Crumbs', which was a gossip column, stories and jokes about people at the university, students and dons, sometimes too clever by half. Not all readers understood who or what it was about. Which saved us from being sued.

I saw myself mainly as a comic writer, that was the bit I enjoyed most. I loved the post-war American humorists, James Thurber and Robert Benchley, discovering them rather late, as Benchley was long dead and Thurber was by then pretty old. I used to read their short stories, working out how they did it, how they laid jokes and situations, so I could anticipate the payoff they were working up to. I admired their word play, turning clichés round unexpectedly. I never liked P. G. Wodehouse, I thought he was whimsical, but mostly I think I disliked the people who liked Wodehouse, considering them affected.

I could do serious stuff as well, if need be. I got into trouble with the authorities for running a front-page story about King's College, Newcastle being separated from Durham to become a university on its own. They officially denied it, but I still ran it, and of course it came true. I also ran a story about Durham itself having a new college, which might be called Cromwell. That led to lots of controversy, people objecting to a college being named after such a baddie.

I got a letter from someone called Anthony Sampson on the *Observer*, who was writing the 'Pendennis' column. He asked me to ring him, reverse charges, as he wanted to write about the Cromwell story. I had not realised outsiders would be at all interested in our purely local content. Then I was told by Michael Bateman, my friend on the local rag, that there was money in it, national papers would pay just for a tip-off, even posh papers. The *Observer* would have paid, so they said, but they never actually ran the story.

I rang the *Daily Express* one week, after I had done a piece about a women's boat club, St Hild's, which at the last moment in a regatta had replaced one of the women rowers with a man. The woman at bow had suddenly fallen ill, just as the race was about to begin, so they substituted their male coach, who did have rather long hair. I got two guineas for the tip-off.

However, whenever I felt pleased with my own little

journalistic efforts, I only had to read some of the student newspapers that started coming in from other much bigger, wealthier, more famous universities. I remember the Leeds one as being superbly professional, with loads more pages than ours, better layout, great photos, none of them cut up. The London ones were also excellent.

But the one that really depressed me was *Varsity*, the Cambridge student newspaper. The Oxford one, *Cherwell*, was fairly boring and predictable, but *Varsity* had a column by someone called Michael Frayn. It was so brilliant, so imaginative, so funny. Whenever it arrived, I used to think, why do I bother, I will never be in the same league.

My final exams were coming up, but I wasn't too worried, even though I had done so little work, being up to my eyes with *Palatinate*. I was sure I had done enough. What I was more worried about was getting a job. I still had no idea what I was going to do.

I went to the appointments board, who are usually a joke in any university – what do they know about the world of work, sitting there shovelling leaflets? They asked what I liked doing and I said, 'Well, journalism,' and they opened some filing cabinet, turned over a few folders, then shook their heads. The computer says no, or whatever it was jobsworths said in the fifties. They had no record of anyone from Durham going into journalism, and had no application forms.

I mentioned this to my moral tutor, at his once-a-term sherry party, and he said it was not quite true. About eight years ago, he remembered that there had been a Castleman who also edited *Palatinate*, name of Harold Evans, who had gone into journalism. No one knew where he was now, or if he was still a journalist. So that wasn't much help.

But the appointments people did give me lists of graduate training schemes, such as with ICI, Metal Box, Marks and Spencer. They were apparently offering management training to graduates, but they mostly seemed to involve sales jobs, which sounded attractive enough. They gave you a car, before sending you out on the road, and you got to stay in hotels. That might be fun. My dad had never driven a car or stayed in a hotel. I filled in a few application forms and was called for an interview by a well-known company called Benzole. They were a British petrol firm, long established, dating back to 1919. There used to be a joke about them: 'She was only a garage man's daughter but she loved the smell of Benzole . . .'

I wrote to Margaret, boasting about landing an interview, thinking I had done well. 'What the hell are you thinking of,' she replied, 'you will be useless selling petrol.' I said, 'Yes, but that's just the beginning, learning the ropes, then I will be a manager one day, you'll see. Anyway, I will get a car.'

The interview was in Newcastle. I can't remember what they asked me, or what I said, or how long I was there, but the answer came pretty quickly. Sorry, no thanks. They had obviously seen at once that I would be pretty useless.

The other thing hanging over me was national service. There had been two periods of forcible conscription in the UK for fit young men – during the First World War, from 1916 to 1920, then in the Second World War, when it lasted from 1939 to 1960, going on so much longer than the actual war itself. Around one and a half million were called up after

1945 – when supposedly it was all over. After the war we got into a series of post-colonial local wars and rebellions and fit young men were needed as fodder, to fill up the ranks. Conscripts, called up straight from school, found themselves fighting and killing in Korea; against the Mau Mau in Kenya and terrorists in Cyprus and Malaya.

You were called up at any age from eighteen, regardless of class and family background, so there was very little fiddling or evading, though of course it did go on, with false medical reports or hiring ringers to take the medical tests for you. There were three exempt occupations, deemed to be essential to the national good: coal mining, farming and the merchant navy. Students and apprentices could defer it if they were in full-time study or training, but they still had to do it, either before or after graduation or qualifying. All healthy young men got called up, sooner or later.

There were lads who loved military service, enjoyed the camaraderie, excited by the chance to see the world, fire guns and drive tanks and shoot at people. The majority, however, seemed to spend most of their time either square-bashing or painting cobbles with white paint. There were some good courses, a chance to learn new skills, such as the Russian course that many of the clever conscripts – such as Michael Frayn and Alan Bennett – went on.

I didn't fancy any of it, so I began to think of doing some sort of postgraduate course, which would keep me as a student for at least another year – and possibly out of national service forever. We knew by 1957 that national service would soon be coming to an end – but we had no idea when. I would have been furious to be called up – and find I was in the last ever batch.

Also in my mind was the desire to remain as a student. I wanted to have the same vacations, and concerns, as Margaret, who was about to start her first year at Oxford. I felt somehow this would help me to stay in touch with her and her world. I then heard that Ian Johnstone, my friend from school, was applying to Oxford to do a year's diploma course in something to do with overseas administration, which would equip you for work in the colonies. He wanted to go abroad and work in what was left of our empire.

I did not know such one-year specialist postgraduate courses existed, so I got a list and applied to do one in social sciences at Oxford, the sort of course that prepares you to be a social worker. You had to apply to the social sciences department at Oxford and also to a college. I applied to St Catherine's, knowing Reg was headed there after his national service. I got an interview with the master, Alan Bullock, who was very friendly and chatty with a strong northern accent, which was reassuring. Looking at my CV, he noticed that I was editor of *Palatinate*. 'That will be useful. *Cherwell* needs improving.' He said he would take me in St Catherine's, if I went on the course.

I then had an interview with the social sciences department, but they turned me down. My heart was not in it anyway. I was just looking for an excuse to be in Oxford for a year, near Margaret.

In desperation, or at least thrashing around for something to do, to cover myself for the next year and avoid national service, I decided I had better stay at Durham. So I applied for a one-year Diploma of Education. It would please my mother. And if all else failed, I would at least have some sort of qualification to get a job. They always want teachers.

The other attraction of staying at Durham for another year was that I could carry on editing *Palatinate*. Towards the end of the last term, before my final exams, I happened to be talking to Michael Bateman, my friend who was on the local paper. He asked why I had not applied to be a graduate trainee journalist. I told him I didn't know there were such things. The appointments board had never mentioned them or given me any applications. He explained that there were two – the one he had joined, run by Westminster Press, which had local papers all over the country, including the *Durham Advertiser*. The better one, with bigger, more important papers, was Kemsley Newspapers. He had applied for their scheme, but had been turned down.

I immediately contacted both of them for further details and got the application forms, but alas, I was just too late for this year. They had taken their quota for 1957. But I could apply in due course for next year, if I was still interested, after I had graduated.

I passed all my final exams and was awarded a second-class degree. When I went to look at the results board on Palace Green, for one moment I allowed myself to think I might get a first, which of course was pure fantasy. How could I have done, spending all that time on *Palatinate*?

My mother came for the graduation ceremony in Durham Cathedral, the first time she had been to see me. One of my sisters, Annabelle, came with her. They sat next to the parents of my friend John Davies. His father, the electrician who worked for Kemsley Newspapers in Newcastle, turned to my mother and said, 'This is the proudest moment of my life.' And then he fell asleep.

To celebrate being a graduate, I did what most other new graduates did – I got myself studio-photographed. In Durham this was always done by Daisy Edis, an elderly woman who had cornered the market in university photographs. I thought she made me look really good, sitting solemnly in my graduate gown and white-fur-trimmed hood, and so did my mother. I showed it with pride to Margaret – and she burst out laughing. 'Your spots!' she exclaimed. 'She's got rid of your spots!'

She thought the result was phoney, effeminate, unreal, not at all attractive. It is true that in this photo – see back cover of this book – I do appear to have the most perfectly lovely skin. In reality, at the time, I was always a mass of spots. During the first year going out with me, Margaret says she never saw me without a sticking plaster on my face. I had either squeezed a spot which had then left an awful, ugly blemish or I was trying to hide a fresh spot.

'Daisy Edis must be a miracle worker . . .'

In the long vacation, I decided I should try to get some sort of journalistic experience, as it would obviously be a help if I applied for the training schemes. I wrote to John – later Sir John – Burgess, the editor of the *Cumberland News*, Carlisle's main paper. He saw me in his office, and I flashed some copies of *Palatinate* to impress him, and of course he had never heard of it. He told me to slow down, start again, he couldn't understand what I was saying. 'You will never make it as a journalist if you speak so quickly.'

He showed me out, saying sorry, there were no vacancies, neither for trainees nor temporary staff. Awfully sorry. So that was someone else I was going to sack, once I was lord of the universe.

I then went across the road to the *Carlisle Journal,* a much older, more old-fashioned newspaper with a small circulation. It had been founded in 1798, so was much older than the *Cumberland News.* I got an interview with the editor, Fred Humphrey OBE. He had received his award for some wartime work in the Ministry of Information. He seemed about a hundred years old and dozy but very kind and gentlemanly – and he agreed to take me on for the summer.

I would not get a salary, as such, but I would work as a reporter in the newsroom. For every story I got in the paper I would be paid one and a half pennies a line. It does seem incredibly low, even for the times, but there were two issues a week, mostly using the same stories, so if my stuff was repeated, I got more lines and more pennies. The money did not matter, of course. I was thrilled to have a chance to be working on a real newspaper.

The offices were beside the City Picture House, in English Street. They had a shop window on the street, filled with dusty stationery, envelopes, lavatory paper, which was apparently a sideline of one of the directors. You entered by a side alley. The print room was on the ground floor, editorial was upstairs through lots of ancient bare rooms with wooden floors.

The two editions came out on Tuesdays and Fridays, with Friday's paper being the main one. It often ran late because the head printer had been refreshing himself at the Sportsman inn. He would come back striding around the office and shouting, 'Fuck the Duke of Edinburgh!'

There was a news editor and about five staff in editorial, plus a photographer, but I did get to sit at a desk and have access to a rickety old typewriter, which I bashed with one finger (today I am hugely advanced and can manage two fingers). I mainly rewrote press hand-outs and announcements, or lifted stories from other publications. When I was allowed out, it was usually to school prize-givings and flower shows. You had to include the names of as many people as possible, the theory being that they would then buy the paper.

One day I was sent out of town, to a place on the Scottish border called Penton, to report on their agricultural show, the furthest away I had been on a story. It seemed a huge honour, to be allowed out on what was practically a foreign story. I would have to go on the bus, for which I could charge expenses. I boasted to Margaret about it, who was now back from France, waiting to go up to Oxford. She had found a holiday job for herself, in the Carlisle laundry, which sounded far worse than the labouring jobs I had done in earlier summers, and smellier.

I had two entrance tickets for the Penton show and told her I would pay her bus fare, if she came with me. So off we went, into an area of north Cumberland, almost in Scotland, which not even Margaret had visited before.

I dutifully made a list of all those who had won prizes for the flowers, vegetables, lambs, cattle, all the usual things that happen at local agricultural shows, plus the winners of the races, the tug-of-war and other competitions. It included pony-trap racing, which I noticed was a bit more exciting than the other events. It involved young men on little two-wheel carts being pulled by a pony, racing each other, doing a lot of shouting.

When the *Journal* came out, I got a good show, big space, with long lists of people, and included a boring quote from the show secretary saying what a grand day it had been. When the *Cumberland News* came out, their headline was 'Horse Runs Amok at Penton'. I had not realised anyone was there from the *Cumberland News*, nor had I seen any horse running amok. It is true that at the end of the pony-trap race one horse had rather reared up, but that was all.

I got a bollocking from the news editor for having missed it, especially when he found out that my girlfriend had gone with me. He suggested I had probably not been concentrating properly and had missed a dramatic incident. Which wasn't true. What a fibber the *Cumberland News* reporter had been, exaggerating such a minor event.

Or was that how professional journalism worked? Did you have to do a bit of fibbing and flamming and taking things out of context to make a story? Which was a bit worrying. Perhaps I would never make it, at least not as a news reporter.

My other worry was Margaret. I stayed working on the *Journal* till the end of the summer, then it was time for me to go back to Durham, for my very last year, while she went off to Oxford, for her first year. Would this be our last summer? I feared she might move on and away from me, once she reached the dreaming spires of Oxford.

20

DREAMING SPIRES

Margaret went off to Oxford in October 1957. We wrote all the time, of course, but I did fear we would begin to lose touch, once she was meeting all these new gilded and sparklingly clever friends, seeing new wonderful and beautiful places, falling in love with the whole idea of Oxford.

But the opposite happened. In her letters it soon began to emerge that she wasn't enjoying Oxford, that she disliked the braying people, living in college and the history course she was having to study. It sounded as bad as mine had been in my first year. Their idea of modern history seemed to finish about 1815.

The first term doing my DipEd was all lectures, based in Durham, on Palace Green, so handy to get to. Or not, as the case soon became, for I was bound up with something more enjoyable and fun and stimulating than lectures on the history of education or the Montessori teaching system.

I was editing *Palatinate* again, part of the real reason for staying on for this extra year, and was trying to recruit some decent writers and increase the circulation. For years, in the hands of the Hatfield mob, *Palatinate* had been looked down upon, particularly in Castle, as a joke, a pathetic, ill-written rag, so it was hard to change the image, but I managed slowly to find some good new columnists.

Two of them went on to careers in journalism – Dan Van der Vat on the *Guardian*, and author of many books, and Colin McDowell, who was our waspish film critic, later turning himself into one of the country's leading fashion experts and writers. I also managed to recruit quite a few women, notably Jill Burtt, who was at St Aidan's. Not sure what happened to her.

Dick Evans, another of my contemporaries, who was a friend at my college, did no journalism at Durham, yet went on to be news editor of the *Financial Times*. Which shows you don't have to do student journalism to get a job in real journalism – and also disproves my belief at the time that Durham was a total wilderness, cut off from the mainstream of media life and aspirations.

Palatinate was doing so well that I decided to enter it for the annual students' newspaper of the year awards, run by the NUS and sponsored at the time by the *Sunday Times*.

We were very pleased to be told we had been put on the shortlist for one of the awards and I was invited to London to the presentation ceremony and to meet the judges. Bailes, our printers, as a little present, offered to print six copies of *Palatinate*, the ones we had to enter, on better-than-normal glossy paper. It did look rather posh and impressive, so I was sure we would win a prize.

In fact, it was held against us. And we won nothing. The judges said we were being unnecessarily wasteful, printing on such expensive paper. Not knowing that only six copies had been printed like that. Students' papers should be on bog paper, or similar.

One of the editors from the *Sunday Times* who presented the awards was Kenneth Pearson. He looked so distinguished, tall and silver-haired, unlike the rather untidy, not to say scruffy, journalists I had met on the *Carlisle Journal*. I was told he had been a wartime pilot, winning some medal or other. I wondered if all London journalists looked as sophisticated and elegant, or just on the posh papers.

I eventually received the application forms for the Kemsley Newspapers and Westminster graduate schemes and filled them in, though with not much hope, convinced it would be carved up by the clever young things currently writing for *Cherwell* and *Varsity*.

I also wrote off to the *Observer*, having felt I had acquired a vague contact through Anthony Sampson asking me to ring him (even though nothing appeared in his 'Pendennis' column). In March 1958, I got a fairly nice letter from Frederick Tomlinson, administration editor of the *Observer*, who said they had no suitable vacancy. 'But if you are coming to London in the near future, I shall be glad to have an informal chat with you.' I took that as the bum's rush. He added that I would be better off applying to Kemsley and Westminster. 'Let me know how you fare.'

People in the fifties did bother to write fairly decent letters, letting you down gently, even if you were a young nobody at some provincial university. Today, the normal reply is silence.

I did get my first payment from a national publication for actually writing something, as opposed to the two guineas from the *Daily Express* for a tip-off. I had been contacted by someone called Peter Dickinson on *Punch*, who was writing to a selection of student editors – possibly those on the NUS shortlists – explaining that they were doing a student edition and would like any humorous offerings. I sent something off, which was accepted – but, bugger it, the issue never came out.

I did receive a cheque for six guineas, which I immediately cashed, and pinned the covering letter on my wall in my rooms on the Norman Gallery. That was a bit of name-dropping. The reference to the Norman Gallery will be totally meaningless to any but a handful of Old Castlemen.

When I got back to Castle in the autumn of 1957, I was elected Senior Man – i.e. president of the JCR. It meant that when I started my DipEd year, 1957–58, I had two jobs – editing *Palatinate* and Senior Man.

When I wrote and told Margaret, she was totally derisive, pouring scorn on the silly title. It is true that whenever I have mentioned being Senior Man, anywhere outside that tiny, isolated peninsula in Durham, people just laugh. (The title lives on: even though University College, Durham became co-ed in 1987, the Senior Man of the JCR is still called Senior Man, even if she is a woman.)

There were three big attractions of being Senior Man. One, you got the best rooms in the house – in this case a suite of rooms on the Norman Gallery, which were stunningly situated, on a wide, handsome corridor filled with statues and pillars. At the end of my previous year, I had found a room to rent on South Street, outside the peninsula but overlooking the river, probably the nicest street in Durham City. I had been so thrilled to acquire it for my DipEd year, thanks to a friend from St Cuthbert's, Peter Gilbourne-Stenson, who'd lived there the previous year and put in a good word for me. But when I was elected Senior Man, right at the beginning of term, I gave it up, so I never actually lived there.

Secondly, as Senior Man I got a sherry allowance. I couldn't believe it, and of course kept it quiet. The theory was that the SM would be having meetings in his rooms, inviting officers of the JCR, entertaining Senior Men from the other colleges, so naturally he had to offer them a quiet sherry, keep up the status and standards of Castle.

Thirdly, and perhaps best of all, I got access to a typewriter, the JCR's very own machine, a sit-up-and-beg Remington. Technically, it was for the use of the JCR secretary, Alan Flint, who lived in the rooms on the Norman Gallery next to me. His job was to make notes during JCR meetings, then type them up afterwards. I said he could still have the honour of keeping the minutes of the meetings, but the typewriter would reside in my room from now on.

In my first year, I had considered the Senior Man as almost a demigod, so mature and impressive and organised. By the third year I realised it was an act, playing a part, looking as if you know what you are doing. All I mainly had to do was walk into JCR meetings, followed by the secretary. They would all stand up and I would announce solemnly, 'This is a meeting of University College, junior common room. Gentlemen may smoke.' I would sit down. Everyone else would sit down. Then I would take the meeting through the agenda, copying the system and phrases I had heard the Senior Men trot out in my previous three years, asking gentlemen to vote 'aye' or 'nay', but doing it all as quickly as possible.

There were no rows or dramas during my year in office, but an awful lot of time was spent on boring problems to do with the college bar, buttery and the Undercroft, and then finally Castle Day and the June Ball, the two big events at the end of the academic year. It was hard keeping a straight face all the time, as if I cared about some of the more piddling stuff, and not appearing a total fraud, but now, aged twenty-one, I was at least a graduate. That meant I wore a BA gown to prove it.

I went down to visit Margaret at Oxford a few times, as soon as she appeared to have settled in and I could get away. I hitch-hiked, which took forever, as I did not want to spend money on trains. Everyone hitchhiked in those days. It was what you did. I suppose the war had helped to make it acceptable and commonplace, as there were few cars and vehicles, petrol was rationed, so you helped each other.

Margaret and I did a lot of hitchhiking together, to the southern Lakes, Yorkshire and Scotland. I used to say I had a lucky thumb, which I would only put up in the air if we were desperate. You hid your luggage, if you had a lot, pulling it out of the dyke when the car has stopped. It was usually much easier with a girl than another boy, so you made sure she was most visible. I went off once to have a pee in a barn, leaving Margaret by the roadside. Into the barn stormed an angry farmer yelling, 'You hard-faced bugger!' I ran like hell, the farmer still shouting after me, just in time to jump into the car which Margaret had stopped. 'You hard-faced bugger' went into our repertoire of phrases whenever I did something vaguely unlawful.

I liked to think I gave good chat, helped the driver of the car or the lorry to pass the time by being amusing, interesting or, most of all, interested in him and his life. I can't remember a woman giving me a lift. It was always male drivers. Sometimes the rides were posh Jaguars or Daimlers. Mostly, though, they were scary bashed-up, rattling lorries and you were glad to get off. Sometimes they said they were just going to the next town. If you suspected that was a fib, you tried doubly hard to be interesting, hoping they would say, 'Actually, I am going all the way to London.' So you felt doubly grateful to humanity and the world and of course yourself, for having sold yourself.

I still think that hitchhiking is the most adventurous form of travelling. You don't know where you are going, how you will get there, with whom, or when, if ever. You are at the hands of traffic, fate, the whims and decisions of others. It can be frightening, worrying, freezing, sweltering. The conversation can be fascinating, annoying, non-existent. The thing to keep telling yourself, when no one has stopped for hours and you are totally losing heart, is that bastards never stop.

Hitchhiking was huge in the UK and USA in the post-war years, right up to the 1970s, part of most people's young lives. Now ordinary people, ordinary students, don't seem to do it, only dossers or vehicle delivery drivers carrying their plates. Once cars became more common it was less necessary. The arrival of motorways made it harder, as you were not allowed to hitchhike on them. But I suppose social attitudes have discouraged it – and horror films. Risk-averse parents do not let their little treasures climb into a strange vehicle with a strange man.

When I visited Margaret, I would aim to do it in a day, though it was an awkward cross-country route, Durham to Oxford, so I would often arrive in the dark. To begin with I slept on Mike Thornhill's floor in Balliol, but eventually I was able to stay with the parents of Margaret's new best friend, Theodora Parfitt. Her home happened to be in Oxford, in Northmoor Road. Both her parents were doctors. Theo and her sister had gone to boarding school while her younger brother Derek was at Eton. On the surface, they appeared to be terribly posh and well off and upper class, yet some of the carpets were threadbare and they seemed to eat a lot out of tins or packets. One room was filled with old newspapers, which the father was saving up to sell for salvage.

Margaret, being a scholar, had a very good room in Somerville and seemed to me to be the centre of quite an admiring group. They were from the best public schools and were charmed by this forthright northerner who knew her mind and had an opinion on everything.

When I went to various Oxford gatherings with her and her friends I fell silent, feeling provincial and lumpen and tongue-tied, awfully inferior, convinced they were all looking down on me for being a northern grammar school boy at a provincial university. None of them, of course, looked down on Margaret because of her background, for she could easily match them in conversational cut and thrust. But her girlfriends were all very friendly and interested in me. It was the men, they just ignored me, as if I wasn't there. So I would go all sullen and resentful.

We were not sleeping together, certainly not. It's 1957–58 – sex, as we know, did not arrive till 1963. I would go all that way to see her just to hold hands. But there was a bit of what was called heavy petting – as illustrated on swimming-pool notices of the time, warning patrons against it. There was sometimes the occasional anguished tussle, but none of that appalling, shocking physical intercourse nonsense, which we had only ever read about, half-believing it was not true. When we went hostelling for the weekend in the Lake District, we made it clear to Margaret's parents that youth hostels were segregated, which they were, male and female dormitories, so all above board, but during the day, on our long walks, we tried to find somewhere dry and preferably with a roof on in which to crouch.

Getting anywhere indoors and alone was such a struggle in the fifties and sixties. Even if you had a regular girlfriend or boyfriend, no parents would let you sleep together, or even stay the night. So in the early days of our courtship, going youth hostelling, spending all day and most of the evening together, was exciting.

I was never as good a walker as Margaret. She walked straight and upright while I slouched the way Baden-Powell said every Boy Scout should never do, for it clearly smacked of slackness and abuses. I got her to carry our rucksack, except when we passed through villages or met anyone. So I didn't appear a total seven-stone weakling. I did, when I was younger, before I had girlfriends, look at those adverts in *The Hotspur* and *Wizard* and wonder if I should send off for a muscle-building course, but I couldn't afford them. By the time I did have the money, I seemed to have girlfriends anyway.

We had stayed one night at the youth hostel in Penrith, after a day walking round Ullswater. In the morning, she counted up the pennies of our joint money and worked out we had enough for one more night in the hostel, for the two of us, or we could walk all day, have a good meal in the evening, and then go home. Which would I prefer? I paused, for probably ten seconds, and opted for the good meal and going home. I was never forgiven.

Another time, sitting in romantic contemplation on the top of Place Fell after a lovely day, she asked what I was thinking. Which is what couples do, when young and courting. I foolishly told the truth. 'I was just thinking I could really do with a pint and pie.'

We spent a good holiday youth hostelling in Scotland. First of all, we went to Cambuslang to stay with my Uncle Jim and Aunt Linda. I wanted to show off Margaret, the Oxford scholar, and also show them off to Margaret, that I did have half-decent, artistic relations with their own house. In my mind, they were very bohemian and ever so liberal, so I had assumed and expected that we would be allowed to sleep together, in an actual bed. The moment I even hinted at this, we were not even allowed in the same house, never mind the same bed. They suddenly announced that Margaret was being accommodated up the road, in the house of my other aunt, Aunt Jean. They said they didn't really have room for the two of us, but Aunt Jean would be delighted to give Margaret a bed.

And she was. She brought Margaret breakfast in bed each morning, on a lovely tray, with flowers and fresh fruit. Margaret was charmed. Down at Aunt Linda's, I had cold porridge, left behind when they went off to work.

Then we headed off to Skye, over on the ferry, and walked and hitched to the very top at Uig, where we booked into the youth hostel. We took a stroll in the evening and sat in the heather on some little hill, from where, in the distance, we could hear a bagpiper practising. Very moody, very romantic, for us Scottish-born folk.

Also staying in the hostel was a woman in her forties with a gawky, overweight son of about ten, over whom she constantly fussed. On the hour, she would say to him, 'Here's your ten o'clocks, Michael', and shove some awful pie down his throat. 'Here's your eleven o'clocks, Michael.' And he would be given a packet of biscuits. It went on all day long. The phrase entered our lexicon, another meaningless banality, said to each other satirically when being given something.

Next morning in the hostel, we had words. Can't remember now what it was about, but the upshot was that Margaret poured a bowl of cornflakes over my head. The hostel dining room was quite full, with half a dozen other couples who pretended not to notice what Margaret had done. For the next few days, arriving at other hostels, working our way up the west coast to Ullapool, we kept on meeting couples from the Skye hostel who would point at us, then whisper and start giggling. Not that Margaret cared, but I was black affronted, as my mother used to say, or 'shanned to deeth', as we said in Carlisle.

On one of my visits to Oxford, I overstayed my time in her room in Somerville. Chucking-out time for all male visitors was six o'clock, just as it was for female visitors at Durham. I don't know how we made a mistake, as nothing all that exciting was happening, just talking probably, but we suddenly realised it was eight o'clock. How was I going to get out?

I didn't know my way round the college, how to find a back door, and didn't want to do myself damage by climbing any walls. We decided the best way was the most direct and brazen way – to go out the front gate, through the porter's lodge. But disguised as a woman. Somervillians could go in and out till ten o'clock, so there were always women leaving or coming back.

I rolled up my trousers, put on Margaret's blue raincoat and wrapped her college scarf round my head, partly obscuring my face. Like me, she had bought a college scarf in her first year, before she decided it was naff. I got through the college gates okay, striding out boldly, then walked up Woodstock Road till I came to an alleyway. I went into it, looked around, took Margaret's scarf and coat off and rolled down my trousers. It was then I noticed that a couple were standing in the alleyway, kissing against a wall. I was aware that the man had seen me, and noticed his look of surprise at my hairy legs.

I got back to Balliol and spent the night on Mike's floor. Next morning I hitchhiked back to Durham. It was a few days later that I discovered that the person in the alleyway who had spotted me was the editor of *Cherwell*. He did a front-page story about a man escaping from Somerville disguised as a woman. Some helpful person at Somerville then told him Margaret's name, and he flogged the story to the *Daily Sketch*, a popular tabloid of the time, later taken over by the *Daily Mail*.

Margaret was summoned before the principal of Somerville, Dame Janet Vaughan, who reprimanded her for bringing the good name of the college into disrepute, especially being a scholar. Her punishment was being gated for the rest of that term. Which wasn't too severe. It was already quite near the end.

In the second term, I had to start my teaching practice, which meant that, in December 1957, at the end of the autumn term, I resigned as editor of *Palatinate*. I managed a bumper edition to celebrate, and we sold 1,500 copies – which was saturation point, as the number of students in Durham was still only around that mark. It was by then about to start expanding, with new colleges being planned, such as Grey College, which opened in 1959.

Jill Burtt did a profile of me in my last *Palatinate*, in which she described me as 'a laughing mischievous devil with a rapid way of speaking so that it seems impossible he could ever be in repose'. I got some stick for that from my Oxford scholar friend.

21

READY FOR ACTION

My teaching practice was at a secondary modern school in West Hartlepool, reputed to have about the highest unemployment and poverty rates in the country at the time. It wasn't all that hard. It was just that I was useless.

The teacher looking after me was very pleasant and helpful and I did admire him, for his wisdom and maturity, still trying his best, but well aware he wasn't doing much to improve the lives of his pupils. He sat at the back during most of my lessons marking exercise books, as if unaware of what I was doing, but it was comforting to know he was there, in case world war three broke out. I was teaching history, not a full load, just a couple of periods a day to so-called easy classes. I would prepare each lesson, as we had been taught, spending ages following the format we had been given about the aims of each lesson, then the achievements, but they never seemed to go to plan. I could never decide whether to be friends with them, talk about pop music and football, or be a right bastard and somehow get their respect.

I once had to meet a parent who had come in to talk to someone about her son Nottingham. Naturally, I eventually asked how he came to have that name. 'That's where I had him,' she replied with a smile. She also had a girl called Scarborough and another called Sheffield. I never found out if she was on the game or a long-distance lorry driver.

In the staffroom you soon discover all the petty squabbles and personality clashes you are never aware of as a pupil, which in my case had been only four years earlier. There were chairs you could not sit in, mugs you should never use, whose turn for biscuits, who hated whom, which topics never to discuss. It was interesting, but not much use, as I couldn't really write about it in *Palatinate*. I did describe the teachers at length in letters to Margaret, just as she had described the complicated family she had lived with as an au pair in Bordeaux, none of whom I had met.

I still went down to Oxford at regular intervals to see Margaret. She was still not in love with Oxford, deciding she hated living in college, with girls all the same age and roughly the same type, all their voices, all the noise and the jolly JCR camaraderie. Like many girls, she had loved boarding-school stories when young, read all of Angela Brazil, and fantasised that she was not Arthur's daughter living in a council house but an orphan who gets sent by a rich distant relative to spend her whole school life in a wonderful boarding school. But she found she much preferred to be on her own, away from groups and gangs and regimentation. So she started making plans to go into a flat in her second year, along with her friend Theo.

I told her she should at least try to make the most of Oxford, try new things, take part more, then give it up if it turns out boring and the people awful, but give things a go. Which is what I had done. Being two years older, I did like to think I was wise to the world, well, Durham's little world.

One of the things Margaret eventually decided to get into was acting. She was given the lead part in a student production of *The Caucasian Chalk Circle*. She played Grusha, the heroine, and Dennis Potter was the judge. The director was Ken Trodd. I went now and again to rehearsals, and could see how good Margaret was, and how they all thought so. But Dennis was the real star, a legend in his circles. He had a coterie of posh public school girls, all supposedly left wing, members of the Oxford Labour Party, who hung on his every word, especially if he started telling stories about living in a hovel, had dripping for breakfast, kept coal in the bath, had worked down the pit from the age of ten. Or similar stories. I suppose in a way Margaret held the same fascination for these sorts of girls as well, with her father in his boilersuit going to his factory on his bike. So different from the dear parents they had. But, unlike Dennis, she did not go on about it.

Margaret gave up acting after one play. It was well reviewed but one production was quite enough, thank you, so she said. Later she became the film critic of *Isis*, which was useful. When I went down to see her, she usually had free tickets for the latest French films at the Scala cinema. Somewhere to go together in the evenings.

Teaching practice succeeded in convincing me that I had to make a proper stab at getting into journalism, something I did feel at home with, so I was desperate to hear if I was going to be interviewed by either Kemsley Newspapers or the Westminster Press. Eventually the call came – and I had secured interviews with both of them at their head offices in London. I managed to arrange both of them on the same day, so needed only one trip to the capital, taking the train this time, not hitchhiking, in case I was late, or dirty or smelly.

The Westminster Press office was in Fleet Street, so that was exciting, being at the heart of the newspaper empire, but the office was a bit dusty and ramshackle. I walked down Fleet Street and was amazed by the *Daily Express*'s glass black palace, the home of the newspaper I had read all my childhood. The *Telegraph* building was imposing in another way, rather ancient and grand and looked like a posh hotel. Fleet Street seemed so romantic and historic, the home of national print for hundreds of years. I looked up at the famous names on the buildings, titles I had delivered as a boy, and through the windows of the pubs which looked more like gentlemen's clubs, with men in pinstriped suits and roses in their lapels, not like the State Management pubs in Carlisle. I wondered if I would ever work there.

Kemsley's HQ was several streets away, at 200 Gray's Inn Road, not near anywhere famous I had heard of, or any other national newspapers, but its building was large and imposing with uniformed doormen. I passed the entrance to Gray's Inn itself, which seemed very like Oxford, but I assumed it was private, so I never ventured through the gate.

Westminster Press was a large group, scattered right around the country, but all its papers were small, like the *Durham Advertiser*, while Kemsley had fewer but bigger, all with large circulations, the dominant papers in their city or region, such as Newcastle (with the *Chronicle* and the *Journal*), Manchester (the *Evening Chronicle*), Sheffield (the *Telegraph*), Aberdeen (the

Press and Journal) and in Wales they had the *Western Mail*. There were others I have forgotten, but all important papers.

Unlike the Westminster Press, Kemsley also had national papers, so that was a huge attraction, notably three Sunday papers – the *Sunday Times*, the *Empire News* and the *Sunday Graphic*. Lord Kemsley (1883–1968), formerly Sir Gomer Berry, was part of a newspaper and business dynasty that had made its money in South Wales, going on to control a large part of the national press. Kemsley's brother was Lord Camrose. They had co-owned the *Telegraph* at one time, till Kemsley took the *Sunday Times* and Camrose the *Telegraph*. Their Berry descendants and relations are still powers in the media to this day.

I presented myself at Kemsley House and was interviewed by a red-faced, pockmarked, tough Scotsman called Jimmy Fraser. When I heard his accent I immediately dragged in my Scottish background. His Westminster counterpart, whose name I have now forgotten, appeared wishy-washy, as if he did not know what he was looking for, almost as limp and useless as the appointments people at Durham, who I considered were all impotent idiots.

Jimmy Fraser seemed decisive, and to carry some authority, and a week or so later I was invited for a second interview. I was sent a telegram calling me this time to Kemsley House, Manchester to see Mr Goulden, editor of the *Evening Chronicle*. He was small, thin, very pale-faced, emotionless, buttoned up in a suit too big for him. He didn't appear anything like my image of a journalist – I had imagined they were all outgoing, interested in people, inquisitive, on the ball, quick. He was more like an accountant or undertaker.

He explained he was interviewing me generally for the group training scheme, not for any particular job, or on any particular paper. I assumed he was merely a clerical figure, doing his job. So I gabbled madly away, to fill up the silence. He gave nothing away, seemed not interested in me. But at the end of our brief chat, he said that Mr Fraser would in due course be in touch with me, after they had finished interviewing all the applicants. Oh God, perhaps there were hundreds of them.

I was back in Durham for the last term of my DipEd course, supposedly going to lectures and swotting for the exams. But mainly I was busy being Senior Man. Then I found myself devoting a lot of my time to work on a film.

Several years previously, some postgraduate education students had got the money and backing to shoot a film about Durham, highlighting all its wonders, to be shown to sixth-formers round the country, thus encouraging them to think of coming to study at Durham. They had been able to buy proper cameras and equipment. The project had never been finished; the keen students who had made the film had left and no one else since had appeared interested. It was all complete, except for one vital missing element – sound.

So the silent film had just lain there in some cupboard, till one of the lecturers discovered it, realised how much had been spent on it already, and asked if anyone knew how to finish it off. I volunteered – despite the fact that I had no knowledge or experience of filming, and had never even used or owned an ordinary camera.

I managed to get the projector working, watched the film

over and over, wrote a script, found a recording machine and microphone, and then looked for a suitable narrator. I talked Hugh, my first roommate, into performing my voice-over. Which he did very well. I then found an editing machine and matched it all up, with a bit of cutting. The department had all the gear, only no one had been either interested or able to work out how to use it.

I have always suspected it was working on this film, saving the department's embarrassment at having spent so much for nothing, that got me my Diploma in Education, rather than displaying any knowledge or aptitude for actual teaching. My education tutor, B.B. Hartsop, gave me a decent reference in April 1958 in which he wrote that I had 'tackled my teaching problems with enthusiasm and vitality' and that, by the end of my teaching practice, I was able 'to teach my young pupils satisfactorily'. Not exactly a rave review, but he said I would make 'a competent teacher to the junior forms of a grammar school or throughout a secondary modern school'.

I still have that reference, and my diploma, all those years later. It gives me a warm feeling, even at this great age, to think if all else in life fails, I can surely get a teaching job, somewhere.

It did go through my mind at the time that, as I had heard nothing about the journalism traineeships, I should perhaps investigate how you get into films. But figuring out how journalism worked had taken me long enough, so I decided not to bother looking into the film world. For the moment anyway.

As the end of term approached, and the end of my final final year at Durham, I eventually got my call-up papers. My mother managed to get to a phone box somehow and rang my college to leave a message with the dreaded news. John Lennon, as an art college student in Liverpool, around that same time, used to dread the same news. When he was lying in, after a late gig with the Quarrymen, his Aunt Mimi would shout up to him, 'John, get up! Your call-up papers have come!' But that was a joke. They never did come for him, being four years younger than me.

I filled in the forms, which included giving the name of my GP in Carlisle. I was called to a board in Newcastle. My Carlisle GP had records of all the years I had suffered from awful asthma, which I had almost forgotten about, having been almost totally free of it for some time. When the national service doctor was reading through my history of asthma, and asked how I was now, I immediately remembered and said, oh yes, I still did get attacks. The upshot was that I was declared unfit to fight for Her Majesty.

So, I was free, not liable to be called up any more. I would have been among the last to do national service, which finally finished in 1960. But I could now start seriously planning, or seriously worrying, about how I was going to enter the world of work. Teaching, or otherwise.

With the end of term approaching, I'd still not heard from Kemsley and I was getting desperate, so on 13 May 1958 I wrote to Mr Fraser, asking him if they had made up their minds yet about this year's graduate intake. On 15 May, almost by return, I got a reply: 'I am just on the point of leaving the office on business for a few days, but this is a very short note to say that you are definitely fixed with us, although I cannot say yet in which office. I shall be writing you a more detailed letter later.'

I studied this note for ages, trying to read between the lines. No starting date, no contract, no wage, no actual job, no place, no newspaper named. It seemed to me they could easily get out of it, or change their minds. I read it all out to Margaret for her opinion, and she said it seemed to be definite – I was being taken on. Hurrah!

It therefore gave me some pleasure to write to Westminster Press, from whom I had heard nothing, to say sorry, chum, I am fixed up with Kemsley. No need to make me an offer. That last sentence was, of course, in between the lines, not overt. No need to be rude to someone I might need a job from some day.

I got a very decent letter back from them, from someone called Philip Duncan, saying he had a feeling this would happen and it was their fault for not having their selection board earlier. 'I am bound to say I am sorry because we do not often find graduates who take as much trouble as you have done to fit themselves for newspaper work. There is no need to apologise. With best wishes for your career in journalism.'

The big event at the end of the college year was the June Ball in Durham Castle – which I wanted Margaret to attend as my partner. I had known from the moment I met her, or didn't meet her, that she hated dances, and hated even more the idea of having to wear a posh ball gown or fancy frock. But I nagged on, explaining that as Senior Man I had to be there, with my official partner, which of course was her, as we had now been going out for two years.

I also got an invitation from the master, Len Slater, and his wife to have drinks with them in July in the master's garden after Congregation in the cathedral, after receiving my diploma. The invite was addressed to me, my parents and Miss Foster. I must have told him I had a girlfriend – though he did not spell her name properly. She refused to come to that and I did not tell my parents. My father, increasingly feeble, could not have come to that either.

But Margaret did agree to come to the June Ball – complaining all the time. She made herself a very posh, long ball gown, in red taffeta. She was handy and quick at making clothes, but not very well, getting bored quickly, taking short cuts for the hems, dashing off the stitching, which meant things often came to pieces while she was still wearing them. We had to have the first dance, as Senior Man of the college, which led to even more sighs, but after that she was allowed to sit down and chat to people. I still have the programme for that June Ball, which was held on Friday 27 June 1958. I see there were forty dances listed, from a quickstep, through a St Bernard's waltz, slow foxtrot, Gay Gordons, Dashing White Sergeant, eightsome reel, strip the willow, charleston, tango, rumba and samba. It went on until the wee small hours when the dancing finished with 'The Last Waltz'. It sounds more like 1938 than 1958, or even 1888. Hard to believe that rock'n'roll had arrived and couples all over the country were throwing their partners around and jiving wildly, while we were in our evening suits sedately doing the Gay Gordons. It was, of course, a formal ball at a traditional college, not one of the more casual 'informals', which we did have. All the same, in 1958 rock'n'roll was still seen by many as pretty subversive.

Music was provided by Bob Potter and His Orchestra with cabaret by Cerberus. Supper was served in the Undercroft from 9 till 11.30pm; breakfast from 1.30 till 3.30am. I did not stay up for breakfast. By that time, Margaret and I were in bed in my room on the Norman Gallery. Which, of course, was illegal. But term was over, my student life was finished forever, that was it. She was so pleased to take off her taffeta frock and chuck it away – never wearing it again.

Nothing untoward happened. I was Senior Man. I did have standards to maintain, oh yes, examples to set the younger, more infantile members of college, the sort who got drunk and threw things at medieval windows. So it was a chaste evening. Both of us were totally knackered anyway, as it was hours past our normal bedtime. That was something else we found we had in common. Going to bed at ten o'clock. Oh, the mad young.

That summer we had fixed up to join some of my friends from Durham in Holland on a sailing holiday. Neither of us had ever sailed before, or even been in a boat. But we thought how wonderful, how exciting, this might be the perfect romantic situation in which to try something else we had never done.

Thanks to Margaret's Oxford friend Theo, whose parents were doctors, Margaret secured an appointment in London, in Weymouth Street, near Harley Street, with a woman called Dr Helena Wright, a birth control specialist, the sort of doctor, apparently, who fitted up the young daughters of progressive, middle-class, intellectual parents, probably from about the age of fourteen, judging by some of the stories we had heard.

I hadn't realised at the time just how eminent and well known Helena Wright was, in the UK and on the continent. She was born in 1887, had met Marie Stopes in 1918, and went on to open her own birth control clinic, lecture on contraception, sex education, sex therapy, and write lots of books. She had while younger been involved in various controversies and legal cases with the Catholic Church, as one might imagine. She did not die till 1982, aged ninety-four, but in 1958 when Margaret had her appointment with her she already seemed incredibly old. She was also rather brusque and no-nonsense.

Now I look up her biog, I see that in her early life she was a missionary in China along with her husband, also a doctor – which is what both of Theo's parents had also done in their younger days. Perhaps that was how and when they met Helena.

Margaret never wanted to go over the full horror and intimate details of what happened in her one-to-one inspection by Helena Wright, how she had to be thoroughly examined, pushed and pressed, measured, mortified and embarrassed, till eventually she was provided with her very own, personalised diaphragm. It was like a large, round rubber cap, which a very small child might use for swimming, with a bendy, metal edge. You could fold it, then insert it, and it would spring back into the correct place – or so you hoped. It came in a round tin, painted a dinky pink, indicating, presumably, that it was for use by females.

They were illegal in the USA, where anti-contraception laws were in place for many years. In the decades before the Second World War, Margaret Sanger, the American birth control activist, fought a long battle to legalise family planning.

After the war, the diaphragm became the most popular form of contraception in the USA, with a third of married American women using this method. It was still difficult, in the USA and in the UK, for an unmarried young woman to be given a birth control device. I did not realise at the time, even in 1958, how avant-garde it all was, at least for people like Margaret, young and unmarried, and from her social class, to manage to get fitted up, ready for action.

Why did I not take birth control into my hands? Fair question. A condom was what my father and his generation had used. I think I could not have been trusted, that was one reason. Margaret wanted to be in control of it herself. And, yes, I wasn't really keen to get involved or investigate or discuss such things. Though I was certainly very keen for it to happen, and the quicker the better, in time for our Dutch holiday with our Dutch cap.

Just before we set off, Margaret was contacted by Dr Helena Wright herself. The bill was ten shillings more than Margaret had actually paid. Dr Wright, rather bad-temperedly, instructed Margaret to send her a ten-shilling postal order, prompt.

22

WATER DRAMA

We did have our romantic moments, even before we set off for Holland, but of course did not draw attention to them, or reveal anything in public. I should think not. None of that soppy stuff.

But there was one occasion on which Margaret did excel herself in soppiness, which totally surprised and amazed and delighted me. This was on Valentine's Day 1958 when she sent me a list of 101 reasons why she loved me, beautifully handwritten in ink on the front and the back of a homemade Valentine's heart.

After she had given me this list of 101 things, and I was reading some of them out, and smirking, she went mad and said she wanted them back, she was going to tear them up. She said it was all a joke, didn't I realise? I said some were jokes, I got them, such as my eyes lighting you up, but some of them were true, surely. No, it was all an amusement. On no account had I ever to show them to anyone. And whatever happened, I had not to keep them. Which of course I did. Forever.

*

There were six of us, all students, going to Holland, all from
Durham, except Margaret from Oxford. I did not really know
any of them, as they were all at other colleges, except for
David Foster, who was from Carlisle, a friend of Margaret's
and mine. I think he was the person who told us about the
trip, which was being organised by someone at Cuthbert's,
who happened to be a friend of some student in Holland who
knew about sailing. Allegedly. We were all very vague about
where we were going and what would happen, and most of
all about the art of sailing.

We got the boat train to the Hook of Holland and met
up with the Dutch student and his girlfriend, all eight of us
staying the night at his house. Then we set off next day to
Friesland, in the north-west of the country, an area of lakes
and canals and waterways, famous in Holland for winter sports
but in the summer for sailing. And also for Friesian cows, the
black-and-white ones, but I don't remember seeing any of
them ...

Our Dutch friend took us to a yacht haven, which was very
pretty and lively, full of young people messing around in boats.
He had booked four little sailing dinghies for us. I never knew
the names or type, just little boats with two sails, a big one in
the middle and a small one at the front, about eighteen feet
long. We had to sign various forms, pay a deposit, and confirm
that we could sail. We had never sailed before, had no idea
what to do, but our Dutch friend said not to worry, just sign,
and he would tell us what to do as we went along.

He came on board after we had pushed off, explained
about the sails, the ropes and the thing you steer with, then
he hopped back on to his boat where his girlfriend was

waiting – and left us to it. We managed somehow to follow him, as he led our little armada. There were some arguments between me and Margaret about which ropes to pull, which sail to alter, who was in charge, but it was all so attractive and wonderful. What a way to start the next stage in our romantic life.

For five nights we stayed in tiny yacht harbours, securely mooring our boats, then going into the town for a drink, mixing with all the yachties, buying some food to take back on board and making our own meals on our little boats, ever so sweet. There was no cabin as such on our boat. At night we had to erect an awning under which we slept in our sleeping bags.

Then during the day we pottered up and down various lakes, along canals, through reeds and waterways, not quite sure where we were heading. It was all one continuous wonderful waterland.

And at night, well, that was not quite as wonderfully wonderful as we had hoped and expected. Margaret found it hard to get the hang of the contraption, wondering all the time if she had done it properly, while I looked away, or went for a walk on the harbour, returning when I thought everything was in place. It all seemed so cold and artificial and contrived and not at all romantic. Added to which, at night, a wind always seemed to get up, the boat started rocking and we felt a bit seasick.

Not having done it before, neither of us really knew what it was all about, how you went about it, what was meant to happen, how it was meant to feel. Would the earth move – would you enter into a state of bliss, leave your conscious self, as so many novelists had led us to believe? The only thing that did move was the bloody boat.

After waiting all these years, I was far too quick, that was my excuse, all over before she had hardly got out of her sleeping bag. I felt guilty and ashamed and embarrassed, ruining everything. Next morning, we didn't discuss it. She didn't talk about how she felt, how disappointed she must have been, and nor did I. What should we do next time to make it better? What were we doing wrong? You felt that such a natural act should happen, well, naturally, humans had been doing it for centuries, though of course the awful pink metallic tin ruined any notion of natural naturalness. You didn't discuss such things, did you, not even with the person you had just slept with. It was as if it had never happened. An unmentionable.

I only hoped that back on dry land, when Margaret returned to Oxford and moved into the flat she had lined up with Theo, or when I got my own flat, or room, if I ever did, in some town, place still unknown, that then we would be able to do it in comfort and seclusion, in our own bed, in our own time.

On the sixth day we were sailing quite well, getting the hang of it, if not the hang of anything else, and were tacking up a broader canal than the ones we had been on so far. The canal was full of much bigger boats, rather than other sailing dinghies like ours, huge professional barges, working barges, heading full speed for the open sea, I presumed, or for the Rhine. I could see one monster barge behind us, blaring his foghorn. We had been told when setting off that sail must always give way to steam, if the steam was working steam, such as barges transporting stuff, plying their trade, as opposed to people like us, messing around.

I told Margaret to tack to the left, to get out of the way, and she decided tacking right would be quicker and safer. While we argued and tussled over the ropes and the rudder, shouting at each other, the monster barge behind, which could not stop because it was going so quickly, smashed right into us.

It was a strange sensation. Our little boat was lifted right up in the air, breaking in two. Margaret fell into the water on one side. I fell the other side. Miraculously, neither of us was really hurt, just bashed and thrown into the water.

The barge man had clearly put his brakes on, or whatever they do, but could not stop at once, so glided for another 100 yards. Boatmen leaned over and shouted and gesticulated, waved poles and arms and things at us. Eventually they got both of us out of the water with grappling hooks and hauled us up on board. Then they used a winch to lift the remains of our boat up out of the water and on to the deck. We were given hot drinks, food and dry clothes. They looked after us very well, dropping us, and what was left of our boat, at the next yacht harbour. In my mind, it was a place called Sneek on a lake called Sneekermeer.

We left the smashed boat on the harbour side and spread our belongings among the other boats. David Foster, our Carlisle friend, was in a boat on his own, so we both joined him, which made it cramped, especially sleeping at night, and was obviously the end of any of our sexual activity. Such as it had been. Wasn't much fun for him either. He had bought a supply of a local Dutch drink called Chocomel, which we all loved, but we had no money left to buy any. As we sailed slowly back to our starting point, we watched with envy every time David opened another bottle of the delicious chocolate-flavoured milk.

We got to the yacht harbour where we had hired our boat. The boatman gave a welcoming smile at first, then became furious when he saw we were missing one boat. We tried to explain its condition, and where it was now lying in a crumpled heap on a quayside. He said the cost would be at least £120 – which was an enormous amount, about £1,500 in today's money. We did not have any money, not more than a few shillings, either with us or at home. It had all gone on the holiday. Then he calmed down and said we were very lucky; we would not have to pay that full amount. On the forms we had signed we had taken out insurance. All we would have to pay would be thirty shillings, which we managed to find.

We finished the sailing holiday days earlier than we had planned because of the accident, so it meant we ended up back in The Hague at the house of our Dutch friend's parents unexpectedly, two days early. But they were absolutely marvellous. His mother took all eight of us in at once, gave us all beds, and fed us. She made us the most delicious pancakes, as many as we could eat, cheerfully keeping on making them till we were sated. She gave us all breakfast the next morning – which turned out to be more pancakes. I didn't mind as they were so wonderful.

I remember thinking that if I ever got married, had a house, children, I hoped I would be as hospitable and generous to total strangers as she had been. She had never met us before and was never likely to see us again. We just happened to be vague friends of her son's, whom he didn't really know either.

The other thought I came back with from that trip was that, dear God, there had to be a better form of contraception than that awful diaphragm. It had taken all the pleasure out of our first experience of sex, making it a deliberate, premeditated, contrived and controlled event rather than a moment of sudden, mad, wild passion.

Fortunately for later generations, things changed quite quickly. Around 1960, the coil arrived, inserted inside permanently, so no need for all that calculated, cold-blooded faffing. This was followed, of course, by the pill, the wonderful and simple birth control pill, which changed everything, life and death, morals and behaviour, for everybody, forever. Now we also have emergency contraception, in the shape of the morning-after pill. Who would have imagined that all you might need one day was to take a simple little pill the morning after?

I did get something out of that awful sailing accident. Afterwards, while at home in Carlisle, waiting to hear from Kemsley, I read a piece in my mother's *Sunday Post* asking for summer holiday stories – either good ones or bad ones that had gone wrong. I sent off my account of our sailing holiday, giving my Carlisle address but saying I was Johnstone-born. My story eventually appeared, top of the page, in the *Sunday Post* on 5 October 1958. I received two guineas. So that more than covered the thirty shillings I had had to pay on the boat's insurance.

It also set me off on a course that has never stopped. Ever since, I seem to have managed so often to get copy out of almost every experience, however apparently trivial or fleeting, bad or good, passing or lasting, boring or ordinary.

*

In Carlisle, during the summer of 1958, still waiting to hear from Kemsley, there was great excitement in the city about the imminent arrival of the Queen, to celebrate Carlisle's 800th anniversary. Its first charter had been granted in 1158 by Henry II and there had been lots of octocentenary events going on in the city all year.

My small contribution was editing a magazine called *Octopie*, a one-off student production, a bit like a rag magazine, on behalf of all the students in Carlisle. It was another of my attempts to build up my portfolio to impress prospective editors who might hire me, and also gain experience.

There was no university in the city at that time, though there had always been proposals and suggestions that we should have one. But there were quite a lot of students whose hometown was Carlisle, plus there was an art college and a tech college – probably around about 200 student types altogether. I asked around for contributions, jokes and stories and cartoons, and we got some good ones, particularly illustrations by students at the art college and also a short story in Cumbrian dialect by Mary Hale, who had been head girl at the high school and was now at London University. My own contribution consisted mainly of parodies.

I produced a mock-up of the *Cumberland News*, the paper that had turned me down, calling it the *Cumberland Spews*, copying the layout and contents of its front page, writing pretend court reports and news stories. I also put together a cod classified ads page, aping the sort of notices that used to appear locally in 1958. In those days there was always a large number of jobs available for agricultural workers and farm lads. Most of them began with the words 'Strong Lad

Wanted'. Or 'Experienced Lad Wanted'. My versions read 'Strong Lad Wanted for Strong Lass' and 'Experienced Lad Wanted for Experienced Lass'. And then I would give the genuine-sounding farm where they should apply. The ads were laid out like the real thing, so you didn't realise at first they were a joke. Another counterfeit ad read 'Cowman wanted at Candlemas – bring own candle and cow'. Well, it amused me at the time.

I also included cod letters to the *Octopie* magazine from famous people of the day, pretending we had invited them to Carlisle for its celebrations. There was one from Mr Khrushchev in Moscow that said he was sorry he could not land a Sputnik on the Old Town Hall, but he looked forward to having a drink in our State Management pubs and meeting Robert Burns.

Arthur Miller declined, saying he had to stay behind with his wife. 'She has a lot in front of her at the moment, I guess she always had, and I would be a sucker to leave her alone with guys like Liberace.' Naturally, I would not make such sexist remarks today (his wife was Marilyn Monroe) and would also be more aware of Liberace's preferences.

The arrival of the Queen, the focal point of all the events, was timed for 11 July 1958 – but she never came. The Duke of Edinburgh, who had turned up, on the way from Scotland, announced from the steps of the Old Town Hall that the Queen had been taken ill and had to go straight on to London. Loud groans could be heard throughout the streets of Carlisle from the thousands who had been waiting. The Queen did turn up, some weeks later, but I was not in Carlisle by then. I was elsewhere. My call had come.

*

On 29 July 1958, I got a letter from the news editor of the *Manchester Evening Chronicle*, Bob Walker, telling me to report to the paper at nine o'clock on Monday 1 September, to 'take up my duties'. I had to present myself to his deputy, Harold Mellor, as he – Mr Walker – would unfortunately be away on holiday at that date, but in his letter he welcomed me to the staff and 'wished me every success and happiness in my activities'.

My salary was going to be £14 a week. It seemed enormous, which it was. When I showed the letter to my dad lying on his sickbed, and told him my wages, he could not believe it either. It was a bigger salary than he had ever earned in his whole working life. It was, of course, some years since he had actually had a working life, but even so, I felt so incredibly fortunate.

23

HELLO MANCHESTER

When I arrived in Manchester, on 1 September 1958, as directed, it was just a few months after the Munich air disaster. Manchester was still very much a city in mourning, among the footballing community of course, but also in the world of journalism. I had read about it, seen all the headlines, all the photographs, all the famous players, as had the whole nation, but I had never taken in just how many journalists had died.

It happened on 6 February 1958 when British European Airways flight 609 crashed on its third attempt to take off from a slush-covered runway at Munich. On the plane was the Manchester United football team, the famous 'Busby Babes', returning from a European Cup match in Belgrade, against Red Star. The plane had stopped to refuel in Munich because a non-stop flight from Belgrade to Manchester was out of the aircraft's range.

Manchester United were attempting to become the third club to win three successive English league titles and were currently six points behind league leaders Wolverhampton Wanderers with fourteen games to go. They had just defeated Red Star on aggregate and advanced into their second successive European Cup semi-final. The team had not been beaten in eleven matches.

Twenty-three people died, including players, crew and journalists. Among the fatalities, the best known was the young halfback Duncan Edwards, already a Manchester United and England star, despite his age. He was born the same year as me, 1936, and was only twenty-one when he died. He survived the actual crash, but died in hospital fifteen days later. The other well-known players who lost their lives, all names I had followed, included Roger Byrne, Eddie Colman and Tommy Taylor.

Eight journalists also died, among them the famous ex-footballer Frank Swift, a boyhood hero of mine when he kept goal for England and Manchester City. He had become a sports journalist, and was reporting on the game for the *News of the World*. I had also heard of Henry Rose, for he worked for the *Daily Express*, which my parents took at home. But I didn't really know the names of the six other journalists who perished, nor presumably did most of the population.

The *Manchester Guardian*, *Daily Mail*, *Daily Herald* and *Daily Mirror* all lost one of their star writers. Then there were two leading footballer writers from the two Manchester evening papers, neither of whom I had ever read, or even heard of, until just before I arrived. Both men were still being talked about, remembered and mourned. There was Tom Jackson of the *Evening News* and Alf Clarke of the *Evening Chronicle*, the paper I was about to join. He could well have been one of my colleagues. It might even have been me.

During my first week, I was totally overwhelmed by the sheer size of my workplace – the noise, the bustle, the people, the round-the-clock activity. Kemsley House in Withy Grove was said to be the biggest newspaper office in Europe, possibly in the world, though there was rumoured to be one in Brazil that was said to print more newspapers.

Withy Grove printed and produced all the northern editions of the national papers in the Kemsley empire, which included the *Sunday Times*, *Empire News*, *Sunday Graphic*, *Daily Sketch*, *Sporting Chronicle*. It was also the home of the northern editions of the *Daily Telegraph*, *Daily Mirror*, *Sunday Mirror*. The printworks were in the basement, which was why the traffic in and out and all around the surrounding streets was constant and the incredible noise never stopped. In that building were said to work 4,000 people. Every week ten million newspapers were disgorged. I found it incredibly exciting, just to be a small part of all this tremendous commotion and creation, bustling and rushing, shouting and yelling, hooting and honking.

Today, northern editions of most of those national newspapers hardly exist. But in 1958, the northern offices – printing and editorial – were just as big and important, with all the same facilities, as their London HQ. Most of the Manchester media considered they were on a par with Fleet Street in every way, if not better, and their basic-wage rates reflected what their London counterparts were receiving. Many of the older and more senior editorial staff, on all these papers, had at one time worked in London, and had returned to their northern roots, not feeling it was in any way a backward step. Of course, the younger ones were still dreaming of one day working in Fleet Street – if just to boast they had been there, done that.

The feeling, mostly, was that they were at the top of their

tree. Almost all of them had worked their way up from local papers in their home area, little old-fashioned weeklies like the *Carlisle Journal*, then moved on to an evening paper in a bigger town in Yorkshire or Lancashire, before eventually reaching Manchester. Few were graduates, as not many people had been to university in those days, but several had gone to grammar schools. Many had started as boys of fifteen, straight from school, as copyboys or messenger boys.

On the masthead of the *Evening Chronicle* it said 'ONE MILLION READERS EVERY NIGHT'. I could not take in that number. It was about a hundred times the population of Carlisle. It took me a while to understand that 'readers' did not mean 'copies', which is always a confusion when looking at any circulation figures. Readership is usually based on the notion that there are three readers for every copy of a paper printed – while 'circulation' should mean the number of copies actually printed and sold. All the same, were there really going to be one million people reading my lovely polished prose?

One reason for the thousands of workers was the archaic printing methods, though at the time the process was considered to be state of the art. Basically, however, it had hardly changed since the days of William Caxton. It was really much the same as at *Palatinate*, just several thousand times greater and more complex.

Each piece of type, each letter or figure on every page, was originally a piece of hot metal, produced by a linotype machine. It then got laid out in a metal frame, with the blocks placed in, in the shape and size and layout of the finished newspaper page. It was then copied on to a mould, before being turned into a sheet of rounded metal, fixed on to a cylinder which revolved at fantastic speed, with ink being pumped in, and these were the printing presses. I think I have that roughly right, if not the correct terminology. It was so large scale and industrial, like a nineteenth-century steam factory, yet everything was under the same roof, so you could follow or watch the whole satanic process, from start to finish, the raw paper coming in, the massive bundles of newspapers trundling out on monster vehicles.

Editorially, things were a little more complicated and labour-intensive than they had been on *Palatinate*, where we published just once a fortnight. For a start, on the *Chron*, we had about eight different editions – a day. They began first thing in the morning, coming out almost on the hour, all day long. The front and back pages would be slightly different each time, depending on the time of day and any new news that had happened since the last edition, while inside four pages at least were devoted to a particular area or town. The earliest editions went the furthest away, to far-flung parts of Cheshire, so their inside news would be all about the latest excitements in Crewe or Bakewell. Then there would be editions for Eccles, Warrington, Wigan, till eventually, as the day progressed, there would be the Salford edition and then a central Manchester one.

Today, in newspapers, the process is totally different, almost like a different industry. So much is created and laid out and transferred on screen, the physical presses divorced from the editorial. And, in the world of print, only one edition a day is being produced.

One of the things that always strikes me about modern printing technology, of newspapers and magazines, is how slow it often is. We could be on the streets in an hour with a different edition, and then keep it up every hour. Today it takes them all day long for one edition of a newspaper, and by then you have usually heard or read about most of the news already online. (Online news is, of course, a different animal.)

The Saturday afternoon pink 'uns or green 'uns, the special football editions that came out in most big cities in the UK, could be had and read even as you were leaving the match. The result and some details of the game you had just watched would be there, in print, in your hand, as you walked home. Mind you, the blurry, inky, abbreviated words might be hard to read, printed sideways in the fudge – which was what that gap at end of the back page was called. And any report might not make a lot of sense, as the reporter had been sending it over from kick-off on a crackly telephone line, without knowing what was going to happen. Goodness, football reporters have it easy today, with laptops, iPads, computers, mobile phones and other technological wonders.

I reported to Harold Mellor that first day, the deputy news editor. My first reaction was – is it me or is he a bastard? Or was it my paranoia? I was informed by a senior reporter, with some obvious relish, that Harold did not like graduates, especially those with poor spelling. But he was feared by almost all the reporters for his bad temper, shouting and dressing people down in front of the whole newsroom. He was fond of mockery, very much like that awful maths teacher I had at the Creighton School who would read out and ridicule your dreadful mistakes. He was, of course, almost always right, knew exactly where you had ballsed up, what you should have done, what you had missed, how you had cut corners.

Even at the time, he was considered old school, how hard-faced, loud-mouthed newsroom editors used to behave – the inference being that they had now improved, we were all so much more civilised. But the fact is they had not. And have not. It was the first time I had experienced such a character, but they do still exist on national newspapers. And elsewhere – the bastard boss from hell, driving everyone to a breakdown. In newspapers, it is still often the news editor, or sometimes, on a tabloid, the editor, who is the foul-mouthed ranter, feared by all, but also admired for his professionalism.

The actual news editor, Bob Walker, when he appeared, was kind and gentle, silver-haired and avuncular, addressed everyone as 'mister' and never raised his voice. There was also an assistant news editor plus a female secretary, who were very pleasant too, and they all sat behind a glass-panel partition, keeping an eye on everyone. The only baddie was Harold Mellor. The sight of his finger in the air through the glass panel, pointing in my direction, made me tremble.

The dozen or so general reporters sat at a very long wooden table, cheek by jowl, each with our own sit-up-and-beg manual typewriter. We didn't have a phone each, but there were enough to go round in the middle of the table in front of us. When all twelve of us were clattering away, the din was like a cotton mill. Or how I imagined a cotton mill must have sounded, with all the spools and spindles, the banging of the bobbins, the bells and the carriage changes.

Behind us at an equally long table sat the subeditors, much older, more worn and weary, middle-aged gents who smoked all the time. Their heads were permanently down, frowning, looking miserable and long-suffering, clearly too good for this job, for this world, with one arm poised, about to strike. Pots of paste (for cutting up copy and sticking it back together) were lined up in front of them, and a spike on which they would be about to impale a particularly useless piece of copy, then whoosh, the arm would come down, the offending page had had its life and guts ripped out of it.

The copy paper came in pads, flimsy, cheap, yellowy typing paper, smaller than today's copy paper, a bit under A4 size. If there was an emergency, and several were working on a Big Story, all contributing, and all being shouted at by Harold, you would often type out just one sentence. It would look strange and wasteful, so few words on a whole page, but by then it would have gone, a copyboy having whisked it to the news-desk. It would then be rushed to the subs, marked up with cuts and corrections, headlines attached, sizes indicated, and then even more swarms of copyboys would appear to speed it on its way to the men on the linotype machines, where all the letters and words would be turned into hot metal. The roar of the machines, combined with all the manic running about, the noise and shouting, the mad panic to catch the edition, made the whole process appear like controlled chaos. Gosh, it was exciting. Don't tell me a laptop provides just as much fun and atmosphere.

On our floor, around the sides, were several offices, with other editorial departments, but I never got to enter most of their preserves. I presumed they housed the feature writer, sportswriters, specialists, women's page, plus lordly folks like assistant editors with their secretaries. I never saw the editor, Mr Goulden. He seemed totally unaware that I had joined them.

I was the youngest by far on the reporters' table. It was only months later that I discovered that another graduate trainee had joined the very same day as me, but she had been placed elsewhere. Something to do with the women's pages, I think. Perhaps business. It was ages before I even spoke to her.

I sat between a rather gruff, middle-aged man in a tweed jacket called Mac, who smoked a pipe all the time and hardly spoke to me, and a middle-aged woman, the only woman reporter, called Beryl, small and rather dumpy. She was the most incredible typist. She sat there all day, bashing away thousands of words, yet never seemed to go out on stories. I eventually discovered, by sneaking a look at her copy, that she was mainly working on so-called news features. They were partially disguised advertising features, with the editorial 'news angle' being the launch of some new product or depart-ment of a big local store. Still goes on today. Even more so.

I was very surprised to discover she was a Cambridge grad-uate, the only graduate in the newsroom. I wondered why she had never moved on to higher things, and seemed content to remain here, doing this sort of humdrum work. I didn't ask her, of course. That would have been very condescending, coming from somebody who knew nothing about anything and had just arrived.

There was a senior reporter called Stan who had worked in Fleet Street, as he told me, several times, and a handsome, thirtysomething man about town called Terry Cringle, who always signed himself TC, as everyone would know him. Then there was a tall, affable, tweedy, well-spoken rather dishevelled reporter who later became a priest. And an old hack in a wide boy's shiny suit called Arnold Field, who worked funny hours, including Sundays, manning the news-room in case any stories broke. He was Jewish, which was why he was prepared to work Sundays. He was the first Jewish person I had ever met. There had been none in Carlisle, nor any at Durham, that I was aware of.

Being a graduate trainee was a joke, in that there was no formal training, nothing you had to learn, no exams you had to pass. So unlike today, now they have tried to turn it into a profession, like a doctor or lawyer. Almost all aspiring journalists have first of all to be a graduate, then they have to do a postgraduate year on a journalism course, at places like Cardiff, City University, Preston and elsewhere.

Someone in the newsroom suggested, in passing, that I might learn shorthand, as they could all do it, having mostly learned it while young, starting on local papers from school, but it was not insisted on and no one had checked whether I could do it. I found a shorthand teacher who charged only half a crown. I went to her house each week along with about five teenage girls, who had just left school. They were all eager and quick and bright and I was put to shame by my slowness and incomprehension. I did eventually learn a few gramma-logues, but gave up totally after a few months. I decided that if I wrote things down in my own sort of scribbled shorthand notes, and then typed them up quickly, I would capture most of it. But if I left my notes for a few days, I found I could not understand a word.

No mention was made of going to any legal lessons, about libel and slander and copyright, which I suppose would have been helpful. Nor was I taught anything about sub-editing, about layout, production, measuring and marking photographs or the technical side, which today I am sure all young journalists are expert at. You were just meant to pick it all up, on the job.

It was hard in a way to see what the advantages of the grad-uate trainee scheme were – apart from the good fortune of being on it, allowed straight on to a professional paper without having any experience. I did hope that one extra advantage, unless I fell out totally with the dreaded Harold, was that I might be fast-tracked, moved around, given the chance to try different sorts of journalism. That's what I thought Mr Fraser had led me to believe. But it seemed, in those early Manchester months, that I had imagined this. I was being left to make my own way, in my own career.

The first story I remember getting into the paper, after just a few weeks, which I had done, was all mine, as opposed to rewriting or following up something, was headlined 'CRUMPSALL VANDALS STRIKE AGAIN!' I am not sure now, and wasn't clear even then, where Crumpsall is. I was taken there in a photographer's car, as some reader had rung in about panes of glass being broken on a local allotment. Who was behind it? Was it an orchestrated campaign? We got there to discover an angry old man, who had arrived at his greenhouse to find all the windows broken. He was ranting and raving, vowing what he would do, and was more than happy to stand, gesticulating and looking furious, over and over again, till we had enough suitably dramatic photographs to stand up the story.

But I did get some really first-rate on-the-job training when I was given what we would now call a mentor, a senior reporter, who turned out to be of enormous help. He was called

Barry Cockcroft, tall, dark-haired, endlessly enthusiastic, who came from Rochdale, where he still lived. He had gone to Manchester Grammar School, a fact which was hard to escape as he usually wore their old boy tie and managed to draw attention to it, which of course was a great help in Manchester where for decades it had been, and still is, an excellent school. He had become a journalist from school and worked firstly on the *Rochdale Observer*. He was only four years older than me, but seemed much more experienced and knowledgeable.

I went out with him on jobs for some weeks, trailing in his wake, watching and admiring his expertise, whether on a murder, a serious road accident, a big fire or some other local news event. He would work out what had happened at once, identify the main characters, then grab the chief policeman on the case, get some quotes from him which he scribbled in his notebook, then perhaps the chief fire officer, or a doctor, all of whom he seemed to know by name. Then he would find an eyewitness, someone involved in the incident, get some sentences from them, then it was a mad dash to the nearest telephone box, hoping to get there before the *Mail*, *Mirror* and *Herald*, but most of all our deadly rival, the *Evening News*.

I would stand outside the phone box, my foot in the doorway to keep out anyone else, and listen in total wonder as Barry dictated 750 words in perfect English, in well-formed paragraphs, the whole story, with a beginning and end, doing it instantly, yet he had not written down a thing, apart from the quotes. How did he do it? He must be a genius. I am never going to manage it.

After a few weeks, when I was at last sent out on my own on some news story, I managed the quotes-gathering okay, worked out who the bigwigs were, and even tracked down locals for the next slip edition. What we always had to do on any half-decent story was find participants and witnesses from different parts of the region, get a quote from them, with their age, job and street. 'Anybody here injured and from Wigan?' we would shout, going round the wounded and the bleeding. If they said no, they were from Chester, you would move on quickly. The Chester edition would have gone ages ago. Who needs them now?

Having got all the details and suitable quotes for the next edition, I would crouch *behind* the telephone box, rather than stepping inside and putting in coins. Then I would start desperately scribbling down my whole story, with crossings-out, changes, by which time I had lost about an hour. When I eventually got through and dictated it to copy, Harold would come on and scream at me, 'What the fuck have you been doing? The *Evening News* has already got it on their front page, get back at once and update it, you dozy sod.'

I got better, but I was never very good at immediate news stories, too concerned with trying to write them, bring in a bit of colour and character. Eventually I realised that Barry's amazing skills were partly a trick, honed over years of doing the same sorts of stories. He had a format for a traffic accident, a fire, an assault, a murder, which he could repeat almost every time, just changing the names and details.

For the first few months I was not in fact allowed out very often. I was stuck on the desk, answering the phone, following up piddling stories, getting quotes, rewriting hand-outs and releases. One of the daily duties I seemed to be landed with was the dreaded calls. They had to be done each morning, as early as possible. You had a list of about ten numbers, for the local police stations, fire stations and main hospitals, and a contact in each who was supposed to answer questions. You would ask about an incident overnight, and hope they would tell you, and check on any running stories, such as people who had been taken into hospital earlier in the week – were they stable, coming out soon, or had they relapsed? Then you would write up a little paragraph, hoping Harold would not go mad because you'd forgotten to ask the one vital thing.

Obviously I can spell, do spell, but I am always in such a hurry, even now, that I bash on without checking. I rarely look back to see how I spelled a place or a person's name the first time, so it can vary, all on the same page. I tell myself I will go back and correct, but I don't always. I suppose it is like leaving my clothes lying around. I expect others to go round and tidy up the spelling after me.

'This John Smith,' Harold would bawl at me. 'Are you sure it is not Smythe? And did you check he is not Jon, short for Jonathan? You didn't? You think you did? You're bloody lying now. Then ring him back, at once, you ...'

Making a phone call out of the Manchester area was a minor event in itself. It had to be legitimate, and not a personal call, and you had to go through the switchboard, so they would always record it if, say, to take an example at random, you had rung Somerville College, Oxford, JCR phone box.

I never got expenses, as such, not for meals or buying people drinks, though I am sure the more senior reporters, especially the crime reporters, had generous expense accounts. I had to go almost everywhere on the bus, which I could claim, but now and again, if it was fairly important, I was allowed to go in an office car. I loved that. It felt like 'hold the front page'. Even better, more impressive, if I zoomed off down Withy Grove, tyres screeching, with a photographer. They were always local, knew their way around, the short cuts, the back entrances, the tricks to pull to get into places, whereas for me Manchester was still a vast alien land. I could hardly understand the accents, never mind the maps.

My first proper out-of-town story was about some Manchester University students on a rag-week stunt. It involved them pushing a pram or perhaps a fridge, something stupid anyway, all the way to Edinburgh. For charity, of course. I was allowed to go with them, travelling there on the bus, a day trip, and met the students up there. I fancied the older hacks on the desk were a bit jealous. One of them did say afterwards, 'Lucky beggar, you'll make some expenses there.' I had never thought of that and forgot to acquire any receipts.

I was trying to set myself up as the reporter on the newsdesk who covered university affairs. I had worked out that was a way to gain promotion, one of two directions for getting on. Become a specialist, of any sort, and you would have your own little field where Harold, however smart he was, would not know everything and not always know where you were.

The specialist area I really, really fancied was football reporting. Alf Clarke, who had died at Munich, had covered Manchester United for the paper and was a big star on the paper, and in football. He had been an amateur in his youth, on the books of Man United, and always had great contacts during the Busby era. He was credited as being the first reporter to spot the potential of young Duncan Edwards, giving him a rave review in a minor game. Obviously, I could never compete with Alf Clarke, his contacts or his knowledge.

His replacement on the paper, covering Man United, was Keith Dewhurst. Man City was covered by Ray Wergan. I so envied both of them, the job they did, the access they got, or I imagined they got, meeting all the stars, the free tickets to games and most of all their white raincoats. They were possibly not quite white, just off-white, and were perhaps not even raincoats, but in my mind's eye I can see them leaving our floor in the middle of the morning, while I was still struggling with the wretched calls, their collars up, their white raincoats flapping, off to Old Trafford or Maine Road, to join the team bus or the reserved train carriage, travelling with our heroes down to Arsenal for the big match. Meanwhile, Harold would be screaming at me for the calls.

I never actually talked to Keith or Ray, not properly, as they were both older than me. I was never sure where their office was, though eventually I became quite friendly with Ray. It was only much later, when Keith Dewhurst went on to become an eminent scriptwriter, for films and TV, and an author, that I realised he had not been all that much older than me – just five years – and he had been to Cambridge. I think Ray Wergan had been there as well. So both had probably been graduate trainees on the paper, just like me.

One day, however, Harold Mellor called me into his office and said he was sending me to Old Trafford for the Big Derby against City. Stand by in an hour for an office car, which I would need in order to avoid the traffic. This was a sure sign of going on a big story. I was thrilled.

But I never got inside Old Trafford, or even saw the game. When he properly briefed me, it turned out that my job was to stand *outside* the ground, before, during and after, then file a colour piece about the atmosphere, with quotes from the fans. I was so disappointed, having imagined it was going to be the start of my great career as a specialist, a football reporter no less, the most glamorous and desirable speciality of all.

The other career move, so it seemed to me, looking round the newsroom, working out who everyone was and how they got there, was to be a subeditor.

Subbing seemed to be an expertise worth mastering and many of the assistant editors seemed to have been subs. One of my fantasies in those early months, which I discussed with Margaret, was that one day, when I was really old, say about forty, wouldn't it be great to retire to Carlisle and be editor of the *Cumberland News*, be someone in the community, with status and position, with a nice house not far away in the country, such as Wetheral? I would need to have had subbing experience to do that job properly.

On the other hand being a sub meant working inside all day long, not going out and interviewing people, which is what I enjoyed most. And, above all, it would presumably mean being able to spell properly . . .

24

MANCHESTER LIFE

I had no one in Manchester to ask for advice on where to stay. I knew nobody, nor any of the streets or place names or districts, their images or reputations.

Even names I thought I did know, such as Northwest, were confusing. In the *Chron* and the *News* there were often stories about 'Northwest couple win the pools' or 'Northwest woman in holiday tragedy'. I would turn to the story expecting it to be about somebody from Carlisle or at least Cumberland, thinking I might know them, or where they live. In Cumberland we always considered ourselves to be the Northwest of England, which it is, if you look at the map. But here in Manchester they considered themselves, and the whole of Lancashire, to be the real, true Northwest, as if unaware of the map of England, which any fool can see goes on for another 100 miles before it reaches Scotland.

When I came to look at the map of Manchester for somewhere I might stay, I did not know where to start. Withy Grove seemed to be in the heart of the city, perhaps just slightly on the northern side, full of businesses and big office buildings, so I looked for any local bus routes that would take me directly to work. Which is how I ended up in Cheetham Hill. What a mistake. I took a room in Heywood Street, the first place I looked at. What a dump.

The area appeared to be filled with decaying houses, many of which had been turned into sweatshops, with European migrants making raincoats, mostly sleeping on the premises. Cheetham Hill had traditionally been an immigrant area for decades, starting with the Irish in the nineteenth century and the Jews in the twentieth century.

I had a single room on the ground floor, at the front, crammed with elderly brown furniture, with a kitchen in an alcove in the communal hall. I shared the bathroom and WC with the rest of the occupants, none of whom I saw for a long time, though I heard them at night, banging around.

Margaret came to see me as soon as I was vaguely settled, but I had to keep her away from the landlord. I had taken the room as a single man, so I would have had to pay more as a couple, but as we were not married, it would have been difficult if not impossible. Landlords, even dodgy landlords in scruffy areas, did not want to encourage unmarried couples to live together.

One evening, when Margaret was staying, the landlord did turn up unexpectedly, wanting his rent. I could hear him in the hall, so we jumped out of bed and I pushed Margaret into the wardrobe and closed the door. I managed to keep the landlord talking in the doorway to my room, then behind me I heard a crashing noise and a small scream. The bed was an old and battered let-you-down sofa bed, which you folded up during the day. It had suddenly decided to jackknife itself, presumably because we'd jumped out of it so quickly, and had sprung up against the wardrobe, giving Margaret, trapped inside, the most awful fright. I managed to keep the landlord out of my room, as he was busy counting the rent, and ushered him to the front door.

Another time, in the middle of the night, when we were in that awful bed, we suddenly felt a draught coming in through the window beside us. Margaret wakened in alarm. And then she woke me up, whispering in my ear.

'Don't worry,' I said, 'it's just the wind, go back to sleep.'

'It's not the wind, someone is there, outside.'

I vaguely glanced at the window, and could see nothing, so turned over and pulled the blankets over my head.

'He's trying to get in!'

'He'll go away, don't worry.'

'He's coming in!'

At this point I was forced to sit up and, sure enough, a figure was clambering through our window, rather unsteadily, as if he had been drinking. I didn't quite get out of bed, half-crouching under the bedclothes, but I did manage to shout at him, asking him what the hell he was doing. He realised his mistake, that he was climbing into the wrong house, and retreated, muttering some sort of apology in what sounded like Polish, and staggered on to the pavement again. I might well have muttered something in reply, such as, 'That's all right, pal' – and then went back to sleep.

Margaret, of course, never returned to sleep – and next morning she went on about my useless behaviour, just lying there, when we could both have been murdered in our beds. Which is what my mother always used to say. What I was supposed to have done, got up and punched him?

After several visits, Margaret managed to make my awful

room a bit more habitable, cleaned it and dusted, bought some end-of-line fabrics to cover the revolting bedclothes and nasty chairs. And one evening we gave our first dinner party. It was our first bit of entertaining as a couple, a couple who had their own place, just one room, it is true, but it was ours, as opposed our parents' council houses.

I invited another journalist, Harry Evans, whom I had recently met, and his wife, Enid. This was the Harold Evans I had been told about at Durham, who had been at my college then gone off to be a journalist, but no one at Durham had a contact for him. I had bumped into him while covering some Manchester University event, which he was covering as well for our rival paper, the *Evening News*.

The *Evening News* was owned by the *Manchester Guardian* and considered itself higher class than the *Chron*. They were a broadsheet and we were tabloid, but really, I could see little between them in terms of general content. They both had a massive readership. The *News* was more the business paper, strong in the centre of the city, while the *Chron* was strong out in the suburbs and local Lancashire towns.

The *News* staff, in their appearance and working habits, were very like us, competing for the same pastures. The *Guardian* journalists, despite being part of the same company, appeared a different breed. Whenever I came across them on stories, I so envied their casual confidence. I was at one event where Terry Coleman was holding forth, cross-examining some official as if he, Coleman, was in charge of the press conference, doing them a favour by being there. I never spoke to him. I knew my place.

I admired the casual clothes of the *Guardian* reporters, often just open-necked shirts, whereas we had to wear jackets and ties and look smart. I suppose that proves we were a tabloid paper. On the whole, then and now, the lower class the paper, the smarter, better dressed, more presentable their reporters felt they had to be. But the *News*, being an evening paper, was neither low class nor high class. Too busy to worry about that. A bit like us on the *Chron*, so I liked to imagine.

Harry had recently been promoted to assistant to the editor on the *Evening News*, whatever that meant, but was still going out doing university stories. He was eight years older than me, much more advanced in his career, and was married to Enid, who had also been at Durham. They lived in Altrincham, Cheshire, which I knew by then was very smart, as was anything in Cheshire.

Harry was born locally in Eccles, had left school at sixteen, got a job on a local paper, then did his national service in the RAF. After that, he passed various exams and applied as a mature student to all fourteen universities in England, which was the total number at the time. Durham was the first to offer him a place. At Durham, he had gone on to edit *Palatinate*, so was clearly highly talented.

Margaret had decorated the room most artistically, with flowers and candles, and had made a lovely meal of fresh herring and oatmeal, very 1950s. The moment Harry started eating his fish, he was fussing about the bones. He then suddenly jumped up and switched on all the glaring, vulgar overhead lights, the better to see what he was eating. By doing so, he immediately revealed the full horror of our crummy, nasty, dingy room which Margaret had worked so hard to disguise. Margaret was mortified.

Harry and Enid did, however, invite us back to their place, which turned out to be only half a semi, but even so, I was well impressed. He knew so much about Manchester and Lancashire, having been brought up there, and also about journalism. He became a valuable help when I was asking about local people, places and institutions.

I met Harry by chance a few months later at Piccadilly railway station. He was rushing for the London train. He was small and thin, but fit and athletic-looking, and seemed to be in a continual whir, full of action and ideas. Sometimes he could be evasive, speaking out of the corner of his mouth, as if he knew stuff he could not reveal. I did, though, ask him where he was going and eventually it came out. He was going to London, so he said, to be interviewed for a job as the BBC's economic correspondent. But I had not to mention it. Nobody knew at the *News*.

He never got that job. A bit afterwards I heard he had moved to Darlington, on the *Northern Echo*. That seemed a bit of a comedown, going back to the provinces, compared with the media heights of Manchester.

Darlington was where I might well have moved to, just a few months earlier, straight from Durham, had I not got the Kemsley training scheme. At the end of my very last term, I received a letter from Mr Harrop in the education department saying he had been approached by Queen Elizabeth Grammar School, Darlington, who were looking for a teacher for the lower forms and would recommend me, if I was interested. I wrote and said thanks, but I was fixed up. I did not reveal what I was going to do instead, that I had wasted their time and the government's money training to be a teacher, and then never intending to practise. Or so I hoped.

I had no contact with Harry after he moved to Darlington, nor saw him for several years, till by chance we met again. But he did okay as a journalist – becoming Sir Harold Evans, editor of the *Sunday Times* and *The Times*.

It was much more fun and more convenient visiting Margaret in Oxford at the beginning of her second year, October 1958. She and her friend Theo moved out of college and into a flat in Winchester Road, round the corner from a row of shops called North Parade, not far from Somerville. Iris Murdoch was pointed out to me one day, walking along Winchester Road, as she lived there or nearby, but I had no idea who she was. She had her head down, rather untidy, as if in a dream, or thinking great thoughts.

Margaret and Theo had a room each and shared a bathroom on the first floor of a little terrace house. I could sleep there with her during the day and the evening till quite late, but not stay the night, as Mrs Brown, the landlady, would have been very upset. I usually stayed overnight with the Parfitts in Northmoor Road, not far away.

Mrs Brown, who had taken in Oxford students for some years, wore a lace cap and a shawl, straight out of Jane Austen, and was very formal and severe-looking. Living with her was Fanny, who was untidy and wild-looking, always cursing and mumbling, rather volatile, but jolly and smiley. She had a pronounced accent, possibly rural Oxford, or West Country, while Mrs Brown sounded posh and refined. I was not very good on any accents south of Manchester and still confused Yorkshire and Lancashire.

Fanny wore a white pinny that reached down to her heavy

black shoes and seemed to do all the cooking and domestic work. She always addressed Margaret as Miss Margaret and Theo as Miss Theodora, and was always gracious and friendly to them, but you sensed she had a sharp tongue behind their backs.

Then there was Reg, who lived somewhere up in the attic. He did any heavy lifting, such as bringing in the coals. Fanny shouted at him all the time and bossed him around, thinking no one else in the house could hear her scolding him – 'Bring them damn coals in!', 'Get on with them potatoes!' On a Saturday evening, Reg could be heard in his attic room, singing to himself, getting louder and louder. 'Yo-ho-ho, and a bottle of rum!' We presumed he did have a bottle up there for company.

All three were old, probably about seventy, but neither Theo nor Margaret ever found out their history. They were apparently sisters, despite their different accents, but was Reg a brother or a lodger who had stayed on? I would have found out quickly, seen it as a challenge, made it my business to get the gen about them, but I was warned not to cross-examine them.

Despite having five people living so tightly in a small house, plus a regular visitor, there was an air of formality, with Fanny pressing herself against a wall should I pass her. Mrs Brown had taken in generations of students, and no doubt was wise to their ways, but kept her distance, if all seemed well.

I never abused the situation by staying the night, or becoming too inquisitive, for Margaret absolutely loved living there. She didn't want to lose it. It made Oxford worthwhile, so she said. In her room was a gas fire on which she toasted crumpets on the dark autumn evenings. We would then go to bed for a few hours, till it was time for me to creep out and go to Northmoor Road.

Jessie Parfitt, Theo's mother, grabbed me one evening when I was letting myself into her house. I wondered what she wanted – had I done something wrong, were they fed up with me sleeping there every few weeks? She was holding an advertisement cut out from a newspaper, the *Daily Herald*. It was an advert for a raincoat factory in Manchester which was selling coats half price, all new. She wanted me to personally go to the factory, which would therefore also save her on postage, and buy a raincoat in these measurements. I assumed Derek needed a new raincoat for Eton. Middle classes, eh, they don't waste money.

The moment I got my first £14 wage packet, in cash, in a brown envelope, Margaret insisted I send £1 home to my mother. I said I'd like to wait, till I knew where I was with the rent and living expenses. I also wanted to buy a portable typewriter and I needed some decent clothes. She said no, I had to do it now, at once, or I would always have reasons to put it off.

She was right, of course. My mother had given me so much, sacrificed so much, paid for so much when she had so little herself. So I sent her £1 every week, with a scribbled note about what I had been doing. I did think of sending her a postal order, but that seemed a faff, having to go and buy one. So I sent it in cash, a pound note. Never once, in all the years that I sent her cash, did any go missing. While I basked in a nice warm glow of righteousness.

Margaret did help me eventually to get some decent clothes.

When she came through to Manchester one weekend, to stay in my horrible room, she insisted that I went to Kendal Milne's in Deansgate, Manchester's smartest shop. I would have preferred somewhere much cheaper – Manchester was full of factory outlets, half the price. I know these fancy department stores, with their fancy prices, it's all a con; they just hike the prices. She found a jacket she said would really suit me. It was Danish, in a grey sort of tweed, most distinctive and unusual, with a European air to it, not the sort you saw people wearing in Withy Grove. It cost £14, a whole week's wages. I protested, demanding to look at cheaper jackets, but I still bought it.

I wore it for the first time going through to Oxford the next weekend. Margaret, having such a generous scholarship grant, decided to pay for each of us to have our photos taken by Studio Edmark, Oxford's Daisy Edis. I thought I looked pretty good in the jacket, and in the photo. I had that jacket for years and really did love it. And it was true – if you buy quality, from a quality place, it will last a long time. Not that I have since ever followed that principle. They don't catch me twice.

One of the problems when Margaret came to visit was having somewhere to go, something to do when we were not in bed together. We longed to get out in the country, in real fresh air, to go on long walks, the way we had done in Carlisle, but we could never find any parks in Manchester or even green spaces, apart from a little triangle of grass near St Ann's Square. It was all so busy with traffic and people and industry. Oxford and Durham were clearly much more attractive cities, and even Carlisle seemed greener.

In Oxford, we were still going to the Scala for the latest films, while in Manchester I began managing some evening entertainments for the two us – and getting paid at the same time. The *Chron* was inundated with invitations for the first nights of all the amateur dramatic productions for miles around, and liked to cover the bigger ones, with a big audience and big cast, all of which had to be listed. Most of the older staff did not want to go out in the evenings, having homes and families, but I volunteered, once I discovered you got paid five shillings for every one that made the paper. Some of them were excellent. Many were laughably appalling.

I was then often asked to review the first night of professional shows at the Hulme Hippodrome. This was an old-fashioned music hall, with old-fashioned variety line-ups of jugglers, people whistling bird noises, acrobats, singers, comics and musicians. Now and again there was a strip show, or at least a tableau where two showgirls would pose, having gone through some brief and clumsy dance routine, slowly slipping off their clothes. They would then stand on stage, without moving, the curtain coming down just at the moment they were about to be naked. Then the whole audience stood up and cheered, demanding more.

The Hulme Hip was an historic theatrical building, first opened in 1901, and what it was showing was also part of history. Even I could tell, in 1958, that what we were watching was the dying, rather tatty and pathetic embers of a century-old music-hall tradition. It was never going to compete with the growing popularity and availability of TV. It closed as a theatre in the 1960s, and became a bingo parlour in the 1980s.

*

After a few months in my crummy room in Cheetham Hill, I eventually managed to find something better. I had by now been to various parts of Manchester on jobs, so had more of a feeling for the different areas. I realised the southern bits of Manchester were considered better, especially near the university, so I looked around Victoria Park and chose a room in a street partly because of its name – 43, Daisy Bank Road. I had a proper kitchen and living room this time, and a separate bedroom. Even my own telephone – RUSholme 7570. Margaret approved at once, thank God, and every time she came through to visit she usually did some painting and decorating, while I was at work. The landlady was called Mrs Craddock, but we hardly saw her. I later discovered, though, that she had at one time been a *Guardian* journalist.

In the flat below was a young couple with a little girl aged about three. Every time I came home from work she would rush out of their flat and down the hall shouting, 'SHUNTER!' So I had to play with her. I always considered myself good with little kids, as opposed to secondary modern third-years. A skill I assumed I would never have a chance to use, as Margaret insisted she never wanted children.

Most of the time I was in my flat on my own, as Margaret could only come through from Oxford now and again. I don't remember doing any cooking, either here or in Heywood Street, or anywhere else in my whole life, come to that. What a disgrace. I blame my generation. My father did not cook either. I can't remember what I ate in Daisy Bank when I came home from work in the evening. Toast I should think, perhaps some eggs and some beans, bought on the way home, cheap.

If I had lunch in Manchester with Barry Cockcroft from the office, at one of the local Chinese restaurants (a form of food that still hadn't arrived in Carlisle), I would fill myself up to save any cooking in the evening.

I didn't really socialise with anyone on the paper. I also didn't like going to pubs, or spending my money. So during the day at work, I was always on the lookout for stories where there was a buffet, or some event where I could scoff some food.

While Margaret was in Manchester visiting me, we were once invited out to Rochdale, best part, by Barry Cockcroft and his wife, who was pregnant at the time. He was so proud of Rochdale, saying he would never leave it, it had everything. 'You've got no ambition, Barry,' said his wife, several times, over lunch. She had a singsong Lancashire accent and this boring phrase, 'You have no ambition, Barry', always with the name at the end, went into our lexicon of boring, banal phrases. I always imagined that if we were captured by Russian spies and hidden away in some Gulag for decades, I would just have to say one of those silly phrases and Margaret would know it was me.

We didn't really have 'our songs' – except perhaps *Songs for Swingin' Lovers!*, the Frank Sinatra LP, which I made Margaret listen to and also play on the Dansette record player I insisted she buy out of her first Oxford grant, though strangely enough it ended up in my flat.

The day that Barry's wife gave birth was a work day, but Barry was allowed to go home early. I was in the office not doing very much, so I decided to write a letter to his newborn baby daughter. I described what Barry had done that day, what he was working on, what the office looked like, who worked there, what we all did, our favourite restaurants, how Barry looked and dressed that very day and month in 1958. I addressed the letter to her, the newborn baby, instructing her not to open it for eighteen years. Then, on her eighteenth birthday, I would meet her at a certain Chinese restaurant, which was our favourite. I told her the exact time and address and not to be late.

Eighteen years later, by which time I had completely forgotten that I had ever written such a letter, I got one from Barry's daughter. 'I was there. Where were you?' I was miles away from Manchester by then, in a different world, a different city, a different life, and so was Barry.

In 1968, Barry left the *Evening Chronicle* and moved to the new Yorkshire TV station, becoming a star director, winning lots of national and international awards. One of his best-known series was about an old farming woman called Hannah Hauxwell, who lived in a remote farmhouse with hardly any money. She became a well-known and much-loved character in the seventies and eighties on TV, and in books, thanks to Barry.

I never actually met Barry again, or his daughter, after I left the *Chron*. But his obituary was in all the national newspapers when he died in 2001, aged sixty-eight. It was, of course, not true that 'you have no ambition, Barry'. He did have ambitions, all the time. As did I.

I will always be grateful to Barry Cockcroft for teaching me how to do news stories, passing on his tricks of the trade, generally helping me when I had just arrived in Manchester and everything was new and rather overwhelming.

25

SAD CYPRUS

I got called into the editor's office in November 1958. I hadn't seen John Goulden since he first interviewed me and, as far as I was aware, he had no idea what I was doing, unless of course Harold Mellor had filled him in on my spelling and other weaknesses.

I had only been at the *Chron* for two months, but it seemed like two years. He told me I was being sent to Cyprus and I would be going there by plane. I didn't quite catch the word Cyprus at first, thinking it was a suburb of Manchester I had not been to yet, perhaps near Crumpsall, so it seemed strange to be going there by plane.

Cyprus was in the news and had been for two years, full of dreadful incidents and outrages, killings and explosions, mainly involving our brave servicemen, probably some of the same brave men who had been and were still fighting the Mau Mau in Kenya as well as in other red or formerly red splodges on the global map that we were trying to retain or control or govern, despite the wishes of some elements of the local population who had other desires.

I hadn't followed all the developments closely, although

recently there had been one of the worst atrocities, when seven young RAF men had been killed by a bomb planted in the NAAFI. That had been in all the national newspapers. The word NAAFI, which I had assumed was no longer in use, had of course made me think of my mother.

Cyprus had been under British control since 1878, becoming an official part of the British Empire in 1914. It became a Crown colony in 1922, which it still was in 1958. It was seen as a vital strategic base at the far end of the Mediterranean, handy for sorting out any problems the UK might find itself in anywhere in the region. At the beginning of the last world war, back in 1939, Britain had offered to give Cyprus to Greece if the Greeks would come in on the side of the Allies, but King Constantine of Greece was against it – being partly German himself and married to a German.

Since 1955 there had been a campaign by a group wanting independence from the UK and union with Greece. They were called EOKA which stood for, in Greek, National Organisation of Cypriot Fighters. The British called the EOKA fighters terrorists, as they were attacking and killing our military forces. They were also attacking civilians employed by the British, blowing up barracks, assassinating informers and being generally unpleasant to all the British expat families. There was an added internal complication because EOKA was also fighting against a much smaller independent movement of Turkish Cypriots, who also wanted the Brits out, but in their case they wanted union with Turkey not Greece. None of these internal wars and struggles, then or now, are ever as simple and straightforward as they can at first appear from the outside.

EOKA had around 1,200 fighters, led by George Grivas. In theory, they should not have stood a chance against some 40,000 British troops who were on the island at the height of the fighting – but, of course, EOKA was on home soil, with lots of local supporters and local knowledge. They were not fighting to take over any territory or bases, which might have been harder for them to achieve. Their main objective was to disrupt the British. Grivas wanted headline explosions and dramatic events to draw world attention and support and sympathy for their struggle. The Brits were therefore trying to protect themselves, keep peace and order on the island generally, while EOKA snipers were taking shots at them, ambushing and blowing up British convoys and men. The scenes we were reading about daily in the papers at home, and watching on TV, were much like the urban warfare we saw later in Belfast and Northern Ireland.

I was being sent out to live with the 1st Battalion, Lancashire Fusiliers. They were a local regiment who had been based in Cyprus for about six months.

I didn't quite understand the deal at first, thinking it was the paper that was sending me, till it was made clear that it was an RAF press visit, using their facilities. I would be going on an RAF plane and would live there under canvas, along with the troops. They had also invited a reporter from the *Evening News*. The two of us would go out and report to our million readers in the Manchester area what a great job our lads, their lads, were doing.

Mr Goulden had also said that London – meaning the HQ of the Kemsley group – would expect me to write stories for all their papers, both national and locals, in the group, if anything significant happened which I witnessed, or if I picked up any good stories. I was thrilled. What a chance, what a great job.

I was rather brought down to earth when I came out of the meeting with the editor and told Mac, sitting next to me on the reporters' table. 'You are only being sent because you are young and single and expendable.'

Thanks a lot. I told Margaret my news, and also what Mac had said. She agreed it was probably true. But what she wanted to know was, why did I want to go anyway, why was I so excited?

It just seemed so obvious to me – a massive career move, and so interesting and exciting. I never for one moment thought of any danger. Going on a plane for a start, that was exciting. I had never been on a plane. I had been abroad, to France and Holland, but Cyprus sounded much more exotic. Perhaps my future was not in writing football reports, as I had fantasised, but as an ace war correspondent.

A week before I was due to set off, I thought of a great idea. I would invite all *Chronicle* readers who had lads or relations out there to write a letter to them which they could send to me at the *Chron* – and I would personally deliver each one by hand, to their loved ones. The *Evening News* had not thought of this ruse, so the *Chron* made a big story of it – with my photo in the paper and my name. The first time either of those wonderful things had happened.

I received 250 letters. Bloody hell, I thought, what have I done, how am I going to carry them all, never mind deliver each one? On going through them, I discovered quite a few could be dumped – they were illegible, illiterate or addressed to soldiers serving in totally different regiments in totally different parts of the world, or not even soldiers, not even abroad. It was the first time I learned, but not the last time, that not all readers actually read. They just think they do, skimming and picking up snippets of what catches their interest.

My fellow ace war reporter was going to be Brian Hitchen, born 1936, so the same age as me, twenty-two, and single, but he was more experienced. He had started as a copyboy aged sixteen on the *Daily Despatch* and worked his way up. He had also done his national service, unlike me, spending two years in the Parachute Regiment. He was also better dressed, very dapper, wearing hound's-tooth suits and a jaunty trilby.

He beat me to the first story, which rather compensated him for my 'Letters for the Lads' idea. We flew out on a troop carrier plane, which had been stripped of seats and fittings, so the sides were bare metal. Rows of soldiers in their full kit sat cramped on the bare floor. Over the Med, we hit a tremendous thunderstorm. The plane and all the soldiers and contents got violently thrown around. The howl of the wind and the rattle of the hail on the metal was frightening. I thought we were goners.

'Thank God that's over,' I said to Brian when we had landed safely and had arrived at our base. I was looking round for a drink, perhaps a pie, but Brian was off, searching for a telephone. He immediately sent over a dramatic story about the near-death experience in the air of our local soldiers. When he got back to our tent, and I discovered what he had done, I realised I'd better cobble something together before Harold was on the phone. It reminded me of missing the so-called 'wild horse drama' when reporting the Penton show. Perhaps

I did not really have a tabloid mentality. However, I sent over a similar story, as quickly as I could. Brian, like Barry, had perfected the knack of instantly writing dramatic news stories.

My story, which I had done thanks to Brian, made the paper on 14 November 1958. And, of course, I still have the cutting. 'MANCHESTER TROOPS IN PLANE DRAMA' by Hunter Davies, Evening Chronicle Reporter, Cyprus, Friday.

Manchester servicemen and women were in a 90-seater Skymaster plane which was struck for five minutes of terror 13,000 feet above the Aegean Sea tonight. The plane was caught in a freak air pocket and tossed about like a toy.

I had a few quotes, as on the plane I had by chance spoken to a woman flying officer who had been powdering her nose in the washroom when she was thrown slightly against the wall. In my story, I had her being 'momentarily stunned'. I finished by saying I had received a big welcome from the Lancashire Fusiliers and was about to deliver '200 personal messages to them from Lancashire and Cheshire'.

The heat was the first thing that struck me, the sort of semi-tropical heat I had never encountered before, not in Carlisle of course, nor in France or Holland during my brief visits there. The weather in both those places had seemed much the same as England. But Cyprus felt vaguely Eastern or African, as if I knew anything about them, a clinging, cloying heat that lasted all night. Going on a plane had been a first for me but so was complaining about the heat. I never thought I would ever moan that the weather was too hot.

It did seem properly foreign, the look of the people, their

language, their pottery and food, all so different from mainland Europe. I felt very young and naive, inexperienced and innocent, but did my best not to show it. Or betray any fear, despite being in what was a war zone. I was doing a man's job, a professional reporter, even though I was but a callow youth in my early twenties, fresh out of university.

We were living in a tented encampment, Kermia camp, which was just outside Nicosia. We were offered guns, for use when we went on patrols. Brian was of course familiar with guns, and could use them, having served the Queen, but I did not know one end from the other. However, we made a unilateral decision between us to politely refuse the offer. We both realised that we would be drawing attention to ourselves by carrying weapons. Anyway, we were civilians, newspaper reporters not soldiers.

Technically, for the sake of the exercise, we were classed as officers. And I still have my official papers, issued by the War Office, which were given to me before we boarded the plane. It states that I was 'authorised to travel by air ... from London to Nicosia' and that my 'Status/Branch of Service/Trade was "officer"'.

Because we were deemed to be officers, we were each given a tent, and a batman who brought tea in the morning. We were also allowed entry to the officers' mess. The food was excellent, and the drink. Quite a few of my fellow officers seemed to be pissheads, who could drink all night. Many had drunk their way round other terrorist hot spots around the empire over the last few years. Staying with them was a learning experience in so many ways. For example, in my sheltered life I had never tasted a whiskey sour. It was excellent.

There was a Major Trevor-Roper who was very keen on his drinks, and also very helpful. He turned out to be the brother of Hugh Trevor-Roper, professor of history at Oxford, where of course Margaret was studying that very subject and had even attended his lectures. The Trevor-Roper family came from the Scottish Borders, so we could talk about that as well, over the whiskey sours.

We had to get up early several mornings, which I found hard to do, in order to accompany a patrol of Fusiliers when they went off on what they called 'soft-shoe patrols'. This meant creeping and dodging around the still-darkened back streets of early morning Nicosia. We – or I should say the soldiers, for we tried to keep in the background – were looking for snipers and also knocking on the doors of alleged terrorists. But mainly, like us, their object was to avoid being shot at. One soldier would guard the other, standing with his gun at the ready, looking down the street, while the other would peer through windows and doors or into alleys. I never actually saw a gun fired in anger, fortunately, but the possibility was always there. There had been enough booby traps and deaths of servicemen.

Now I look at some photos I'd forgotten I ever had – presumably taken by a War Office photographer – I see that I travelled in open army trucks, with armed soldiers. We must have been an easy target. I look about fifteen. I am wearing a sort of khaki semi-military floppy hat, not to denote status but to keep the strong sun off my head.

Now and again in the evening we went into Nicosia with some of the off-duty officers, heading for the bar of the Ledra Palace Hotel, which was very swish. Brian and I also wandered around the town centre, looking for stories, interviewing expats who were working there, in bars or playing music, asking first if they were from Wigan, or similar. No point in having people not in our circulation area. Training does work.

I also have a photograph of me with a large group of ordinary soldiers, handing out letters. They also look about fifteen. Most were, of course, about my age. But for my asthma, I could quite easily have been one of them, either in Cyprus or another trouble spot, going round with a gun, getting shot at.

Reading my Cyprus cuttings book now, I see I made no attempt at any political analysis of the situation. But I did interview Sir Hugh Foot, the British governor and commander in chief, and faithfully repeated some of his uplifting banalities about our brave lads. My main job was to write about the soldiers, what they were doing, what life was like for them, who they were. In one story I did manage to drag in a Shakespearean quotation from *Henry V* – the obvious corny one about Agincourt, stiffening the sinews, summoning up the blood. My A-level Eng lit had not been wasted.

I also wrote a little piece about the things the soldiers were constantly asking me: 'How are Man United getting on? Is it snowing yet in Manchester? Tell them to send out copies of the pink 'un.'

But otherwise, I can't believe I wrote any of these stories. They don't sound like me. I also can't believe now, looking at the dates on the articles, that I was only out there for two weeks. Two weeks! It seemed at the time that I had been out there for six months at least, for so much happened, so many new experiences. That, anyway, was the impression I liked to give for the next few years, that I had been out there for months. Oh yes, I have seen service. I have been a war correspondent, you know.

Reporting from overseas, travelling the world, still appears so glamorous and so desirable to many young journalists. But from my observations since, I would say there is a type of war correspondent who is doing it to escape himself, his or her responsibilities and weaknesses. They often have shambolic home lives, bills unopened, taxes not paid, boring paperwork left ignored, wives, girlfriends and children neglected, left behind when the next call comes, which often they engineer, dying to get away, leaving all their daily, annoying problems behind, desperate for the next fix, the next surge of adrenalin. They get depressed when they return and nothing much is happening, when partners nag them; they then drink too much, hang around the office, doing less and less. Not all foreign reporters are like this, of course, or even most, but it does take a special personality to cope with the demands of always being on alert, ready and prepared to fly off – and it does attract a certain sort of character.

And it is true some get killed in the line of duty, or kidnapped. The danger is always there. I have known and worked with several excellent war reporters who never returned.

Being a foreign editor based permanently in some nice foreign capital, as opposed to a war zone, does not of course carry the same risks. And I did fancy that for a few years. It looks a fabulous job, when you are stuck back home on the reporters' desk, going nowhere, answering the phone, while some jammy bastard has a big by-line as our New York editor,

or Moscow editor, his picture on the front page, free accommodation and a generous expense account.

In reality, when I have visited them, they have been full
of moans and petty grievances, worried about things being
schemed and plotted back in London, while they are not in
the loop, out of sight. In the capital where they are based, the
home press get the best invites and the exclusives. They are
just one of the foreign pack, occasionally thrown crumbs,
no officials really know them or care what they write or are
interested in what they are doing.

If I had known all this, or believed it, back in 1958–59, it
might have stopped me fantasising for so long about somehow,
somewhere, getting myself sent abroad again. I also didn't
know at the time, as none of us did in the UK, that some of
our brave lads in Cyprus, and also in Kenya, had possibly,
maybe, in fact probably not been as honourable and honest
as they should have been. And the press went along with it,
turned a blind eye, did not report, or investigate, or were not
aware. It is only in recent years that allegations of torture by
certain British troops, of Mau Mau and EOKA suspects, has
begun to appear – and resulted in court cases.

The British press, and the nation as a whole, were as gung
ho, trusting, obedient and wildly patriotic and flag-waving as
the servicemen and the authorities. Today we have become
more cynical and suspicious of our leaders, in politics, the
police and the military. We no longer naturally assume that
Britain is the home of fair play. Is this because there are more
cover-ups, more corruption? Or is it just that we hear about it
now because we live in a more open society?

*

After my return from Cyprus, I kept in touch with some of the families of Lancashire Fusiliers I had met out there, hoping for any human interest stories for the paper. There was one soldier who had been badly injured while I was there. I went to see his mother once a week, to find out if she had heard anything. She had no phone, so I just arrived, unexpectedly, and ingratiated myself, being sympathetic and ever so concerned about her son, my friend, but of course mainly hoping she had received some news that I could turn into a story.

All reporters have to learn to be two-faced. I liked to think I always did it naturally, and that both faces were genuine. I was and am genuinely fascinated by everyone, desperate to hear their story, their biography, their thoughts, but of course it is also a trick, a ruse. You are conning your way into their trust, their lives, making out you are going to be their best friend, forever. That's what they actually begin to think. But of course you are not. Once the story is over, or comes to a halt, you are off, on to the next.

I remained in contact with Brian Hitchen for a few weeks after we came back from Cyprus, having an occasional drink with him after work, though the *Chron* and the *News* staff rarely mixed. He was telling me one evening about a girl he had been chatting up while doing the calls, a girl on the switchboard at one of the big hospitals, whose job it was to provide updates and answer press queries on injuries. He had been talking to her every morning for a week, naturally trying to ingratiate himself with her, as we all did, in order for her to tell us things she should not. He had chatted her up so well, been so amusing and inter-esting and flirtatious, that she'd agreed to meet him after work.

There were no Facebooks or mobile phones or instant images or dating sites, so until he met her he had absolutely no idea what she looked like or how old she was. I think all she told him was the colour of the hat she would be wearing that evening. Next time I saw him, he told me what happened. He had positioned himself across the street from the hospital exit he knew she would use. He managed to spot her before she saw him – and decided she was so ugly and ill-dressed that he turned round and left, without speaking to her. I thought this was the most appalling behaviour. He argued that it might have been cowardly, but it was best for her. It didn't waste her time on a relationship that would have gone nowhere. So I suppose he had a point.

Brian left the *News* not long afterwards and joined the *Daily Mirror*, becoming their man in Paris and then a war correspondent, covering all the big international events over the next few years. I only ever met him again once, just a few years ago in London, at some event. I could not believe it was him. That slim and dapper young man I had once known briefly some forty years earlier had put on about five stone, had a bull neck and no hair. We had an awkward conversation, in which I tried to reminisce about our time in Cyprus. He didn't seem to recognise me or even remember me. No doubt I too had totally changed.

Brian ended up as editor of the *Daily Star* and then latterly as editor of the *Sunday Express*, and was awarded a CBE in Mrs Thatcher's resignation honours list in 1990.

In 2013, I read that he and his wife had died in Spain, where they had a holiday home. While crossing the road, they were both knocked down, sustaining injuries from which they never recovered.

26

A DEATH IN THE FAMILY

I went home to Carlisle for Christmas 1958, not long after I had returned from Cyprus, taking presents for my parents and also Margaret. She was home for the vacation from Oxford. I had brought them all things I thought were unusual, not to say unique, ethnic gifts of the sort you never saw in Carlisle – small items of decorated pottery, pots and small plates, covered in Greek mythological figures. Rather artistic, I thought. Margaret did not quite agree.

I also brought a present for myself. I had so loved the whiskey sours every evening in the officers' mess that I asked one of the officers how it was made. He said something about Angus Stewart, who I thought at first must be the officers' mess barman, or perhaps the brand of whisky they used. It was, of course, Angostura bitters, which I had never heard of before, an alcoholic drink containing spices and herbs.

The officer very kindly slipped a small bottle into my bag. It had a rather outsize label and I carried it carefully all the way back to Manchester. Margaret was there, on my return home, to welcome our hero. She started to unpack my bag for me – but the smell put her off. The bitters had somehow leaked and every item of clothing was stained pink. It never came out, despite endless washings. Good job I had not taken my best Danish tweed jacket to Cyprus.

Margaret had met my parents quite a few times by then. My father was always at his charming best when she was shown into his bedroom. He hummed and whistled and was on his best behaviour. All a pose, of course. But it had taken a while for my mother to properly warm to her.

The first time I took Margaret home, my mother had naturally offered her a cup of tea. 'No thanks, Mrs Davies, I don't drink tea.'

'You don't drink tea?' my mother said, sniffing, a sure sign of disapproval. 'I've heard it's very good for you.'

'No, Mrs Davies, I hate tea.'

'Oh, just a wee one. Won't do you any harm. It's freshly made, the teapot's on the stove.'

The teapot was on the stove from first thing in the morning till last thing at night, so the latter was true, but it was rarely very fresh, just continually boiled up, all day long.

This pantomime conversation was repeated every time Margaret came to the house. My mother would immediately insist on offering Margaret tea, despite being told often enough that Margaret did not partake. Either she believed there was nobody who didn't like tea, so if she offered it enough times Margaret would see the light, or her memory was going. All three probably.

I did tell Margaret off for saying she hated tea, no need for that, it was provocative. Just say, 'No thanks, Mrs Davies, how kind', as nicely as possible and move the conversation on quickly.

My mother loved everyone, welcomed everyone, but she couldn't understand Margaret. She was also suspicious of Margaret's reputation as a bluestocking and intellectual. My twin sisters, Annabelle and Marion, just a year younger than Margaret, had heard of Margaret's academic achievements while they had been at the Margaret Sewell. I think they half-felt they might be looked down upon, having left school at fifteen with no qualifications, which of course was not the case. They knew that Margaret's background was the same as ours and, in fact, her dad was a blue-collar worker, whereas ours, when he had worked, wore a white collar.

Annabelle had gone from school into the office of book-makers, Downie's, while Marion was working at a tyre factory, on some sort of machine. My younger brother Johnny had become an apprentice electrician. He had a struggle get-ting any sort of apprenticeship, having gone to such a small and basic secondary modern. Fortunately, my mother had pulled strings.

This is a family joke. How could my poor old mother pull any strings, when she knew nobody, knew nothing about how Carlisle worked? But by chance she needed to have a minor electrical job done in my father's room, another plug installed for his radio. It was done by a man in the next street, Mr Kelly. When Johnny was failing to get any kind of apprenticeship, she knocked on Mr Kelly's door and asked him to take on her son. He presumably felt sorry for us, knowing the family circumstance, and so agreed to take on Johnny at fifteen as his apprentice, even though he did not really need one.

Johnny was let go at the age of twenty-one, when he had finished his apprenticeship, as Mr Kelly would have had to pay him a proper wage, which he could not or would not afford. This was normal at the time, and there was no protection. But Johnny did quite quickly get another job, as an electrician for the State Management.

So that Christmas time, 1958, all three of my siblings were still living at home, but at least they were working. Tony McMynn, the lodger my mother had taken in, who had had half of my bed, had moved on. It was a few years later that my sisters and brother, in turn, decided to study at night school, get some qualifications and start proper careers. It was as if all three had been asleep, or had told themselves they were not academic, were no use at learning, had been rubbish at schoolwork, unlike Margaret, and even me. Though I could never call myself an academic role model.

Marion and Annabelle always made faces when I mentioned Margaret. If I happened to say what she was doing at Oxford, such as acting in a play, or that she had made her own gown for my June Ball, they would satirically say, 'Oh, she is so clever, your Margaret, is there nothing she can't do?' Then they would roll their eyes at each other and try not to snigger.

My mother could be just as bad. According to Annabelle, when she and my mother came through to Durham for my graduation ceremony at Durham Cathedral, Margaret and I were ahead of them in a queue to go in. And we were holding hands. My mother exchanged glances with Annabelle, pointed at our hands, then they both made faces and rolled their eyes, while my mother mouthed, 'Oh help.'

On my visits home, ever since going to Durham, I had begun to realise how much I was growing away from my family.

I even started to think that really I had never been close to them, had no intimate relationships, no connections with them, which was worrying. I did not want to think or admit such thoughts. I did love my mother so much, though it might have been pity as much as anything.

I did not fight with them, apart from physical fights with Marion when we were much younger, or argue with them. With my sisters and brother, I never seemed to have anything to talk about. I put this down partly to being the oldest, doing things long before they did them. It probably began at grammar school, when they thought I was now on a different route to them, becoming a different person.

I was relatively closer to Annabelle. She was pretty and presentable, always good in social situations, and everyone always loved her. I did invite her once to a Durham dance, as I had no partner at the time, and enjoyed showing her off. I can't remember inviting either Marion or Johnny to visit me at Durham. Was I ashamed? Oh God, I hope I wasn't.

This was always a problem in an age when so few people went to university from working-class families. You change socially, intellectually, culturally, whether you mean to or not, or whether you are aware of it or not. Those left behind, in your street, in your family, in your town, will often think you have changed, become lost, fancy yourself, have new airs and graces, up your own bum, which you will deny. Your accent changes, mixing for the first time with so many other accents. It's not that you want to disguise your own origins but in order to make yourself clear and understandable. Naturally, I don't think I consciously altered my accent, but going home to Carlisle I was aware, when I heard myself talking to old friends, that I no longer sounded quite like everyone else.

One aim of university is, of course, to change you, educate you, give you fresh perspectives and outlooks and experiences, so you are bound to emerge different at the end, otherwise what was the point?

People of my generation did often have a feeling of alienation from their roots as a result of going to university. It was foreign enough to them when they first arrived, till they acclimatised, but remained totally alien to those at home. I suppose today this does not happen to the same degree. Going to 'uni' is the norm, which the majority of teenagers aspire to, and in turn many of them will have parents and grandparents who have themselves been to university, who don't see it as an unusual experience, remote from normal life. All the same, it must still happen. You are bound to feel cut off from your family, when you move away, emotionally and not just physically.

Over that Christmas of 1958, we had the usual pathetic festivities. My parents, being Scottish, never really celebrated Christmas. We were brought up with New Year's Eve, Hogmanay, being the most important event of the festive season. But I went up street on Christmas Eve and bought a bottle of British port and a small bottle of my mother's favourite tipple, eggnog, now that I was such a big wage earner. My father had not been so well. He had caught a bad cold which was making him weak and fed up. But I bought him a small bottle of Scotch and loads of packets of peanuts.

On the evening of 27 December, I had come home early

from being out somewhere with Margaret and gone to bed. I think Johnny was out late, with a girlfriend at a dance. Sometime in the night, I sensed someone had come creeping into my bedroom. I heard a drawer being opened and what looked like a sheet being taken out. I woke up, looked over, and it was my mother. She shushed me and told me to go back to sleep, not to get up.

I turned over and soon went back to sleep, but subconsciously I had registered something unusual had happened. I didn't know what, or didn't want to work out what it might have been.

In the night, my father had died. My mother might have heard him, a last croak or cry, a turning in the night. His end had probably been half-expected, which was why my mother had gone down to check on him, discovering what had happened and then covering his body with a sheet.

I did not discover what had happened till the morning. My mother had saved me from it. But in hindsight I did know, or suspected, what had happened in the night. I had turned over, turned my back on the reality or possibility of his death, reassured by my mother that there was no need for me to get up. What else could have I have done anyway, in the dead of the night?

In the morning, as the oldest, I took charge of the funeral and all the other arrangements. While I was in town, I went up to Margaret's house and told her. She came back with me to town and we rushed round together, obtaining his death certificate, filling in all the forms and paperwork. When it is your first bereavement, and you have never before had to cope with all the bureaucracy, it can become a nightmare, no matter how clever you might think you are at understanding. I'd never realised there was so much to be done. A further complication was that it was the holiday period, and many offices were closed till after the New Year.

The official cause of death given on his death certificate was complications brought on by pneumonia, but of course it was the multiple sclerosis that had done for him. He had suffered for so many years, been confined to his bed, which had weakened his body and his soul.

We managed to organise the funeral and his burial for the first day after the holiday period and invited all our Cambuslang relations – his family – to come down for the wake, which was to be held in our living room. Meanwhile, his body lay in our front parlour, in the bed in which he had died. The undertaker had dressed him, plumped up his face, put some make-up on him. The effect was to make him look strangely himself, but not himself, a dummy version, but rather serene. It was the first corpse I had ever seen. In a way, I recognised him dead better than I had recognised him alive, as he seemed to have been made younger, more content, and cleaner.

Visitors, when they arrived, were taken in to see his body lying in his coffin. I took Margaret in when she arrived. There was a bowl of flowers beside his bed and a petal had blown on to my father's face. I flicked it off with my finger and thumb. Margaret was appalled, considering this was dreadful behaviour, showing no respect. She believed anyway that I was hardly grieving, that somehow I had risen above it, moved on and away. I explained that I had so much to do, that was why I might have appeared preoccupied. But I suppose, really, I had never known my father. My happy memories of him were few.

I was pleased that at least he had met Margaret, that he had seen me graduate, had seen me get a job, go on my first foreign trip, but of course he was never going to know what happened afterwards, in my life, or in the lives of my sisters and brother.

Our minister came to the house, recited some suitably Scottish funeral benediction. The hearse came, men in black carted out the body of my father in his coffin, all the men piled into black cars and went off to the cemetery. The Scottish tradition, which was new to me but my mother insisted it was the proper thing to do, was that only the men went to the graveside. So I did as she directed.

It was very early January, absolutely freezing in Carlisle cemetery, but when we all came back to the house, to join my grieving mother and all the women relations, Margaret and my sisters had made ready a splendid funeral tea, with lots of cakes, scones, hot sausage rolls. Margaret even poured and gave out cups of tea. And of course there was whisky for the men.

One of our Cambuslang relations said what a fine man John had been, how much they had all loved him, but what a struggle my mother must have had, coping with him all these years.

'Yes,' said Margaret very tartly, 'and all on her own.'

'What precisely are you insinuating by that, Margaret Forster?'

What Margaret meant was that during all those years none of our relations had done much to help, apart from having me on holiday when I was young. She had picked up from the twins how they had never been invited to stay in Cambuslang, nor had any of them come to stay in our house, to look after us, to give my mother a break.

Fortunately, Margaret held back from further barbs or comments. She busied herself offering more scones, realising it was not her place to say such things, and certainly not at this sort of solemn occasion. Which in the end was enjoyed by all. There were no scenes, no words, no further moments of frostiness. We had done my father's Cambuslang relations proud, not skimped on any ceremonies or hospitalities or traditions.

My mother was very grateful for how Margaret had helped. Better and more sincerely than me. After that, she became a champion of Margaret. The eye-rolling and clearing of the throat ceased from then on.

My sister Marion said an interesting thing to Margaret during the funeral tea. 'You are the first person who has ever been interested in our family.' By this she meant involved with us, concerned about us, interested in knowing each of us, not just me, as her boyfriend, getting to understand us all and the family dynamics, listening and reacting with sympathy and insight. Margaret was always very good at empathy and also explaining why people acted as they did, and predicting what would happen.

Marion's comment reflected my mother's attitude that she had been let down by my father's family and also the social services, such as they were. My father's friends from work had all disappeared, once he became totally bedridden. People did not want to know, to get involved. My mother never commented or complained about this openly, but Marion was more outspoken and possibly more bitter.

I can't say I was ever aware of the outside attitude to my family, or if it bothered me. Perhaps I ignored it, caught up in my own world. But Marion was conscious of it. Having been wary of Margaret, they now saw her as a welcome, involved addition to our family. Even something of our champion.

During the funeral, many of the visiting relations took my mother aside and said the same thing to her: 'It must be a blessed relief, Marion, now John has gone.' Every time it happened, she sniffed and shrugged and denied it. She got quite upset and annoyed in the end, indignant at the suggestion that she had wanted him dead. With him being so ill and bedridden, she must now be pleased, or at least relieved, they said. But she would not go along with this. Or at least admit it, even to herself. But of course it was a blessed relief, all round.

My mother's domestic situation then began to improve somewhat, over the next few months and years. She was still without a fridge, a phone or a TV, and still did her washing in the tub in the outside washhouse – no mod cons came her way until 1960. The first one I remember her having was a spin-dryer, which she used when it was too wet outside to hang out the clothes on the line. It was a temperamental little brute which rocked and moved around the lino floor of our kitchen, banging into people and things. Doing a lot of spinning but not much drying.

But she was now free to go out for about the first time in twenty years, started attending fancy salad classes and French lessons, which enabled me to do a bit of eye-rolling. She even joined an amateur drama club in Stanwix and had a part as a Scottish maid. Which of course she had once been. She now had a spare room, the parlour. As happened when I left, vacating half a bed, it was soon filled up.

Mr Watson, the French teacher from the grammar school who had helped me so much with my O-level resit, arrived at the door one day to ask my mother if she could possibly put up the school's new French assistant, who was arriving the next day. The lodgings he had fixed for him had fallen through. Goodness knows how he had found out that my mother now had a spare room.

My mother said of course, no problem, bags of room, be a pleasure. The French assistant was called Michel, at a French university studying English, and he stayed for the whole term. He was replaced by a woman French assistant, Madeleine, who stayed for a whole year. Several others followed.

The surprising thing was that they loved the house, and my mother so much, that they came back to visit, year after year. Madeleine remained a lifelong friend of our family. Annabelle, my sister, still goes on holiday with her. Not long ago I took two of my own grandchildren to Paris for the day on the Eurostar and had a meal with Madeleine. All this new stimulus and interest, and of course a small income, only started after my father had died.

Last year I went back to Carlisle cemetery for the first time in twenty years. And I couldn't find my father's grave. I wandered around for an hour failing to locate it. How shameful is that? Surely I should have remembered where my own father was buried.

I wanted to visit it for several reasons. Down memory lane for a start. It was close to where I did some of my courting, back in the fifties, when Margaret lived opposite the main gates. I never realised back then that the cemetery was one of the wonders of Carlisle, nay the county, perhaps of all England, being a classic Victorian graveyard, dating back to 1855, and covering almost 100 acres with chapels, ancient graves and monuments, hills and woods, little streams and bridges, with wild orchids, wild violets. It was one of the first in England to introduce woodland burials, the graves marked with an oak tree.

It looks immaculate today, with its sad cypresses, the ancient yew trees carefully sheared and shaped, the clippings going off to help make a cancer drug. And yet at the same time it feels wild and natural, a woodland reserve rather than a park.

It was voted the UK's Cemetery of the Year four years running, the last in 2008. The competition has now ceased, but surely they would have won it again.

There are 90,000 bodies buried there. No wonder I couldn't find my father's grave. In the 1950s, the office used to be in a couple of small, poky, dark rooms at the right of the front gate – but it had gone. It has now become a café. Never been to a cemetery café before.

The owner was taking scones out of the oven when I arrived. They looked so enticing I decided to have one, even though I never eat between meals, certainly not. She'd had to convert the old offices into a café herself, when she took on the lease. Helpful friends suggested some jokey names for it: Death By Chocolate, Last Orders, Dead Delicious, Coffin Cake, Mourning Coffee. Or jokey signs to be hung by the counter such as 'Please Let Us Know If You Suffer From Any Elegies'. She wanted the name to be respectful, so she has called it simply the Gatehouse Café.

I found my father's grave in the end – after I had located the office, now behind the crematorium — and was given a map with his plot number, 17-P-57. I had to pull some ivy and ferns away to read his details: Born 1906, died 1958. Reading his name gave me a shock, as it contains my name, JOHN HUNTER DAVIES. Even more of a shock reading it on a gravestone.

When he died in 1958, he was aged just fifty-two. Every year since I turned fifty-two has felt like a bonus.

27

LONDON CALLING

During 1959, I ceased to be employed by Kemsley Newspapers. I didn't get the sack. I didn't leave the company. It was just that Kemsley Newspapers left me – and everyone else. They suddenly got taken over by someone from Canada, of whom most of us had never heard. Kemsley Newspapers, then the biggest newspaper group in the UK, ceased to exist.

Kemsley had been part of the national media, and of politics, for most of the century. Today, when I mention the name, and say I began life as a graduate trainee with Kemsley Newspapers, I have to explain who they were. Or I just omit the name Kemsley and say I was a Thomson trainee, which technically I was. I had been in Manchester for just under a year when the takeover took place, so I was still being trained, in theory, for my contract had been for two years.

The newcomer was Roy Thomson (1894–1976), a Canadian with Scottish roots, who made his first fortune selling radios in Ontario. He had bought the *Scotsman* in Edinburgh a few years earlier then swooped and gobbled up the whole of the Kemsley empire in 1959. The Thomson name is, I suppose, still known today, unlike Kemsley. Lord Thomson, as he became – almost all press barons did in those days become real barons – was a power in the land as a newspaper mogul for the next few decades, and also branched out into other businesses still going, such as Thomson Holidays.

Unlike Lord Beaverbook and so many of the press lords who had gone before, Thomson had no real interest in self-promotion, or newspapers and politics, and meddled in neither. His only interest was in the bottom line – did his papers make money, could they make more money?

So it made not a jot of difference to those thousands of wage slaves slogging away in the various major cities that had a Kemsley House when overnight every one became a Thomson House. We were scared at first for our jobs – what would happen, would he start selling off papers? But life then carried on, as per normal.

I was called down to London in early 1959 to see Mr Fraser, the man who was in charge of the company's training scheme. I assumed it was just a routine catch-up meeting, for him to meet each of the current trainees. It was on the train to London that I met the other graduate trainee who had started with me on the *Chron* six months or so earlier, back in September. It was the first time I had properly spoken to her. We walked round the streets behind Gray's Inn Road before our respective meetings, as we were early. Afterwards we came back to Manchester together. But now I can't remember her name. Not much of a reporter.

On the train down, she asked me how I was getting on. I said I loved it, really good. 'Yeah, well, you have done exciting things,' she said. Meaning, of course, going to Cyprus.

She had done very little, just a bit of rewriting and was now starting to learn subbing. Her home was in the Manchester area, somewhere in Cheshire, and she was an Oxford graduate, but she didn't appear to have done anything at Oxford, such as student journalism. That surprised me. I assumed every would-be journalist would be like me, busying themselves on student papers, accumulating cuttings, showing journalistic enterprise.

It then transpired that she had some local connections with the company through her family. Either her father or some friend of his was a director of the Manchester paper and, when she didn't seem to have much idea about what to do on leaving Oxford, an interview had been arranged with Mr Goulden, the editor, and she'd been accepted.

I had no idea how many graduate trainees were taken on each year, but probably about six. I imagined they were all high-powered and well motivated, and also Oxbridge graduates, apart from me, so I did feel it was a bit unfair that somebody had apparently managed to get on the scheme without having shown much real hunger or interest in journalism. But then that was my idealistic, romantic vision of journalism, when I was starting out. Later on, I did meet perfectly happy, successful journalists who seemed to have no interest in people, or in writing, or even in newspapers. How could this be so? I used to think. But of course it happens in other so-called creative careers. You meet publishers who never read books, or reviews, or know about other publishing firms, their history. Or people who work in television who never watch TV.

I now know of course that journalists come in many forms, which is true of many other professions and occupations.

Newspapers need management people, business people, subs and editors, graphic artists and photographers, ideas and organisation people not just writing people. You don't have to produce any journalism to succeed in journalism. Or need to have what I imagined was the journalistic character and temperament.

My young female colleague could presumably have carved out a good career in some aspect of journalism or newspapers, not necessarily as a writer – but she left soon after we got back to Manchester. I never saw or talked to her again.

Mr Fraser said how well I had done in Cyprus, lots of good stories, several of which had been used by some of the group's newspapers, though, of course, I had never seen them. Then he told me, in confidence, that a bloodbath was expected in South Africa soon. The *Sunday Times* had no staffer out there, and were thinking they should have one, in which case the group would be represented by the same person. Would I be interested? It was all in the air at the moment, still being discussed.

The ANC – African National Congress, founded in 1912 – were becoming more militant against apartheid, moving on from peaceful demonstrations to active opposition, under their so-called Defiance Campaign. In reply, the South African government had started banning and arresting ANC leaders and the police were using more physical means of suppressing any demonstrations. All the political experts, in South Africa and in London, were predicting there would soon be bloodshed.

I said yes, of course, I would be interested, but promised I would keep quiet about what he had said. I told Margaret as soon as I could. She wasn't at all impressed. She couldn't understand my pleasure in being asked and willingness to go off and live in Jo'burg – as I was already beginning to call the main town. She personally would never want to live there.

Back in Manchester, I was on the calls again, boring news stories, press conferences, hanging around the Manchester University Students' Union, while I waited for word from Mr Fraser. Nothing came. I couldn't badger him as he had made it clear it was still at the discussion stage and I would be informed, if it ever came to pass, and if ever I was in the running.

Meanwhile, I was given a features series to do called 'Teenagers Talking', which ran in the *Chron* for a whole week, every day, from Monday 6 April 1959. The idea was to investigate and reveal this new phenomenon of teenagers, their life, thoughts and culture, which the adult world had still not quite come to grips with or understood. Who were they? In Manchester, so the paper estimated, there were 30,000 teenagers, mainly just hanging around. What did they think, what did they believe in, where did they hang out?

I was given free rein and several weeks to go out and report – and could write as much as I liked, go where I wanted, see how it went. Mac, the older journalist I sat next to, thought it was a nonsense, calling it an 'investigation' was phoney, where was the story, what was new about it? This passion for stuff about youth was getting out of hand. A cry which has been heard for decades ever since.

At the same time, knowing how keen I was to do it, he warned me not to interview any teenagers I might know personally.

I couldn't understand this piece of advice. Obviously it would be handy and quick to use people you already knew.

As I wasn't from Manchester, I didn't actually know any teenagers, so it wasn't an issue, but it took me a few years to understand his main point, which on the whole is correct.

It is always liable to rebound on you if you write about people you know, such as relations and friends. If you want to interview a nurse, find a nurse you have no connection with. Human interest, real-life interviews can so quickly escape your control, once you have written them. They get altered, cut, the wrong things get highlighted, vital stuff missed out. The person gets upset, does not understand the process, their own friends are either jealous of the attention or critical, hurt by quotes that the person has supposedly given. The same principle applies even more to television. The object in TV is often to set you up from the beginning, force you into the roles and stereotypes they have already decided upon.

Mac gave me another piece of advice, during my early months, which I ignored then and have ignored ever since. I had been sent to a flower show, and spent a lot of time working on how to get into the story sideways, looking for an offbeat introduction, a funny angle or amusing quote, and was probably straining too hard to find one. He said readers just wanted to know the list of winners, no point trying to be a clever bugger. I argued that if you could make the story interesting and unexpected, then more people would read it, even if they then gave up when they found it was just a list. Surely this applied to all stories. I think he told me to shut up and get on with it.

I never heard any more about South Africa, but the predictions and fears turned out to be justified. Just a year later, in 1960, came the Sharpeville Massacre, during which sixty-nine people were killed. I was never posted to South Africa. Or anywhere else abroad.

I did get called in one day by Bob Walker, the news editor. He said I was being moved to a new position. I thought for a moment it might be somewhere exciting, if not as scary as either Cyprus or Jo'burg. The answer was Wigan.

I was being sent to work in our branch office there, one of the *Chron*'s many offices round the region where they produced each day four pages or so of local news for the different editions. The local *Evening Chron* office normally consisted of just one journalist, sitting in a little room above the shop, usually on a high street, plus some sort of business person, who acted as the local advertising and circulation manager, and a woman on the front counter where you could drop in your classified adverts.

I was not going to live in Wigan, but travel out on the train every day to help our Wigan editor. It felt like an awful demotion, after the highs of being a foreign correspondent and feature writer, with my face and name in the paper. I was now back at the beginning. Even worse, I was out in the sticks, having to learn about local stuff that I had never been expected to cover when based at HQ in Kemsley House. Such as court reports.

I had given up my shorthand lessons quite quickly, convinced it was a skill I would never need. Now I was being sent to the magistrates' court in Wigan, and in nearby Eccles, so I had somehow to get down what was happening and make sense of it. I had never heard of the local streets and shops and institutions where apparently heinous crimes were being committed every day.

In each place, there were old sweats, regular court reporters who had worked there for years, either as freelances or for a court agency, supplying all the Manchester papers, and London, should anything unusual or with human interest value arise in their particular magistrates' court. They were all helpful, willing to tell me how they did their work, what to look out for. None seemed jealous that I might be taking their court reporting jobs from them. Some chance.

I couldn't understand how they stood it, every day of their working lives, sitting on the same seat in the same place, taking down notes, then phoning in stories, often no more than a paragraph long.

It was interesting for me, of course, seeing the law in action, watching lawyers working, the court officials, listening to the police reading out their statements as if they were speak-your-weight machines. I did learn something. But, oh, the boredom.

The worst part was knowing nobody, especially at lunch-time, as they all had their own roles and routines, so I would wander off looking for a cheap caff or a pub. The floors of the pubs seemed awash with spilled beer. The sandwiches were always soggy, especially the tinned salmon variety. I don't think they poured any liquid out of the can before emptying the contents on the sliced white bread. The regular *Chron* reporter, in theory my boss, never seemed to leave the office, typing all day long, only pausing to tell me which courts I should go to, meetings I should attend. At least he was nothing like Mr Mellor, shouting out instructions. So that was a pleasant change.

I was in Wigan during Whit week in May, which was very

colourful, with all the local children parading around in their best frocks and outfits. I can also remember wakes week, when the whole town seemed to close. Each of the Lancashire towns had a different wakes week, which dated back to the early Industrial Revolution, when all the factories closed and the workers had their annual holiday, going to the pubs or more likely to Blackpool. Such events have disappeared, and the cultural life and traditions that went with them, once the factories closed forever and manufacturing moved on.

I did try to find Wigan Pier, thinking I might get an offbeat story, the place made famous by George Orwell in his 1937 book *The Road to Wigan Pier*. But I failed to locate it. I had not realised it was a very old Lancashire joke, not known in Cumberland, which was to pretend Wigan was some marvellous, idyllic seaside resort. There was originally a wooden staithe, where coal was landed on the canal, but it was never a pier. George Formby used to joke that he had just been to Wigan Pier – 'And the tide was in'. (The area has now been redeveloped and the old nickname has become a marketing tool, with visitors invited to join the 'Wigan Pier Experience'.)

In my mind, I seemed to have been stuck at Wigan for months and months, all on my own. I can see myself sitting slumped on the empty train going out to Wigan first thing in the morning from Manchester, as everyone was going the other way. I was alone in my Daisy Bank flat when I got home in the evening. I did try to review as many amateur plays as possible, for the extra income, unless I was visiting Margaret or she was coming through to see me.

*

She had a bit of excitement of her own. She had written a piece for *Isis* called 'A Woman's Very Own', in which she described how she much preferred reading any of the women's magazines, such as *Woman* and *Woman's Own*, rather than boring, dreary publications like the *Manchester Guardian* and the *New Statesman*, which all her friends and tutors were reading.

As a result of this, she got a letter from someone called James Drawbell, who was apparently the boss of the magazine empire which included *Woman's Own*. He invited her to London to have lunch with him and talk about possibly working on women's magazines when she graduated. She decided to go for the lunch, thinking it would be amusing to meet him, hear what he had in mind.

When she got to the restaurant, Jimmy Drawbell had another man with him, who was the actual editor of *Woman's Own*. After a lavish lunch, they all jumped into a cab and went to the Guards Club, where they had more drinks. Nothing untoward took place in the cab, or was suggested, for I did ask, except she was invited to come and see them again when she left Oxford in another year and they would give her a job. Doing what, she asked? One of the things they dangled before her was interviewing Pietro Annigoni, then a famous and fashionable artist who had painted the Queen. Back in Oxford, she wrote and declined their offer. She said her interests did not lie in that direction.

I thought, of course, it was totally unfair – being offered a job on the strength of one silly little article, just because she was at Oxford writing for *Isis*.

*

Stuck in Daisy Bank Road on my own, one of the things I started trying to do was 'write'. I don't know why I decided to have a go at what we all now call creative writing, as opposed to simply writing. I had always been mocking about anything that smacked of purple prose, so I usually did it secretly, telling no one. While at Durham, I did write a sensitive piece about a lovers' quarrel – i.e. about me and Margaret – for the student literary magazine, *New Durham*. They accepted it, and printed it, but I didn't put my name on it – embarrassed, perhaps, that someone who fancied himself as a humorous writer was trying to be serious.

I also wrote eighteen pages of a play, though I had no memory of doing so. It has just fallen out of my *Evening Chronicle* cuttings book, which I had not opened since 1959. It appears to be a searing domestic drama, clearly about my father's illness and death, and the effect on his family. I still haven't read it all. I don't like that sort of heart-wringing, weepy, family realism. I may be obsessed by my own life and entrails, but even I can't bear to read that sort of juvenile rubbish.

But I did get one so-called creative article published: 'Like Swans Asleep' appeared in the *Manchester Guardian*. It was about being in Cyprus, sitting looking at the sea and the ships and thinking of that poem by James Elroy Flecker (1884–1915) which we had all learned at school: 'I have seen the old ships sail like swans asleep.' It is set in Cyprus and mentions Famagusta, which I visited while I was there. I did not reveal in the piece what I was doing in Cyprus, the reason why I was there. I hope I cleared it with the *Chron*. It was an awfully sensitive and moving piece of fine writing. Well, my mother thought so.

*

Looking back through my 1959 diary, I see I was based in Wigan for only about a month, from May to June. It is just in my mind I was there forever. As you get older, the past does tend to grow bigger. The further away, the clearer it all becomes.

And my total time in Manchester was in all only nine months. Manchester is still vivid and visible in my mind, yet it all happened almost sixty years ago. Remembering what I did last year, that is a struggle. Or ten years ago, that's equally jumbled and faded. I have a new routine for when I am recalling something. When I hear myself beginning 'I bought this/ did this/went there, oh, I think it must be, hold on, must be five years ago ...', I stop myself, mid-flow, and change it to ten years. Five years seems to be about right when I launch into the memory, but I then double it, knowing I now always underestimate the passing of recent times.

My diary entry for Thursday 11 June 1959, written in large letters, reads 'FAREWELL!' I have also added '5', presumably indicating the time, and 'entrees at 9', whatever they might have been. Could I have been treating some of my chums from the *Evening Chronicle* offices, such as Barry and Beryl and Mac, to a drink and possibly a nibble? What a spendthrift. Or show-off.

The editor of the paper, Mr Goulden, had called me in just two days previously to inform me I was being moved at once from Wigan. This time I was going to London.

28

LONDON LIFE

I think it was the smell of London that hit me. Not a nasty smell, just a hot, sticky, semi-tropical cockney smell. Of course, cockneys don't have a smell, but cockney-land did seem a place apart, with its own aromas and sounds and sensations. It was midsummer, the middle of June 1959, and it was very hot, far hotter than in the North, which you never believe, living in the North, but alas it is true.

They all seemed to be archetypal cockneys, or at least local Londoners, cheerful, chirpy, quick, witty, the sort I had seen in British post-war movies. They made me seem slow and lumpen and very northern. In 1959 there were few recent migrants, from Asia or Europe, and the ones from the West Indies, who had been encouraged by our government to come here with the offer of work, kept to themselves, or were kept to themselves. Most of them had settled quietly in the Brixton area.

I had no idea where Brixton was, or where any of the different parts of London were in relation to each other. I did know some of the names, like Mayfair and Park Lane and the main railway stations, but that knowledge came from playing

Monopoly, not from real life. They might well have been fantasy places for all I knew.

The tube was frightening, and of course the relationship between the stations on the map bore no resemblance to their situation above ground. Buses were even scarier, with people jumping on and off all the time, pushing and shoving, all knowing precisely where they were going.

In Manchester I had got a map and wanted to live anywhere near the office. This time I had slightly grander ambitions – a flat of my own, self-contained, with my own front door, where Margaret could stay without any of the faff of sneaking her in, hiding her, pretending she wasn't there.

Suddenly landing in London at twenty-three, out of the blue, seemed to be part of a pattern in my life. I'd gone to the Creighton School at eleven at the last moment, unexpectedly moved to the grammar at sixteen and got into Durham at eighteen in a way that felt as if it had nothing to do with me. How have I come to be here, and where am I anyway?

At Euston I clutched the address of Squire Barraclough, someone I had never met, just a name. He was my only contact in the whole of London. He worked on the London desk of Thomson née Kemsley Newspapers and I had occasionally spoken to him about stories on the phone. His name, of course, was unforgettable – a better by-line than mine. But I knew nothing about him, his age, circumstances, where and how he lived or with whom. When I happened to tell him on the phone a few days earlier that I was being moved t/ Thomson House, and had nowhere to stay, he said, no pro' lem, I could spend the night on his sofa.

Hs address was in Archway, in a side street of Vic^rian

terrace houses, near Archway's suicide bridge. He shared a small ground-floor flat with another Thomson journalist. The one night turned into ten days, which was a bit embarrassing. The sofa was in their living room, so I had to put away my things, such as they were, behind the sofa every morning. I tried to get up early and leave before they did and come home late, so as to inconvenience them as little as possible. I didn't eat with them, except on Sunday when we all walked over to Highgate and had a pub lunch. Highgate looked attractive and affluent, but totally out of my range. They seemed so knowledgeable about pubs and areas, and buses and tube stations. The barmaid knew them. They understood it when cockney persons affected mock fury or rudeness. I wondered if I would ever master any of it.

I felt under such pressure to find somewhere of my own to live. Margaret could not stay on that sofa, so my need was urgent, yet I was working every day. They moan about renting in London today, what hell it is to find any place to live, but I am sure there has never been a good or easy time. Only the rents change.

I discovered that it was vital to get the first edition of the *London Evening Standard*. Like the *Chron*, they had lots of editions all day long, the first one being full of dull stories about people out in the Home Counties. In those days, there were three London evening papers. At every tube station and busy corner you could hear the different vendors shouting out the different titles. The *Evening News* was a broadsheet, strong in the suburbs, while the *Star* was a tabloid with banner headlines. The *Standard* was also a tabloid, but considered more upmarket, strong on the City and the West End, with good literary pages. That was the paper, so I was told, that had most of the central London flat adverts. But if you didn't get the first edition, they would all be gone.

So I got the first edition on the way to work all week and started ringing surreptitiously on the office phone, trying to book viewing appointments, but of course I could not physically see them till the evening. Straight after work, armed with my tube map and an *A–Z*, I rushed to see flats, full of excitement at first, then despondent when most of them had been taken by the time I got there.

I eventually narrowed down my search to north London. I could see Highgate looked nice, and I heard Hampstead was even better, and Hampstead Heath was said to be amazing. Northerners, over the centuries, when they have come to London, usually arrive at either Euston or King's Cross, which is why they start looking roughly around those areas. So northerners end up in north London. Going over the river is seen as passport country.

I eventually found a self-contained flat I liked – at 6a Kingscroft Road, Shoot Up Hill, just north of Kilburn High Road. A fairly nondescript area, but quite attractive, I thought, full of converted semi-detached houses. It was a long way from the areas I really wanted, but I worked out I could walk to the heath in about an hour. I had my own front door, leading to the upstairs of a semi-detached. I had a living room, a bedroom, kitchen and bathroom. The living room had a proper fitted carpet, off-white, which I thought was awfully luxurious. We never had fitted carpets at home in Carlisle or in the two flats I had rented in Manchester.

The rent was six guineas a week. I had to give the landlord, a Mr Polak, endless references and bank statements. On 19 June 1959 I paid him a deposit of £25 and got the flat. I was thrilled. I could now leave Squire Barraclough's sofa and concentrate properly on my new job, which I had rather neglected in the first ten days with trying to find accommodation.

I rang Margaret and she came the first weekend I moved in. She declared at once that the road and house were nasty and suburban, the furnishings dreadful, including the fitted carpet of which I was so proud. The whole flat was awful and poky. I was so upset, especially after all the hours I had spent traipsing to places that had gone when I got there. 'You should have seen the flats I turned down,' I said. 'Okay for you to criticise, you didn't have to go through it all.' She said it was just the sort of awful Carlisle suburban semi she had hoped never in her life to have to live in.

Mike Thornhill, our friend from Carlisle, still at Balliol, later came through to London for a weekend with a college chum and asked if they could stay. I said no problem, of course, after all the times I stayed with him. It felt wonderful having my own place and being able to give hospitality for a change. The chum he brought with him was a young man with floppy fair hair, same age as us, called Angus Douglas-Hamilton, later the 15th Duke of Hamilton.

I didn't realise his background till later, but when I told Margaret that the aristocracy had stayed and had not complained, she said, 'So what, it's still a horrible flat.'

My new job was on the *Sunday Graphic*, a paper I knew of but had never read, one of the two popular Sunday papers that Roy Thomson bought in 1959, the other being the *Sunday Times*.

The *Sunday Graphic* began in 1915, and at one time was the sister paper to the *Daily Graphic*. It was a homely, unsensational tabloid, at least when I joined, a bit like an English version of the *Sunday Post*, a paper all the family could read and not be offended by. The *Empire News*, Thomson's other popular Sunday paper, was founded in 1884 in Manchester as the *Umpire*, when it mainly covered sport. Edward Hulton bought it in 1917 and it became a mainstream national newspaper. It was a broadsheet, with rather heavy type and big headlines, full of crime and sex and scandals and was competing hard with the *News of the World*.

The *Sunday Graphic* offices were upstairs at the back of Thomson House, all a bit dusty and cramped. When Roy Thomson took over, changing the building's name, he slowly revamped the main entrance, making it much more modern, and built himself a penthouse on the top floor, with his own lift. He wore pebble glasses and was known for being canny with his pennies.

The first day he arrived to move into his penthouse, a rival newspaper sent a photographer to hang around all day, waiting for his Rolls. The photographer had thrown some pennies in the gutter, where he knew Thomson would alight. Sure enough, as Roy got out, despite his bad eyesight and heavy specs, he managed to spot the pennies and bent down to pick them up. Good trick. Snap, snap. It amused all the rest of Fleet Street. I don't think Thomson himself was at all bothered.

The big worry for the staff was that having bought all these papers, plus the provincial ones, he would start pruning, but slowly, as the months went on and nothing happened, everyone began to relax. Best of all, he did not interfere edi-torially, being primarily interested in studying balance sheets.

I sat in the *Sunday Graphic*'s main newsroom, as I had done in Manchester, a big open space, with the news editor and his deputy at one end, keeping an eye on everybody. Like the paper itself, the atmosphere was homely, good-natured, nobody shouted at you. Lots of people seemed to float in and out, freelances bringing stories or gossip. Around the news-room were offices where the editor and assistant editors and star writers lived.

There were two male reporters, just a few years older than me – Eric Tyson, who was always busy, making endless notes, seemed very efficient, and Gordon Jackson, who was more laid-back. Then there were three older women reporters, feature writers really, who specialised in the sob stories and anything human interest. The paper did have a lot of heart-breaking stories about candlelit vigils for dead grannies or missing children or runaway pets.

I sat next to Dorothy Harrison, a very experienced Fleet Street woman reporter, who had spent many years on various magazines and newspapers. I thought she was pretty old, but she was probably little more than fifty. She wore a lot of make-up and perfume, flowing clothes and was always pumping up her bosom, as if checking all was well, that she was still intact, busty and blooming. She took me under her wing and was endlessly helpful, telling me how the paper was run, who was who, which pubs to go to. She always had a glass or two of wine at lunchtime, which I thought very cosmopolitan. I didn't know anyone in Manchester who drank wine at lunchtime.

I would join her as she sat on her high stool at the bar and after two glasses she would be full of gloom about the future of the paper. And about herself. At her age, this would be her last job, she would never get another. She was very matter-of-fact, not really moaning. Yet she constantly reassured me. I would be okay, she could tell, things would work out for me, trust her, she had been around. I suspected she was simply trying to cheer me up.

I never discovered where she lived, whether she had been married, or had children, but I met quite a few of her friends, including a gay journalist called Freddie. I never knew journalists could be gay. He and his boyfriend lived in a very small flat in Hampstead over the Coffee Cup in the middle of the High Street. It seemed to me like the Left Bank.

The news editor of the *Sunday Graphic* was John Ralph, an ex-RAF officer type, with a trim moustache, hearty laugh, posh accent, who was always bubbling with new ideas, most of which seemed potty to me. In the first week I had to go with a driver out into deepest Surrey to observe the effect of new road markings on traffic. I think either red lines had come in or double yellow lines on main roads. There was no story. Even if I had found a line, or something amusing, it would not have kept from Tuesday to Sunday.

Another time he called me over and said, 'Quick, get to Heathrow airport, Frank Sinatra is coming in – you might get a word with him.' I jumped on the first bus to Piccadilly, knowing that was the heart of London, got out and asked people the way to Heathrow. I had absolutely no idea where it was, what direction, how to get there. It took me took two hours, by which time Sinatra had long gone. If, of course, he had ever come. Which I always doubted.

The first useful thing I learned was to fill in your expenses. In Manchester you were lucky to get your bus fares back. Fleet Street was so different, and also the regime of a Sunday paper. Sunday paper journalists begin their week on a Tuesday and work Saturday. The whole of Tuesday morning every week was taken up by one thing: filling out your expenses. Once you had done that, you could go off for lunch. Perhaps never come back that day.

I was instructed to make sure I claimed £5 every week – that was the rate for my level. Not official, nothing written down, but the editor and the management knew all about it, because they had their own agreed level. If you didn't claim your agreed weekly expenses, it would muck up the whole system.

I was told how to write down that I had had lunch with a contact, and if not lunch, describe it as social expenses or entertainment. Any name would do of some sort of contact. And enclose a bill, any old bill, but you did need bills when claiming for any meals. Didn't matter who the meal was with or what for, personal or otherwise, you just needed a receipt. Friendly restaurants and pubs would give you blank bills to fill in.

If you actually spent real money, on a real job, going somewhere, then of course you claimed this to the hilt, over and above your normal, agreed £5. Each week, if you were hard up, you could get what was called a 'pink slip', an advance on your expenses. You named some contact you needed to meet, some story you were going on, and as long as an assistant editor signed it, you rushed off to accounts, handed it over and got the money in cash, always crisp pound notes, as if they had just printed them. Fleet Street's version of quantitative easing.

The problem was to remember what you had claimed on a pink slip and make sure your next expense sheet covered it all. There were several semi-contract freelances who totally abused the system, living entirely on pink slips for months and never filling in their claim forms. Then a heavy from accounts would come round and issue dark threats.

After two weeks of being sent on dopey non-news stories, I discovered the real purpose of my sudden transference from Manchester. I had been taken on to work on a new gossip column, 'The World of Peter Raymond'. There was no such person. He was like William Hickey, a fictional character, to cover whoever was writing.

I was working under the watchful eye of Terence Feely, an assistant editor. He was very debonair and handsome, pinstriped suit, always a flower in his buttonhole, part of the paper's officer class. Another was Robert Robinson, a prematurely balding, confident man who was the film expert, interviewing Hollywood movie stars who were over here. I thought his life was incredibly glamorous. He always got a massive spread in the paper, yet he moaned all the time about his job, saying he was embarrassed by it, when clearly he was so clever and gifted. He had been to Oxford, quoted Oscar Wilde all the time. He obviously never thought he would end up doing this, on this sort of paper. But he was funny and caustic and I got on well with him.

My job was to write little gossip paragraphs about so-called well-known people, or at least people well known in other gossip columns. In the beginning, I had hardly heard of any of them. But once I got into the swing of things, I contacted all the theatre and film PRs, leading restaurants and posh hotels, all of which, to my surprise, had their own designated press officers, wanting you to write about their clients or mention their hotels or shows. I had not come across such people in Manchester. So the invitations were soon flooding in. There were also dozens of Chelsea freelances hanging around the King's Road, who rang up all day trying to sell you tittle-tattle tip-offs about someone with a title. All gossip columns were obsessed by the aristocracy, more than they are today, now that the stars of reality TV have taken over as the true celebs.

The *Sunday Graphic* was hardly a major paper, and felt to me fairly folksy and harmless, so I was surprised that it was still considered worth courting by all the PRs, on the list for invites, first nights and press conferences. It was because we were a national paper. PRs needed their clients mentioned anywhere nationally, to get their contracts renewed.

When I first joined the paper there was some trouble with the National Union of Journalists, which was very powerful. I was still only twenty-three, and had been in journalism just eighteen months. The NUJ normally insisted on Fleet Street staffers being at least twenty-four, with two years' provincial experience – but the management sorted it.

In my diary for July–December 1959, my first six months in London, kept for expenses purposes, I have a most impressive list of star names, famous people I must have seen or met or been in the presence of or at least observed across a crowded room. A lot were at press conferences, such as Noël Coward at the Savoy, so I was probably in a scrum of about a hundred press people and photographers at the launch of his new play. Then there was Bob Hope, Benny Goodman, Jayne Mansfield, Harry Secombe, Connie Francis, Lonnie Donegan, Otto Preminger, Julie Andrews, Yves Saint Laurent, Olivia de Havilland, David Niven, Alicia Markova. Oh yes, I met them all, sort of, got a sentence from them, more or less, then written a couple of pars in which it appeared they were talking just to me, personally.

As I got more space, and into my stride, and Terence let me get on with it, I did now and again do one-to-one interviews with people I really wanted to meet, such as Arnold Wesker, Tommy Steele, the Boulting brothers, who were well-known British film producers. I went to see Shelagh Delaney, who had just had a surprise success with her play *A Taste of Honey*. She lived in what appeared to be an old Victorian mansion block, possibly council owned, in a side alley off Charing Cross Road. I never knew such blocks existed in the heart of the West End. It was not just meeting Londoners but getting to know London that was endlessly interesting.

Now and again I managed to interview more offbeat people such as Frank Richards, the creator of Billy Bunter. I was surprised he was still alive. And that his real name was Charles Hamilton. He was in his eighties, unmarried, and living alone out in the country near the coast in Kent, so that gave me an excuse for a nice day out. He was funny and jolly and insisted on singing to me '(Won't You Come Home) Bill Bailey'. In Latin. He had translated it himself. I was entranced by it, the daftness and cleverness of what he had done. Being, of course, someone who had passed O-level Latin. Afterwards, he gave me a typed transcript, signed, which I still have. He died just a year later.

Another excursion I arranged for my own personal interest was going up to Wolverhampton to interview Billy Wright. He had just retired after a long career as a Wolves player and as England captain. Every English schoolboy for generations had admired him, our blond, comic-book hero. I must have been cheeky about him, or written something disobliging, for his wife Joy, one of the Beverley Sisters, wrote to the editor and complained afterwards. I never worked out what remark or quote had annoyed her. It can often be simply by saying someone is well built, which they take to mean fat, or untidy, i.e. scruffy, which can upset them or, more usually, their loved ones.

I also went to see Teasy-Weasy Raymond, a celebrity hairdresser, very well known at the time, who lived in a smart flat in Sloane Square. I happened to tell him I had recently arrived from Manchester, and this was my first job in London. He made some remark about my provincial clothes, then took me into his dressing room and threw open a large wardrobe. He then insisted on giving me one of his suits. It was in a very loud check, so I looked like a bookie on the way to Ascot. I showed it with pride to Margaret next time she came to visit – and she threw it straight out, saying it was an awful suit and I looked ridiculous. 'But it's free,' I cried. 'All free.'

Terence Feely, as my boss, would often drop his own stories into the column and would also arrange for me to meet well-known people, such as Fanny Cradock and her screen partner Johnnie, later her husband. She was one of TV's first celebrity chefs, rather grand and imperious, her voice so posh you felt it must be a fake, who bossed around her henpecked partner.

I went with Terence to Fanny's house somewhere near

Greenwich and we were treated to an excellent meal, cooked by Fanny herself. Terence did most of the chatting – but then it turned out I should have been making notes. I hadn't realised that my job was to write it all up. It was PR for her.

I also started a series of interviews, as Peter Raymond, which was called 'Nothing but the Truth'. It was a Q & A format, even more popular in newspapers today, being cheap and simple to do. Once you launch it, PRs put forward their clients, and often write all the answers. I usually tried to do follow-ups on the phone, to get some genuine-sounding answers.

One of my subjects was the boxer Freddie Mills, born 1919, who had started as a fairground fighter and had risen to be light heavyweight champion of the world between 1948 and 1950. He had a bashed-in face, seemed practically incoherent, but was greatly loved by the great British public as a character, a trier. My piece about him had the banner headline: 'FREDDIE MILLS – FIGHTING FIT AT FORTY!' And the first question was – how old are you Freddie?

I was so ashamed by the banality of the piece, but we had to keep it soppy and harmless or so-called celebs would not be put forward by their PRs or agents. I never met him, just talked briefly on the phone. Turned out he wasn't all that fit, mentally, financially or otherwise. He had got himself mixed up with Soho gangsters, including the Kray twins. He shot himself in the head in 1965, sitting in his car behind a night-club, aged just forty-six.

I did one story the following year which made the front-page lead, the splash as we called it. It was just before the marriage of Princess Margaret, which took place on 6 May

1960. We had heard a rumour that their honeymoon, or part of it, might be on the royal yacht *Britannia*, but no announcement was being made. I was sent down to Portsmouth to poke around the docks and speak to sailors, so I went to their pubs, and also met a few of the wives, and it did seem to be true, the crew was secretly standing by to set sail imminently. I wrote the story, desperately hoping I had not misread all the signs, all the gossip, but it turned out to be correct.

When Margaret came through from Oxford for the weekend I now always had somewhere exciting to take her, unlike in Manchester. It was usually to the West End – and all free. She didn't approve of free things, from a free bus ride to free meals. I explained it was work. I would have to write a paragraph somehow. And it involved other people's work. There were PRs whose job it was to get people like me to go to an opening night at the Pigalle or Talk of the Town, stuff myself at the best tables with the best food and drink, and watch Eartha Kitt perform. Not easy.

One freebie consisted of a whole weekend by the seaside, for the two of us – at Butlin's holiday camp in Margate. The *Sunday Graphic* had become sponsors of the Butlin's glamorous granny event, which had been going for some years. As the *Graphic* was involved, we had to supply a judge and I was given the job on behalf of the paper, as Peter Raymond, their famous columnist. I had never been to a Butlin's, or Margate or any other English southern seaside town. Would it be like Silloth?

Margaret and I had a chalet to ourselves, but ate and drank with all the campers. Heats for the glamorous grannies had been running all summer at the various Butlin's all over the country. Now three judges, including me, had to decide on a winner. They were all stunning, amazingly preserved, fabulously coiffured and made up. Some were quite old, i.e. around forty or fifty, but a few were only in their thirties. One, aged thirty-four, said she had had a daughter at seventeen who had now recently given birth.

We chose the winner, there was a grand dinner, with music and entertainment by the Redcoats, then Margaret and I went to bed in our chalet, carefully locking the door, as it looked a bit fragile. We had just climbed into bed when there was a tremendous banging at the door. I opened it to find one of the grannies standing there – one who had not won but who had made it to the final shortlist. She was absolutely furious and blamed me, shouting at me, demanding an explanation for why I had not chosen her.

'Everyone says I look like the Queen Mother, they always do, go on ask anyone. So why did you not pick me? I know it was you, don't lie ...'

I managed to wedge the door with my foot to keep her out but she was pushing and shouting, determined to come in. She might have had a few drinks. Then she got all flirtatious, fluttering her eyelashes, as if jumping into bed with me now would make the judges alter their minds.

I said I had chosen her, she was my number one, but the other judges had overruled me. Eventually I pushed her away before she managed to get into the chalet, and into my bed, where of course Margaret was trying to sleep, praying that she never had to spend a weekend in a holiday camp ever again. Even if it was free.

There was another time we went away together to the seaside, not as a freebie, for a romantic break, just the two of us. She was supposedly working hard for her final exams, or schools as they were then called at Oxford, but we still met most weekends. She either came to London or I went through to Oxford, much nearer now, compared with Manchester, and quick, as I could afford to go on the train.

We looked at a map; I talked to people in the office, asked where the really attractive seaside places near London were. Rye was recommended, and Camber Sands. I rang a pub which had rooms and said I wanted a double. They asked for my name and address – and if I was married. They did not allow unmarrieds to sleep together in the same room. Otherwise I would need to book two rooms. This was a pub, in a remote area, 1959, in the wicked South, or so we Cumbrians had been led to believe. I said of course we were married.

We arrived too early, and the pub wouldn't let us in, so we went for a walk on Camber Sands. We walked for ages, trying to get to the sea, but gave up as the tide was so far out. When we were eventually allowed into the pub, I had to sign us in as Mr and Mrs Davies. It looked strange, written down in the residents' book. Margaret had to write her name as well – Mrs Davies. Which was something she had said she never wanted to happen.

29

Double Thrills

Margaret had always said she was never going to have children. She didn't want to be responsible for bringing another human being into the world, which was a pretty rotten place. So, therefore, why get married? It was logical not to.

She was always very hot on logic, most of it pessimistic, that things would go wrong, and if they went right, it would not be for long. She had reasons and explanations for every eventuality, all quite convincing, except I was never convinced. With people, I always believe the best in everyone. With events and life and all that, I believe the best is yet to come, though really, it is pretty good now.

Our really awful rows and arguments had settled down over the last four years, when I used to sulk or she would storm off. They hadn't ceased, but we had a modus operandi to deal with them. One way was to stop the other going back over who had started it, who had said what. We had always been doing that, arguing about the argument, which always led to more arguments. Another way was not to let it last till bedtime, to call a truce at the end of the day. Strangely enough, the next day's petty disagreements always seemed to follow the same old pattern as the day before.

When we stayed overnight in the pub at Rye, I did buy her a ring – a pretend wedding ring from Woolworths, bought specially for that occasion. She also had a pretend engagement ring she had worn on our sailing holiday in Holland, made of coal, which turned her fingers black when it rained. We were told it was a real stone, which it was, made of haematite. The point of these fake rings was for appearances. It is hard to believe now how difficult society made it for couples to sleep together, even long-established courting couples.

Then, of course, there were her parents. They could not help it, being products of their generation. They had seen and heard of the social and economic devastation caused by having a baby out of wedlock, so they would have been appalled by the thought of their offspring enjoying carnal relations without being married. And of what other people would say, if they ever found out. There was also the fact that 'Jesus would not like it'. Which was how Lily, Margaret's mother, thought. So we always had to keep up pretences in front of Margaret's parents, about how often Margaret was visiting me, and what we were doing.

During the summer of 1959, my first in London, in my own rather des res, Margaret stayed with me most of the time from June, when she broke up, to October – but she could not tell her parents that. Instead, she told them she would be mostly in Europe. All her well-off girlfriends at Somerville were off to exotic places, or their luxurious family villas. Margaret wrote in advance a series of postcards to her parents, showing scenes of Paris, Venice, Rome and elsewhere, depending on when and where her friends were going. They were supposed to post each one on a certain date, following a certain order, so that when Margaret said from Paris that she was having a great time there and next week would be in Venice, the Venice card did not arrive before the Paris one. One of the girls did get the order wrong, which puzzled Margaret's father, Arthur. He loved reading postcards, kept them in an album, examining the stamps and the postmarks, turning them over and muttering, 'Oh aye, oh aye', a sure sign that something was puzzling him. As Margaret explained, the post in France and Italy is useless, not like England. That seemed to satisfy him.

I didn't tell my own mother the true facts about us either, but I didn't worry about her. She didn't really take in such things as arrangements and places and addresses, and, anyway, as far as she was concerned I had gone, flown the nest.

Traditionally, working-class parents don't worry about their sons as much as their daughters.

Nevertheless, all this pretending to her parents, all the complications with booking places, did become annoying. And there was one obvious and easy solution to it. I can't say it was the most important reason for getting married, but it was one of them. It was mainly that we had got to that stage in life and in our relationship when, at that time in the Western world, it was what people did. My generation did marry young, in their early twenties, and it was often really for sexual reasons, to sleep together.

I never proposed. Never went down on one knee, far less asked Arthur for his daughter's hand. I would have got a good kicking, or looks that could have withered. Whenever over the last few years she had said that she did not want to get married, I would always reply, 'Who's asking you?'

Marriage just sort of happened. I know, I am always saying that, or telling myself that, but there was no definite moment when I remember that we agreed, yes, we will get married. It just became sort of inevitable. It seemed obvious that she would come and live with me in London, so why not get married, make it simple and easy?

She was keen to leave Oxford and move to London, but had no idea what she might do, what sort of work or career. She had turned down that *Woman's Own* offer, having no interest in journalism. She felt she did not have the cheek and impudence to ask people questions. As a young girl, she had wanted to be a missionary, and then an MP. Those ambitions had rather faded. All she knew was that she wanted to be independent, earn her own money, not be reliant on a husband, as her mother had been, as almost all mothers had been for centuries.

She had realised in about her second year at Oxford that she was not academic after all, having gone through her school life with everyone telling her she was. She found it tedious having to write essays to a formula, having to be controlled and measured, saying 'on the one hand' and then 'on the other'. She felt she'd had more of a spark, more originality, before she went to Oxford, when no one was trying to knock her into shape, guide her thoughts and her style.

She did, though, apply for one thing, the BBC training scheme for producers. The university appointments board suggested it, and gave her the forms to fill in. She got down to the last six and was interviewed by a panel at Broadcasting House.

Without being asked, or the subject being mentioned, as even then questions of a personal nature were not encouraged, she told them that she was getting married in a week. The atmosphere totally changed. She was never offered a place.

We had decided to get married as soon as possible after she left Oxford. Or even earlier. She discovered she could do it before she had technically left, the day after her final exam was over, before her term was officially finished, if she got permission from the principal, which she did.

We got married on 11 June 1960 at Oxford register office, straight from her last exam. There was no one else there, apart from our two witnesses – Theodora Parfitt, Margaret's best friend in Oxford, and Mike Thornhill, our old friend from Carlisle, still at Balliol.

There was no church ceremony and no reception. After the brief, blank, emotionless, unromantic register office formalities, we went out to the Bear at Woodstock and had lunch. Then we came back to Northmoor Road, the home of Theo's parents. Some snaps were taken in their back garden, among the roses.

I wore my best suit, not quite a new one, and it was becoming a bit shiny round the bum, but pretty sharp for 1960, Italian style, dark blue, faintly pinstriped, low-cut jacket, straight at the back, bought from Cecil Gee in Oxford Street. I did buy a new white shirt and a new Van Heusen collar, which was very tight and hellish uncomfortable. But I looked smart and clean, so I thought, and incredibly young.

Margaret wore, well, clothes, I do remember that. The wedding photos are amateur snaps, very small and in black and white, so it is hard to spot all the details. I can see she was wearing a white cotton sleeveless frock, straight at the neck, for the register office. Then for her going away outfit she changed into a very nice outfit, light jacket and skirt in lilac, I think.

Margaret refused to have any sort of wedding reception. And I agreed with her. We couldn't bear to have all that fuss. Nor did we tell our families or anyone else what we were going to do. We had been going out for four years, so, dear God, getting married could not possibly come as a massive surprise to most of our relations.

But I did get cards printed, which we sent out *after* the event. I was rather proud of them, of the design and the printing. It was a folded-over green card and contained an illustration by Peynet from his *Lovers' Pocketbook*. Raymond Peynet (1908–1999) was a French artist and designer who produced a series of little books about lovers. They featured a thin young man in a bowler hat, supposedly a poet, with his girlfriend. They were enormously popular among students and lovers in the late 1950s and early 1960s. Back then they were considered rather arty and hippy, showing you believed in peace and love, not like the usual corny and soppy romantic Woolworths counter stuff.

I took one of his drawings, which showed the lovers on a bench, holding up a cut-out heart to each other, to a printer. It was only when we got the proofs that someone at the printing firm asked if I had permission. Oh God, I had never thought of that, yet I was supposed to be a Fleet Street journalist who would surely know about such things. I spent ages making calls to Paris to find out who owned the copyright and managed to clear it, without having to pay. It was anyway a private card, not commercial, to give to friends. Just to cover myself, under the drawing, I printed the publisher's details.

The wording on the card was simple: 'IT WON'T BE A STYLISH MARRIAGE', so it said on the front. Inside it read: 'IN FACT . . . JUST HER AND HIM AND NO ONE ELSE'. But it did give details of where and when the unstylish marriage had taken place. And, on the back, it issued a welcome – to our relations and friends to come and visit us at our new address.

Several relatives were a bit upset at missing a do, any sort of family do. I suppose, looking back, we were a bit mean. All our brothers and sisters in due course did the proper thing, and had church weddings with a full reception, which we went to, and they were all lovely and touching events. Did we regret it? Not really.

After the snaps had been taken in the Parfitts' back garden, we were going away on our honeymoon, to a new flat we had acquired in Hampstead. It even had the proper telephone number, HAMpstead 3487. In the Shoot Up Hill flat, my number had been GLAdstone 4788. Numbers did matter in those days and HAMpstead was considered awfully smart. You dialled the first three letters of the phone number, followed by the four figures. I never knew how they managed that. In Manchester, the *Chron*'s number had been BLAckfriars 1234, while at Thomson House in London our number was TERminus 1234. Great numbers, so easy to remember, so easy to give out, not like today when nobody knows their own mobile number.

I had just bought my first car, a 1947 Riley 2.5, which cost £100. I had to save like mad because my bank, the Midland at

King's Cross, would not advance me a loan when I told them it was to buy a car. I never forgave them.

It was a most attractive-looking car, long and racy, with a fabric roof that some vandal had taken a knife to but it had been repaired. Inside it smelled delightful, of wood and oil and age and quality. But it was a total mistake and always breaking down. I got talked into it by Mike. He maintained he knew about cars, and I believed him – when growing up in Carlisle his family had been the only one I knew who had one.

The day before our wedding, I failed my driving test. For the second time. Oh, the ignominy. And embarrassment. It rather ruined my fantasy of driving my bride away to London straight after our wedding, to our new flat, to our new life. Instead, I had to persuade Mike to come with us in the car, on stage one of our honeymoon.

Failing the driving test, on the eve of my wedding, could that be a metaphor for marriage and life and the whole damn thing? No, not for one second did I think that.

Mike, our best man, later became a solicitor and moved to Hong Kong, where he became senior partner in one of the city's major legal firms. I had lunch with him there a few years ago, in the Hong Kong Club, which was very smart, and I got sent out to put on a tie.

Ian Johnstone, also from Carlisle, who went to Durham at the same time as me, joined the Colonial Service, serving the Queen in Africa and then moving to New Zealand where he became a well-known TV presenter and newsreader. He still lives in New Zealand.

My roommate from Durham, John Davies, who was a

chemist, did a PhD, worked at Harwell as a nuclear scientist then moved to the USA and worked for the US government on their nuclear programme, which meant he had to become a US citizen. He still lives in California with his family. And still has a Geordie accent.

Reg Hill, my best friend from Carlisle, whom I had known since I was four, became a teacher after he left Oxford, then a lecturer, before eventually becoming a writer, going on to great success as an award-winning crime novelist, Reginald C. Hill, author of the Dalziel and Pascoe books. He later returned to live in Cumbria with his Cumbrian-born wife Pat and died there in 2012, aged seventy-five.

I have always enjoyed the fact of getting married in 1960. I can always tot up the years since. Being born in 1936, I have to pause, depending on what time of the year it is, to work out my age. My Durham student years began in, let's see, thinking back, oh yes, 1954. But the year of my marriage, I can always remember that without thinking. Hurrah for 1960.

It did seem special at the time, getting married at the beginning of a new decade, though of course we had no idea what a wondrous decade it was going to be.

The year 1960 turned out to be doubly special. The second most important event in my long-legged life also happened to happen in 1960. Not long after our wedding. I joined the *Sunday Times*. Which led on to so many other events and excitements, people and places.

One of the things they say about the sixties is that if you can remember them, you weren't there. It's a joke, of course, the inference being that real sixties people were stoned all the time. As a joke, it is quite amusing. As a fact, it is bollocks.

You also hear people saying and writing that the sixties did not begin till 1963, perhaps 1966, as that was when the real changes began to happen. This is roughly true, more or less. *Time* magazine did not come out with their 'Swinging London' issue till 15 April 1966. Most modern historians, when writing about the sixties today, looking back to a time most of them never experienced, generally agree that the year 1963 was the birth of what we now call the sixties.

But personally, I will always consider that the sixties began in 1960. They did for me, in every way.

If I had to meet myself now, coming down the street in 1960, would I recognise myself, my thoughts, my feelings, my worries? Possibly. But certainly not if I were to meet my 1954 self, going up to Durham, or my 1947 self starting at the Creighton. As for my years in Scotland, they are a foreign country.

One of the things Margaret and I used to argue about was luck. I always maintained that you made your own luck. The more you did, the more you tried, the more goes you had, the more experiences you were open to, the more ideas and suggestions and offers you put up – then the more chance you had of one of them coming off. Margaret never agreed. Life is random, she said, and you can do nothing about it. Bad luck and good luck, they just happen, despite what you do. So you have to face up to it. Hope for good luck, but accept the bad luck, which everyone will have at some time.

Growing up during the war must count as bad luck, but

as children at the time, we didn't think that. We didn't miss what we had never had. Rations and deprivations, no sweets or bananas, were facts of life. Now we are told that rations and restrictions and no cars kept us slim, fit and healthy, far healthier than any generation since. Pity we didn't know that then.

The NHS coming in when it did, that was good fortune, a blessing which our own parents didn't have when they were growing up. Those years I suffered with asthma, that admittedly was bad luck. My father's illness, which dominated the whole of my growing-up years, that was a scunner.

But hurrah and huzzah for the Butler Act of 1944 and the decades of free education which followed. How amazing that was, getting everything for free. And we did appreciate it at the time. Which you don't always do with good fortune. Margaret at Oxford for three years not only never paid a penny, she ended up in profit each year, with about £100 not spent when she finally left. I did marry well. I ended my four years at Durham owing the buttery about £100 in bills, but that was extravagance and dry sherry, which I repaid the minute I started work.

Finding work that I loved, after having had no idea at all what I might do, that was another lucky stroke. Work, any sort of work, was generally readily available, so that was also fortunate. Almost everyone in the fifties expected to get a job, and could move around, change jobs, should they want to. Or they could stay forever, in the same place, the same job. More or less.

Not doing national service, I was always grateful for that. Now aged eighty, I have lived all these years since without serving Queen and country and without the country being in a major war, unlike my parents who suffered the consequences of two world wars.

All lucky breaks, and nothing to do with me. Believers in the randomness of life will point to this as proof that luck and life are down to chance.

The best bit of luck was meeting Margaret and then marrying her in 1960. But even better was yet to come ...